The Lotus Sutra

The Lotus Sutra

Homage To
All the Buddhas and Bodhisattvas

Adaptation by Lance Carter
Translation by Hendrik Kern

The Lotus Sutra
Poetic adaptation by Lance Carlyle Carter
Translation from Sanskrit by Hendrik Kern
Text previously published under the title:
'The Saddharma - Pundarika Sutra'
in the Sacred Books of the East Series,
vol. XXI, Oxford, 1909.

ISBN: 978-1-935057-07-9

Copyright © 2019 by Lance Carlyle Carter

All rights reserved. No part of this book may be reproduced or transmitted in any form or by any means, electronic or mechanical, including photocopying, recording or by any information storage and retrieval system without written permission from the author, except for brief quotations in critical articles and reviews.

Table of Contents

I.	Introductory	1
II.	Skilfulness	25
III.	A Parable	51
IV.	Disposition	83
V.	On Plants	99
VI.	Announcement of Future Destiny	119
VII.	Ancient Devotion	129
VIII.	Announcement of the Future Destiny of Five Hundred Monks	159
IX.	Announcement of the Future Destiny of Ânanda, Râhula, and the Two Thousand Monks	171
X.	The Preacher	179
XI.	Apparition of a Stûpa	191
XII.	Exertion	213
XIII.	Peaceful Life	219
XIV.	Issuing of Bodhisattvas from the Gaps of the Earth	235
XV.	Duration of Life of the Tathâgata	249
XVI.	Of Piety	259
XVII.	Indication of the Meritoriousness of Joyful Acceptance	273
XVIII.	The Advantages of a Religious Preacher	281
XIX.	Sadâparibhûta	297
XX.	Conception of the Transcendent Power of the Tathâgatas	305
XXI.	Spells	311
XXII.	Ancient Devotion of Bhaishagyarâga	317
XXIII.	Gadgadasvara	331
XXIV.	The All-sided One	341
XXV.	Ancient Devotion	351
XXVI.	Encouragement of the Samantabhadra	361
XXVII.	The Period	369
Index		373

Chapter I
Introductory

Thus have I heard. Once upon a time the Lord was staying at Râgagriha, on the Gridhrakûta mountain, with a numerous assemblage of monks, twelve hundred monks, all of them Arhats, stainless, free from depravity, self-controlled, thoroughly emancipated in thought and knowledge, of noble breed, like unto great elephants, having done their task, done their duty, acquitted their charge, reached the goal ; in whom the ties which bound them to existence were wholly destroyed, whose minds were thoroughly emancipated by perfect knowledge, who had reached the utmost perfection in subduing all their thoughts ; who were possessed of the transcendent faculties ; eminent disciples, such as the venerable Âgñâta-Kaundinya, the venerable Asvagit, the venerable Vâshpa, the venerable Mahânâman, the venerable Bhadrika, the venerable Mahâ-Kâsyapa, the venerable Kâsyapa of Uruvilvâ, the venerable Kâsyapa of Nadî, the venerable Kâsyapa of Gayâ, the venerable Sâriputra, the venerable Mahâ-Maudgalyâyana, the venerable Mahâ-Kâtyâyana, the venerable Aniruddha, the venerable Revata, the venerable Kapphina, the venerable Gavâmpati, the venerable Pilindavatsa, the venerable Vakula, the venerable Bhâradvâga, the venerable Mahâ-Kaushthila, the venerable Nanda, alias Mahânanda, the venerable Upananda, the venerable Sundara-Nanda, the venerable Pûrna Maitrâyanîputra, the venerable Subhûti, the venerable Râhula ; with them yet other great disciples, as the venerable Ânanda, still under training, and two thousand other monks, some of whom still under training, the others masters ; with six thousand nuns having at their head Mahâpragâpatî,

and the nun Yasodharâ,
the mother of Râhula,
along with her train ;
further with eighty thousand
Bodhisattvas,
all unable to slide back,
endowed
with the spells of supreme,
perfect enlightenment,
firmly standing in wisdom ;
who moved onward
the never deviating
wheel of the law ;
who had propitiated
many hundred thousands
of Buddhas ;
who under many
hundred thousands
of Buddhas had planted
the roots of goodness,
had been intimate with
many hundred thousands
of Buddhas,
were in body and mind
fully penetrated
with the feeling of charity ;
able in communicating
the wisdom
of the Tathâgatas ;
very wise, having reached
the perfection of wisdom ;
renowned in many hundred
thousands of worlds ;
having saved
many hundred thousand
myriads of kotis of beings ;
such as the Bodhisattva
Mahâsattva Mañgusrî,
as prince royal ;
the Bodhisattvas
Mahâsattvas Avalokitesvara,
Mahâsthâmaprâpta,
Sârvarthanâman,
Nityodyukta,
Anikshiptadhura,
Ratnapâni,
Bhaishagyarâga,
Pradânasûra,
Ratnakandra,
Ratnaprabha,
Pûrnakandra,
Mahivikrâmin,
Trailokavikrâmin,
Anantavikrâmin,
Mahâpratibhâna,
Satatasamitâbhiyukta,
Dharanîdhara,
Akshayamati,
Padmasrî,
Nakshatrarâga,
the Bodhisattva
Mahâsattva Maitreya,
the Bodhisattva
Mahâsattva Simha.

With them were also
the sixteen virtuous men
to begin with Bhadrapâla,
to wit, Bhadrapâla,
Ratnâkara, Susârthavâha,
Naradatta, Guhagupta,
Varunadatta, Indradatta,
Uttaramati, Viseshamati,
Vardhamânamati,
Amoghadarsin,
Susamsthita,
Suvikrântavikrâmin,
Anupamamati,
Sûryagarbha,
and Dharanîdhara ;
besides eighty thousand
Bodhisattvas,

among whom
the fore-mentioned
were the chiefs;
further Sakra,
the ruler of the celestials,
with twenty thousand gods,
his followers,
such as the god
Kandra the Moon,
the god Sûrya the Sun, the god
Samantagandha the Wind,
the god Ratnaprabha,
the god Avabhâsaprabha,
and others;
further, the four great rulers
of the cardinal points
with thirty thousand gods
in their train,
namely
the great ruler Virûdhaka,
the great ruler Virûpâksha,
the great ruler Dhritarâshtra,
and the great ruler
Vaisravana;
the god Îsvara
and the god Mahesvara,
each followed by thirty
thousand gods; further,
Brahma Sahâmpati and his
twelve thousand followers,
the Brahmakâyika gods,
amongst
whom Brahma Sikhin
and Brahma Gyotishprabha,
with
the other twelve thousand
Brahmakâyika gods;
together with
the eight Nâga kings
and many hundred thousand
myriads of kotis
of Nâgas in their train,
namely
the Nâga king Nanda,
the Nâga king Upananda,
Sâgara, Vâsuki, Takshaka,
Manasvin, Anavatapta,
and Utpalaka; further,
the four Kinnara kings
with many hundred
thousand myriads
of kotis of followers,
namely
the Kinnara king Druma,
the
Kinnara king Mahâdharma,
the Kinnara king Sudharma,
and the Kinnara
king Dharmadhara;
besides,
the four divine beings
called Gandharvakâyikas
with many hundred
thousand Gandharvas
in their suite, namely
the Gandharva Manogña, the
Gandharva Manogñasvara,
the Gandharva Madhura,
and the
Gandharva Madhurasvara;
further,
the four chiefs of the demons
followed
by many hundred thousand
myriads of kotis of demons,
namely, the chief of the
demons Bali, Kharaskandha,
Vemakitri, and Râhu;
along with
the four Garuda chiefs
followed
by many hundred thousand

Introductory 3

myriads of kotis of Garudas, namely
the Garuda chiefs Mahâtegas,
Mahâkâya, Mahâpûrna,
and Mahârddhiprâpta,
and with Agâtasatru,
king of Magadha,
the son of Vaidehî.

Now at that time it was
that the Lord surrounded,
attended, honoured,
revered, venerated,
worshipped
by the four classes of hearers,
after expounding
the Dharmaparyâya called
'the Great Exposition,'
a text of great development,
serving to instruct
Bodhisattvas
and proper to all Buddhas,
sat cross-legged
on the seat of the law
and entered upon
the meditation termed
'the station
of the exposition of Infinity ;'
his body was motionless
and his mind had reached
perfect tranquillity.
And as soon as
the Lord had entered
upon his meditation,
there fell a great rain
of divine flowers,
Mandâravas
and great Mandâravas,
Mañgûshakas
and great Mañgûshakas,
covering the Lord
and the four classes of hearers,
while the whole Buddha
field shook in six ways :
it moved, removed, trembled,
trembled from one end
to the other,
tossed, tossed along.

Then did those
who were assembled
and sitting together
in that congregation, monks,
nuns, male and female
lay devotees, gods, Nâgas,
goblins, Gandharvas,
demons, Garudas,
Kinnaras, great serpents,
men, and beings not human,
as well as
governors of a region,
rulers of armies
and rulers of four continents,
all of them
with their followers,
gaze on the Lord
in astonishment,
in amazement,
in ecstasy.

And at that moment
there issued a ray
from within the circle of hair
between the eyebrows
of the Lord.
It extended over
eighteen hundred thousand
Buddha-fields
in the eastern quarter,
so that
all those Buddha-fields
appeared wholly illuminated

by its radiance,
down to the great hell Avîki
and up to the limit
of existence.
And the beings
in any of the six states
of existence became visible,
all without exception.
Likewise the Lords Buddhas
staying, living, and existing
in those Buddha-fields
became all visible,
and the law preached
by them could be entirely
heard by all beings.
And the monks, nuns, lay
devotees male and female,
Yogins and students of Yoga,
those who had obtained
the fruition of the Paths
of sanctification
and those who had not,
they, too, became visible.
And the
Bodhisattvas Mahâsattvas
in those Buddha-fields who
plied the Bodhisattva-course
with ability,
due to their earnest belief
in numerous
and various lessons
and the fundamental ideas,
they, too, became all visible.
Likewise the Lords Buddhas
in those Buddha-fields
who had reached
final Nirvâna
became visible, all of them.
And the Stûpas
made of jewels
and containing the relics
of the extinct Buddhas
became all visible
in those Buddha-fields.

Then rose in the mind
of the Bodhisattva
Mahâsattva Maitreya
this thought :
O how great a wonder
does the Tathâgata display !
What may be the cause,
what the reason
of the Lord producing
so great a wonder as this ?
And such astonishing,
prodigious, inconceivable,
powerful miracles
now appear,
although the Lord
is absorbed in meditation !
Why, let me inquire
about this matter ;
who would be able here
to explain it to me ?
He then thought :
Here is Mañgusrî,
the prince royal,
who has plied his office
under former Ginas
and planted
the roots of goodness,
while worshipping
many Buddhas.
This Mañgusrî,
the prince royal,
must have
witnessed before such signs
of the former Tathâgatas,
those Arhats,
those perfectly enlightened
Buddhas ;

of yore he must have enjoyed
the grand conversations
on the law.
Therefore will I inquire
about this matter
with Mañgusrî,
the prince royal.

And the four classes
of the audience,
monks, nuns,
male and female lay devotees,
numerous gods,
Nâgas, goblins,
Gandharvas, demons,
Garudas, Kinnaras,
great serpents, men,
and beings not human,
on seeing the magnificence
of this great miracle
of the Lord,
were struck
with astonishment,
amazement and curiosity,
and thought :
Let us inquire
why this magnificent miracle
has been produced
by the great power
of the Lord.

At the same moment,
at that very instant,
the Bodhisattva Mahâsattva
Maitreya knew in his mind
the thoughts
arising in the minds
of the four classes of hearers
and he spoke to Mañgusrî,
the prince royal :
What, O Mañgusrî,
is the cause,
what is the reason
of this wonderful,
prodigious,
miraculous shine
having been produced
by the Lord ?
Look,
how these eighteen
thousand Buddha-fields
appear variegated,
extremely beautiful,
directed by Tathâgatas
and superintended
by Tathâgatas.

Then it was that Maitreya,
the Bodhisattva Mahâsattva,
addressed Mañgusrî,
the prince royal,
in the following stanzas :

1.
Why, Mañgusrî,
does this ray darted
by the guide of men
shine forth
from between his brows ?
this single ray issuing
from the circle of hair ?
and why this abundant
rain of Mandâravas ?

2.
The gods, overjoyed,
let drop Mañgûshakas
and sandal powder,
divine, fragrant,
and delicious.

3.
This earth is, on every side,
replete with splendour,
and all the four classes
of the assembly
are filled with delight,
while the whole field
shakes in six different ways,
frightfully.

4.
And that ray
in the eastern quarter
illuminates the whole
of eighteen thousand
Buddha-fields,
simultaneously,
so that those fields
appear as gold-coloured.

5.
The universe
as far as the hell Avîki
and the extreme limit
of existence,
with all beings of those fields
living in any
of the six states of existence,
those who
are leaving one state
to be born in another ;

6.
Their various and different
actions in those states
have become visible ;
whether they are in a happy,
unhappy, low, eminent,
or intermediate position,
all that I see from this place.

7.
I see also the Buddhas,
those lions of kings,
revealing and showing
the essence of the law,
comforting
many kotis of creatures
and emitting
sweet-sounding voices.

8.
They let go forth,
each in his own field, a deep,
sublime, wonderful voice,
while proclaiming
the Buddha-laws
by means of myriads of kotis
of illustrations and proofs.

9.
And to the ignorant creatures
who are oppressed with toils
and distressed in mind
by birth and old age,
they announce
the bliss of Rest, saying :
This is the end of trouble,
O monks.

10.
And to those
who are possessed
of strength and vigour
and who have acquired merit
by virtue or earnest belief
in the Buddhas,
they show the vehicle
of the Pratyekabuddhas,
by observing
this rule of the law.

11.
And the other sons
of the Sugata who,
striving after
superior knowledge,
have constantly
accomplished
their various tasks,
them also they admonish
to enlightenment.

12.
From this place,
O Mañgughosha,
I see and hear such things
and thousands of kotis
of other particulars besides ;
I will only describe
some of them.

13.
I see in many fields
Bodhisattvas
by many thousands of kotis,
like sands of the Ganges,
who are
producing enlightenment
according to the different
degree of their power.

14.
There are some who charitably
bestow wealth, gold, silver,
gold money, pearls, jewels,
conch shells, stones, coral,
male and female slaves,
horses, and sheep ;

15.
As well as litters
adorned with jewels.
They are spending gifts
with glad hearts,
developing themselves
for superior enlightenment,
in the hope of gaining
the vehicle.

16.
Thus they think :
'The best
and most excellent vehicle
in the whole
of the threefold world
is the Buddha-vehicle
magnified by the Sugatas.
May I, forsooth,
soon gain it after
my spending such gifts.'

17.
Some give carriages
yoked with four horses
and furnished with benches,
flowers, banners, and flags ;
others give objects made
of precious substances.

18.
Some, again,
give their children and wives ;
others their own flesh ;
or offer, when bidden,
their hands and feet,
striving to gain
supreme enlightenment.

19.
Some give their heads,
others their eyes,
others their dear own body,
and after cheerfully

bestowing their gifts
they aspire to the knowledge
of the Tathâgatas.

20.
Here and there, O Mañgusrî,
I behold beings
who have abandoned
their flourishing kingdoms,
harems, and continents,
left all their counsellors
and kinsmen,

21.
And betaken themselves
to the guides of the world
to ask for
the most excellent law,
for the sake of bliss ; they
put on reddish-yellow robes,
and shave hair and beard.

22.
I see also many
Bodhisattvas like monks,
living in the forest,
and others inhabiting
the empty wilderness,
engaged in reciting
and reading.

23.
And some Bodhisattvas
I see, who,
full of wisdom or constancy,
betake themselves
to mountain caves,
where by cultivating
and meditating
the Buddha-knowledge
they arrive at its perception.

24.
Others who have renounced
all sensual desires,
by purifying their own self,
have cleared their sphere
and obtained the five
transcendent faculties,
live in the wilderness,
as true sons of the Sugata.

25.
Some are standing firm,
the feet put together
and the hands joined
in token of respect
towards the leaders,
and are praising joyfully
the king of the leading Ginas
in thousands of stanzas.

26.
Some thoughtful,
meek, and tranquil,
who have mastered
the niceties
of the course of duty,
question the highest of men
about the law,
and retain in their memory
what they have learnt.

27.
And I see here and there
some sons
of the principal Gina who,
after completely
developing their own self,
are preaching the law
to many kotis of living beings
with many myriads
of illustrations and reasons.

28.
Joyfully
they proclaim the law,
rousing many Bodhisattvas ;
after conquering the Evil One
with his hosts and vehicles,
they strike the drum
of the law.

29.
I see some sons of the Sugata,
humble, calm,
and quiet in conduct,
living under the command
of the Sugatas,
and honoured by men, gods,
goblins, and Titans.

30.
Others, again,
who have retired
to woody thickets,
are saving the creatures
in the hells
by emitting radiance
from their body,
and rouse them
to enlightenment.

31.
There are
some sons of the Gina
who dwell in the forest,
abiding in vigour,
completely renouncing sloth,
and
actively engaged in walking ;
it is by energy
that they are striving
for supreme enlightenment.

32.
Others complete
their course
by keeping a constant purity
and an unbroken morality
like precious stones
and jewels ;
by morality do these strive
for supreme enlightenment.

33.
Some sons of the Gina,
whose strength consists
in forbearance,
patiently endure abuse,
censure, and threats
from proud monks.
They try to attain
enlightenment
by dint of forbearance.

34.
Further, I see Bodhisattvas,
who have forsaken
all wanton pleasures,
shun unwise companions
and delight
in having intercourse
with genteel men âryas ;

35.
Who, with avoidance
of any distraction of thoughts
and with attentive mind,
during thousands
of kotis of years
have meditated in the caves
of the wilderness ;
these strive
for enlightenment
by dint of meditation.

36.
Some, again,
offer in presence of the Ginas
and the assemblage
of disciples
gifts consisting
in food hard and soft,
meat and drink,
medicaments for the sick,
in plenty and abundance.

37.
Others offer
in presence of the Ginas
and the assemblage of disciples
hundreds of kotis of clothes,
worth thousands of kotis, and
garments of priceless value.

38.
They bestow
in presence of the Sugatas
hundreds of kotis
of monasteries which
they have caused to be built
of precious substances
and sandal-wood,
and which are furnished
with numerous
lodgings or couches.

39.
Some present
the leaders of men
and their disciples
with neat and lovely gardens
abounding with fruits
and beautiful flowers,
to serve as places
of daily recreation.

40.
When they have,
with joyful feelings,
made such various
and splendid donations,
they rouse their energy
in order
to obtain enlightenment ;
these are those
who try to reach
supreme enlightenment
by means of charitableness.

41.
Others set forth
the law of quietness,
by many myriads
of illustrations and proofs ;
they preach it to thousands
of kotis of living beings ;
these are tending to supreme
enlightenment by science.

42.
There are sons
of the Sugata who try
to reach enlightenment
by wisdom ;
they understand
the law of indifference
and avoid acting
at the antinomy of things,
unattached like birds
in the sky.

43.
Further, I see,
O Mañgughosha,
many Bodhisattvas who
have displayed steadiness
under the rule

of the departed Sugatas,
and now are worshipping
the relics of the Ginas.

44.
I see thousands
of kotis of Stûpas,
numerous
as the sand of the Ganges,
which have been raised
by these sons of the Gina
and now adorn
kotis of grounds.

45.
Those magnificent Stûpas,
made of
seven precious substances,
with their thousands
of kotis of umbrellas
and banners,
measure in height no less
than 5000 yoganas
and 2000 in circumference.

46.
They are always
decorated with flags ;
a multitude of bells
is constantly heard sounding ;
men, gods, goblins,
and Titans pay their worship
with flowers, perfumes,
and music.

47.
Such honour do the sons
of the Sugata
render to the relics
of the Ginas,
so that all directions of space

are brightened
as by the celestial coral trees
in full blossom.

48.
From this spot
I behold all this ;
those numerous
kotis of creatures ;
both this world and heaven
covered with flowers,
owing to the single ray
shot forth by the Gina.

49.
O how powerful
is the Leader of men !
how extensive and bright
is his knowledge !
that a single beam
darted by him over the world
renders visible
so many thousands of fields !

50.
We are astonished
at seeing this sign
and this wonder,
so great,
so incomprehensible.
Explain me the matter,
O Mañgusvara !
the sons of Buddha
are anxious to know it.

51.
The four classes
of the congregation
in joyful expectation
gaze on thee, O hero,
and on me ;

gladden their hearts ;
remove their doubts ;
grant a revelation,
O son of Sugata !

52.
Why is it that the Sugata
has now emitted such a light ?
O how great is the power
of the Leader of men !
O how extensive
and holy is his knowledge !

53.
That one ray
extending from him
all over the world
makes visible
many thousands of fields.
It must be for some purpose
that this great ray
has been emitted.

54.
Is the Lord of men
to show the primordial laws
which he, the Highest of men,
discovered on the terrace
of enlightenment ?
Or is he to prophesy
the Bodhisattvas
their future destiny ?

55.
There must be
a weighty reason
why so many
thousands of fields
have been rendered visible,
variegated, splendid,
and shining with gems,
while Buddhas
of infinite sight
are appearing.

56.
Maitreya asks
the son of Gina ;
men, gods, goblins,
and Titans, the four classes
of the congregation,
are eagerly awaiting
what answer Mañgusvara
shall give in explanation.

Whereupon Mañgusrî,
the prince royal,
addressed Maitreya,
the Bodhisattva Mahâsattva,
and the whole assembly
of Bodhisattvas
in these words :
It is the intention
of the Tathâgata,
young men of good family,
to begin a grand discourse
for the teaching of the law,
to pour
the great rain of the law,
to make resound
the great drum of the law,
to raise
the great banner of the law,
to kindle
the great torch of the law,
to blow the great conch
trumpet of the law,
and to strike
the great tymbal of the law.
Again, it is the intention
of the Tathâgata,
young men of good family,

to make a grand exposition
of the law this very day.
Thus it appears to me,
young men of good family,
as I have witnessed
a similar sign
of the former Tathâgatas,
the Arhats,
the perfectly enlightened.
Those former Tathâgatas, &c.,
they, too,
emitted a lustrous ray,
and I am convinced
that the Tathâgata
is about to deliver
a grand discourse
for the teaching of the law
and make his grand speech
on the law everywhere heard,
he having shown
such a foretoken.
And
because the Tathâgata, &c.,
wishes that
this Dharmaparyâya
meeting opposition
in all the world
be heard everywhere,
therefore does he display
so great a miracle
and this fore-token consisting
in the lustre occasioned
by the emission of a ray.

I remember,
young men of good family,
that in the days of yore,
many immeasurable,
inconceivable, immense,
infinite, countless Æons,
more than countless

Æons ago, nay,
long and very long before,
there was born a Tathâgata
called Kandrasûryapradîpa,
an Arhat, &c.,
endowed with science
and conduct, a Sugata,
knower of the world,
an incomparable
tamer of men,
a teacher and ruler
of gods and men,
a Buddha and Lord.
He showed the law ;
he revealed the duteous
course which is holy
at its commencement,
holy in its middle,
holy at the end,
good in substance and form,
complete and perfect,
correct and pure.
That is to say,
to the disciples
he preached the law
containing
the four Noble Truths,
and starting from the chain
of causes and effects,
tending to overcome birth,
decrepitude, sickness,
death, sorrow,
lamentation, woe,
grief, despondency,
And finally
leading to Nirvâna ;
and to the Bodhisattvas
he preached the law
connected with
the six Perfections,
and terminating

in the knowledge
of the Omniscient,
after the attainment
of supreme,
perfect enlightenment.

Now,
young men of good family,
long before the time
of that Tathâgata
Kandrasûryapradîpa,
the Arhat, &c.,
there had appeared
a Tathâgata, &c.,
likewise called
Kandrasûryapradîpa,
after whom, O Agita,
there were twenty thousand
Tathâgatas, &c.,
all of them bearing the name
of Kandrasûryapradîpa,
of the same lineage
and family name,
to wit, of Bhâradvâga.
All those
twenty thousand Tathâgatas,
O Agita,
from the first to the last,
showed the law,
revealed the course
which is holy
at its commencement,
holy in its middle,
holy at the end, &c., &c.

The aforesaid Lord
Kandrasûryapradîpa,
the Tathâgata, &c.,
when a young prince
and not yet having left home
to embrace the ascetic life,

had eight sons,
namely the young princes
Sumati, Anantamati,
Ratnamati, Viseshamati,
Vimatisamudghâtin,
Ghoshamati,
and Dharmamati.
These eight young princes,
Agita, sons to the Lord
Kandrasûryapradîpa,
the Tathâgata,
had an immense fortune.
Each of them
was in possession
of four great continents,
where they exercised
the kingly sway.
When they saw that the Lord
had left his home
to become an ascetic,
and heard that
he had attained supreme,
perfect enlightenment,
they forsook all of them
the pleasures of royalty
and followed the example
of the Lord
by resigning the world ;
all of them strove to reach
superior enlightenment and
became preachers of the law.
While
constantly leading a holy life,
those young princes
planted roots of goodness
under many thousands
of Buddhas.

It was at that time, Agita,
that the Lord
Kandrasûryapradîpa,

the Tathâgata, &c.,
after expounding
the Dharmaparyâya
called 'the Great Exposition',
a text of great extension,
serving to instruct
Bodhisattvas
and proper to all Buddhas,
at the same moment
and instant,
at the same gathering
of the classes of hearers,
sat cross-legged
on the same seat of the law,
and entered upon
the meditation
termed 'the Station
of the exposition of Infinity;'
his body was motionless,
and his mind had reached
perfect tranquility.
And as soon as the Lord
had entered upon meditation,
there fell a great rain
of divine flowers, Mandâravas
and great Mandâravas,
Mañgûshakas
and great Mañgûshakas,
covering the Lord
and the four classes of hearers,
while the whole Buddha-field
shook in six ways;
it moved, removed, trembled,
trembled from one end
to the other,
tossed, tossed along.

Then did those who were
assembled and sitting together
at that congregation,
monks, nuns,
male and female lay devotees,
gods, Nâgas, goblins,
Gandharvas, demons,
Garudas, Kinnaras,
great serpents,
men and beings not human,
as well as
governors of a region,
rulers of armies
and rulers of four continents,
all of them with their followers
gaze on the Lord
in astonishment,
in amazement, in ecstasy.

And at that moment
there issued a ray from within
the circle of hair between
the eyebrows of the Lord.
It extended over eighteen
hundred thousand
Buddha-fields
in the eastern quarter,
so that all those Buddha-fields
appeared wholly illuminated
by its radiance, just like
the Buddha-fields do now,
O Agita.

At that juncture, Agita,
there were twenty kotis
of Bodhisattvas
following the Lord.
All hearers of the law
in that assembly,
on seeing how the world
was illuminated
by the lustre of that ray,
felt astonishment,
amazement, ecstasy,
and curiosity.

Now it happened, Agita,
that under the rule
of the aforesaid Lord
there was a Bodhisattva
called Varaprabha, who
had eight hundred pupils.
It was to this Bodhisattva
Varaprabha that the Lord,
on rising from his meditation,
revealed
the Dharmaparyâya called
'the Lotus of the True Law.'
He spoke during fully
sixty intermediate kalpas,
always sitting
on the same seat,
with immovable body
and tranquil mind.
And the whole assembly
continued sitting
on the same seats,
listening to the preaching
of the Lord
for sixty intermediate kalpas,
there being
not a single creature
in that assembly
who felt fatigue
of body or mind.

As the Lord
Kandrasûryapradîpa,
the Tathâgata, &c., during
sixty intermediate kalpas
had been expounding
the Dharmaparyâya called
'the Lotus of the True Law,'
a text of great development,
serving to instruct
Bodhisattvas
and proper to all Buddhas,
he instantly announced
his complete Nirvâna
to the world,
including the gods,
Mâras and Brahmas,
to all creatures,
including ascetics,
Brahmans, gods, men
and demons, saying :
To-day, O monks,
this very night,
in the middle watch,
will the Tathâgata,
by entering the element
of absolute Nirvâna,
become wholly extinct.

Thereupon, Agita,
the Lord
Kandrasûryapradîpa,
the Tathâgata, &c.,
predestinated
the Bodhisattva called
Srîgarbha to supreme,
perfect enlightenment,
and then spoke thus
to the whole assembly :
O monks,
this Bodhisattva Srîgarbha
here shall immediately
after me attain supreme,
perfect enlightenment,
and become Vimalanetra,
the Tathâgata, &c.

Thereafter, Agita,
that very night,
at that very watch, the Lord
Kandrasûryapradîpa,
the Tathâgata, &c.,

Introductory 17

became extinct
by entering the element
of absolute Nirvâna.
And the aforementioned
Dharmaparyâya, termed
'the Lotus of the True Law,'
was kept in memory by
the Bodhisattva Mahâsattva
Varaprabha ;
during eighty
intermediate kalpas did
the Bodhisattva Varaprabha
keep and reveal
the commandment of the Lord
who had entered Nirvâna.
Now it so happened, Agita,
that the eight sons of the
Lord Kandrasûryapradîpa,
Mati and the rest,
were pupils to that very
Bodhisattva Varaprabha.
They were by him
made ripe for supreme,
perfect enlightenment,
and in after times
they saw and worshipped
many hundred thousand
myriads of kotis of Buddhas,
all of whom
had attained supreme,
perfect enlightenment,
the last of them
being Dîpankara,
the Tathâgata, &c.

Amongst those eight pupils
there was one Bodhisattva
who attached
an extreme value to gain,
honour and praise,
and was fond of glory,
but all the words and letters
one taught him
faded from his memory,
did not stick.
So he got the appellation
of Yasaskâma.
He had propitiated
many hundred thousand
myriads of kotis of Buddhas
by that root of goodness,
and afterwards esteemed,
honoured, respected,
revered, venerated,
worshipped them.
Perhaps, Agita,
thou feelest some doubt,
perplexity or misgiving
that in those days,
at that time, there
was another Bodhisattva
Mahâsattva Varaprabha,
preacher of the law.
But do not think so. Why ?
because it is myself
who in those days,
at that time,
was the Bodhisattva
Mahâsattva Varaprabha,
preacher of the law ;
and that Bodhisattva
named Yasaskâma,
the lazy one, it is thyself,
Agita, who in those days,
at that time, wert ?
the Bodhisattva named
Yasaskâma, the lazy one.

And so, Agita,
having once seen
a similar foretoken of the Lord,
I infer from a similar ray

being emitted just now, that the Lord is about to expound the Dharmaparyâya called 'the Lotus of the True Law.'

And on that occasion, in order to treat the subject more copiously, Mañgusrî, the prince royal, uttered the following stanzas :

57.
I remember a past period, inconceivable, illimited kalpas ago, when the highest of beings, the Gina of the name of Kandrasûryapradîpa, was in existence.

58.
He preached the true law, he, the leader of creatures ; he educated an infinite number of kotis of beings, and roused inconceivably many Bodhisattvas to acquiring supreme Buddha-knowledge.

59.
And the eight sons born to him, the leader, when he was prince royal, no sooner saw that the great sage had embraced ascetic life, than they resigned worldly pleasures and became monks.

60.
And the Lord of the world proclaimed the law, and revealed to thousands of kotis of living beings the Sûtra, the development, which by name is called 'the excellent Exposition of Infinity.'

61.
Immediately after delivering his speech, the leader crossed his legs and entered upon the meditation of 'the excellent Exposition of the Infinite.' There on his seat of the law the eminent seer continued absorbed in meditation.

62.
And there fell a celestial rain of Mandâravas, while the drums of heaven resounded without being struck ; the gods and elves in the sky paid honour to the highest of men.

63.
And simultaneously all the fields of Buddha began trembling. A wonder it was, a great prodigy. Then the chief emitted from between his brows one extremely beautiful ray,

64.
Which moving to
the eastern quarter glittered,
illuminating the world
all over the extent
of eighteen thousand fields.
It manifested the vanishing
and appearing of beings.

65.
Some of the fields
then seemed jewelled,
others showed the hue
of lapis lazuli,
all splendid,
extremely beautiful,
owing to the radiance
of the ray from the leader.

66.
Gods and men,
as well as Nâgas,
goblins, Gandharvas,
nymphs, Kinnaras,
and those occupied
with serving the Sugata
became visible in the spheres
and paid their devotion.

67.
The Buddhas also,
those self-born beings,
appeared of their own accord,
resembling golden columns;
like unto a golden disk
within lapis lazuli,
they revealed the law
in the midst of the assembly.

68.
The disciples, indeed,
are not to be counted :
the disciples of Sugata
are numberless.
Yet the lustre of the ray
renders them
all visible in every field.

69.
Energetic,
without breach or flaw
in their course,
similar to gems and jewels,
the sons of the leaders of men
are visible
in the mountain caves
where they are dwelling.

70.
Numerous Bodhisattvas,
like the sand of the Ganges,
who are spending
all their wealth in giving alms,
who have
the strength of patience,
are devoted
to contemplation and wise,
become all of them
visible by that ray.

71.
Immovable, unshaken,
firm in patience,
devoted to contemplation,
and absorbed in meditation
are seen
the true sons of the Sugatas
while they are striving
for supreme enlightenment
by dint of meditation.

72.
They preach the law
in many spheres,
and point to the true, quiet,
spotless state they know.
Such is the effect produced
by the power of the Sugata.

73.
And all
the four classes of hearers
on seeing the power
of the mighty Kandrârkadîpa
were filled with joy and asked
one another : How is this ?

74.
And soon afterwards,
as the Leader of the world,
worshipped by men,
gods, and goblins,
rose from his meditation,
he addressed his son
Varaprabha,
the wise Bodhisattva
and preacher of the law :

75.
'Thou art wise,
the eye and refuge
of the world ;
thou art the trustworthy
keeper of my law,
and canst bear witness
as to the treasure of laws
which I am to lay bare
to the weal of living beings.'

76.
Then, after rousing
and stimulating,
praising and lauding
many Bodhisattvas,
did the Gina proclaim
the supreme laws
during fully
sixty intermediate kalpas.

77.
And whatever
excellent supreme law
was proclaimed
by the Lord of the world
while continuing sitting
on the very same seat,
was kept in memory
by Varaprabha,
the son of Gina,
the preacher of the law.

78.
And
after the Gina and Leader
had manifested
the supreme law
and stimulated
the numerous crowd,
he spoke, that day,
towards the world
including the gods as follows :

79.
'I have manifested
the rule of the law ;
I have shown the nature
of the law ; now, O monks,
it is the time of my Nirvâna ;
this very night,
in the middle watch.

80.
'Be zealous
and strong in persuasion ;
apply yourselves
to my lessons ;
for the Ginas,
the great seers,
are but rarely met with
in the lapse of myriads
of kotis of Æons.'

81.
The many sons of Buddha
were struck with grief
and filled
with extreme sorrow
when they heard the voice
of the highest of men
announcing that his Nirvâna
was near at hand.

82.
To comfort so inconceivably
many kotis of living beings
the king of kings said :
'Be not afraid, O monks ;
after my Nirvâna there
shall be another Buddha.

83.
'The wise
Bodhisattva Srîgarbha,
after finishing his course
in faultless knowledge,
shall reach highest,
supreme enlightenment,
and become a Gina
under the name
of Vimalâgranetra.'

84.
That very night,
in the middle watch,
he met complete extinction,
like a lamp
when the cause of its burning
is exhausted.
His relics were distributed,
and of his Stûpas
there was an infinite number
of myriads of kotis.

85.
The monks and nuns
at the time being,
who strove after supreme,
highest enlightenment,
numerous
as sand of the Ganges,
applied themselves
to the commandment
of the Sugata.

86.
And the monk who then was
the preacher of the law
and the keeper of the law,
Varaprabha,
expounded for fully eighty
intermediate kalpas
the highest laws according
to the commandment
of the Sugata

87.
He had eight hundred pupils,
who all of them were by him
brought to full development.
They saw many kotis
of Buddhas, great sages,
whom they worshipped.

88.
By following
the regular course
they became Buddhas
in several spheres, and
as they followed one another
in immediate succession
they successively foretold
each other's future destiny
to Buddhaship.

89.
The last of these Buddhas
following one another
was Dîpankara.
He, the supreme god of gods,
honoured by crowds of sages,
educated thousands of kotis
of living beings.

90.
Among the pupils
of Varaprabha,
the son of Gina,
at the time
of his teaching the law,
was one slothful, covetous,
greedy of gain and cleverness.

91.
He was also excessively
desirous of glory,
but very fickle,
so that the lessons
dictated to him
and his own reading
faded from his memory
as soon as learnt.

92.
His name was Yasaskâma,
by which
he was known everywhere.
By the accumulated merit
of that good action,
spotted as it was,

93.
He propitiated thousands
of kotis of Buddhas,
whom he rendered
ample honour.
He went through
the regular course of duties
and saw the present
Buddha Sâkyasimha.

94.
He shall be the last to reach
superior enlightenment
and become a Lord
known by the family name
of Maitreya,
who shall educate thousands
of kotis of creatures.

95.
He who then, under the rule
of the extinct Sugata,
was so slothful, was thyself,
and it was I who then
was the preacher of the law.

96.
As on seeing a foretoken
of this kind I recognise a sign
such as I have seen
manifested of yore, therefore
and on that account I know,

97.
That decidedly
the chief of Ginas,
the supreme king
of the Sâkyas,
the All-seeing,
who knows the highest truth,
is about to pronounce
the excellent Sûtra
which I have heard before.

98.
That very sign
displayed at present
is a proof of the skilfulness
of the leaders ;
the Lion of the Sâkyas
is to make an exhortation,
to declare
the fixed nature of the law.

99.
Be well prepared
and well minded ;
join your hands :
he who is affectionate
and merciful to the world
is going to speak,
is going to pour
the endless rain of the law
and refresh
those that are waiting
for enlightenment.

100.
And if some
should feel doubt,
uncertainty,
or misgiving in any respect,
then the Wise One
shall remove it.

Chapter II
Skilfulness

The Lord then rose
with recollection
and consciousness
from his meditation,
and forthwith addressed
the venerable Sâriputra :
The Buddha knowledge,
Sâriputra,
is profound,
difficult to understand,
difficult to comprehend.
It is difficult for all disciples
and Pratyekabuddhas
to fathom the knowledge
arrived at by
the Tathâgatas, &c.,
and that, Sâriputra,
because the Tathâgatas
have worshipped
many hundred thousand
myriads of kotis of Buddhas ;
because they have fulfilled
their course for supreme,
complete enlightenment,
during many hundred
thousand myriads
of kotis of Æons ; because
they have wandered far,
displaying energy
and possessed of wonderful
and marvellous properties ;
possessed of properties
difficult to understand ;
because
they have found out things
difficult to understand.

The mystery
of the Tathâgatas, &c.,
is difficult to understand,
Sâriputra,
because when they explain
the laws or phenomena,
things that have their causes
in themselves they do so
by means of skilfulness,
by the display of knowledge,
by arguments, reasons,
fundamental ideas,
interpretations,
and suggestions.
By a variety of skilfulness
they are able to release
creatures that are attached
to one point or another.
The Tathâgatas, &c.,
Sâriputra, have acquired
the highest perfection
in skilfulness
and the display
of knowledge ;
they are endowed
with wonderful properties,
such as the display of free
and unchecked knowledge ;
the powers ;
the absence of hesitation ;
the independent conditions ;
the strength of the organs ;
the constituents of Bodhi ;
the contemplations ;
emancipations ; meditations ;
the degrees
of concentration of mind.
The Tathâgatas, &c.,
Sâriputra,
are able to expound
various things

and have something
wonderful and marvellous.
Enough, Sâriputra,
let it suffice to say,
that the Tathâgatas, &c.,
have something extremely
wonderful, Sâriputra.
None but a Tathâgata,
Sâriputra, can impart
to a Tathâgata those laws
which the Tathâgata knows.
And all laws, Sâriputra,
are taught by the Tathâgata,
and by him alone ;
no one but he knows all laws,
what they are, how they are,
like what they are,
of what characteristics
and of what nature they are.

And on that occasion,
to set forth the same subject
more copiously,
the Lord uttered
the following stanzas :

1.
Innumerable
are the great heroes
in the world
that embraces gods and men ;
the totality of creatures
is unable to completely
know the leaders.

2.
None can know their powers
and states of emancipation,
their absence of hesitation
and Buddha properties,
such as they are.

3.
Of yore have I followed
in presence
of kotis of Buddhas
the good course
which is profound, subtle,
difficult to understand,
and most difficult to find.

4.
After pursuing that career
during an inconceivable
number of kotis of Æons,
I have on
the terrace of enlightenment
discovered the fruit thereof.

5.
And therefore I recognise,
like the other chiefs
of the world,
how it is, like what it is, and
what are its characteristics.

6.
It is impossible to explain it ;
it is unutterable ;
nor is there such a being
in the world.

7.
To whom this law
could be explained
or who would
be able to understand it
when explained,
with the exception
of the Bodhisattvas,
those who are firm in resolve.

8.
As to the disciples
of the Knower of the world,
those who have
done their duty
and received praise
from the Sugatas,
who are freed from faults
and have arrived
at the last stage
of bodily existence,
the Gina-knowledge
lies beyond their sphere.

9.
If this whole sphere
were full of beings
like Sârisuta,
and if they were
to investigate
with combined efforts,
they would be unable
to comprehend
the knowledge of the Sugata.

10.
Even if the ten points of space
were full of sages like thee,
ay, if they were full of such
as the rest of my disciples,

11.
And if those beings combined
were to investigate
the knowledge of the Sugata,
they would,
all together,
not be able to comprehend
the Buddha-knowledge
in its whole immensity.

12.
If the ten points of space
were filled
with Pratyekabuddhas,
free from faults,
gifted with acute faculties,
and standing in the last stage
of their existence,
as numerous as reeds
and bamboos in the woods ;

13.
And if combined
for an endless number
of myriads of kotis of Æons,
they were to investigate
a part only
of my superior laws,
they would never find out
its real meaning.

14.
If the ten points of space
were full of Bodhisattvas who,
after having done their duty
under many kotis of Buddhas,
investigated all things
and preached many sermons,
after entering a new vehicle ;

15.
If the whole world
were full of them,
as of dense reeds
and bamboos,
without any interstices,
and if all combined were
to investiage the law which
the Sugata has realised ;

Skilfulness 27

16.
If they were going
on investigating
for many kotis of Æons,
as incalculable as the sand
of the Ganges,
with undivided attention
and subtle wit,
even then that knowledge
would be beyond their ken.

17.
If such Bodhisattvas
as are unable to fall back,
numerous
as the sand of the Ganges,
were to investigate it
with undivided attention,
it would prove
to lie beyond their ken.

18.
Profound are the laws
of the Buddhas, and subtle ;
all inscrutable and faultless.
I myself know them
as well as the Ginas do
in the ten directions
of the world.

19.
Thou, Sâriputra,
be full of trust
in what the Sugata declares.
The Gina speaks
no falsehood,
the great Seer
who has so long preached
the highest truth.

20.
I address all disciples here,
those who have set out
to reach the enlightenment
of Pratyekabuddhas,
those who are roused
to activity at my Nirvâna,
and those
who have been released
from the series of evils.

21.
It is by
my superior skilfulness
that I explain the law
at great length
to the world at large.
I deliver whosoever
are attached to one point
or another,
and show the three vehicles.

The eminent disciples
in the assembly headed
by Âgñâta-Kaundinya ,
the twelve hundred Arhats
faultless and self-controlled,
the other monks, nuns,
male and female lay devotees
using the vehicle of disciples,
and those who had entered
the vehicle
of Pratyekabuddhas,
all of them
made this reflection :
What may be the cause,
what the reason of the Lord
so extremely
extolling the skilfulness
of the Tathâgatas ?
of his extolling it by saying,

'Profound is the law
by me discovered ;'
of his extolling it by saying,
'It is difficult for all disciples
and Pratyekabuddhas
to understand it.'
But as yet the Lord has declared
no more than one kind
of emancipation,
and therefore we also should
acquire the Buddha-laws
on reaching Nirvâna.
We do not catch the meaning
of this utterance of the Lord.

And the venerable Sâriputra,
who apprehended the doubt
and uncertainty
of the four classes
of the audience
and guessed their thoughts
from what was passing
in his own mind,
himself being in doubt
about the law,
then said to the Lord :
What, O Lord, is the cause,
what the reason of the Lord
so repeatedly and extremely
extolling the skilfulness,
knowledge, and preaching
of the Tathâgata ?
Why does he repeatedly
extol it by saying,
'Profound is the law
by me discovered ;
it is difficult
to understand the mystery
of the Tathâgatas.'
Never before have I heard
from the Lord
such a discourse on the law.
Those four classes
of the audience, O Lord,
are overcome with doubt
and perplexity.
Therefore may the Lord
be pleased to explain
what the Tathâgata
is alluding to,
when repeatedly extolling
the profound law
of the Tathâgatas.

On that occasion
the venerable Sâriputra
uttered the following stanzas :

22.
Now first does the Sun of men
utter such a speech :
'I have acquired
the powers, emancipations,
and numberless meditations.'

23.
And thou mentionest
the terrace of enlightenment
without any one asking thee :
thou mentionest the mystery,
although no one asks thee.

24.
Thou speakest unasked and
laudest thine own course ;
thou mentionest
thy having obtained
knowledge and pronouncest
profound words.

25.
To-day a question
rises in my mind
and of these self-controlled,
faultless beings
striving after Nirvâna:
Why does the Gina
speak in this manner?

26.
Those who aspire
to the enlightenment
of Pratyekabuddhas,
the nuns and monks,
gods, Nâgas,
goblins, Gandharvas,
and great serpents,
are talking together,
while looking up
to the highest of men,

27.
And ponder in perplexity.
Give an elucidation,
great Sage, to all the disciples
of Sugata here assembled.

28.
Myself have reached
the perfection of virtue,
have been taught
by the supreme Sage; still,
O highest of men!
even in my position
I feel some doubt whether
the course of duty
shown to me shall receive
its final sanction by Nirvâna.

29.
Let thy voice be heard,
O thou
whose voice resounds like
an egregious kettle-drum!
proclaim thy law such as it is.
The legitimate sons of Gina
here standing
and gazing at the Gina,
with joined hands;

30.
As well as the gods,
Nâgas, goblins,
Titans, numbering
thousands of kotis,
like sand of the Ganges;
and those that aspire
to superior enlightenment,
here standing, fully eighty
thousand in number;

31.
Further, the kings,
rulers of provinces
and paramount monarchs,
who have flocked thither
from thousands
of kotis of countries,
are now standing
with joined hands,
and respectful, thinking:
How are we to fulfil
the course of duty?

The venerable Sâriputra
having spoken,
the Lord said to him:
Enough, Sâriputra;
it is of no use
explaining this matter.

Why ?
Because, Sâriputra,
the world,
including the gods,
would be frightened
if this matter
were expounded.

But the venerable
Sâriputra entreated
the Lord a second time,
saying :
Let the Lord expound,
let the Sugata
expound this matter,
for in this assembly,
O Lord,
there are many hundreds,
many thousands,
many hundred thousands,
many hundred thousand
myriads of kotis
of living beings who have
seen former Buddhas,
who are intelligent,
and will believe,
value, and accept
the words of the Lord.

The venerable Sâriputra
addressed the Lord
with this stanza :

32.
Speak clearly,
O most eminent of Ginas !
in this assembly
there are thousands
of living beings trustful,
affectionate,
and respectful towards
the Sugata ;
they will understand the law
by thee expounded.

And the Lord
said a second time
to the venerable Sâriputra ;
Enough, Sâriputra ;
it is of no use explaining
this matter, for the world,
including the gods,
would be frightened,
Sâriputra,
if this matter
were expounded,
and some monks
might be proud
and come to a heavy fall.

And on that occasion
uttered the Lord
the following stanza :

33.
Speak no more of it that
I should declare this law !
This knowledge is too subtle,
inscrutable,
and there are
too many unwise men
who in their conceit
and foolishness would scoff
at the law revealed.

A third time
the venerable Sâriputra
entreated the Lord, saying :
Let the Lord expound,
let the Sugata
expound this matter.
In this assembly,

Skilfulness 31

O Lord,
there are many hundreds
of living beings my equals,
and many hundreds,
many thousands,
many hundred thousands,
many hundred thousand
myriads of kotis
of other living beings more,
who in former births
have been brought
by the Lord to full ripeness.
They will believe,
value, and accept
what the Lord declares,
which shall tend
to their advantage,
weal, and happiness
in length of time.

On that occasion
the venerable Sâriputra
uttered the following stanzas :

34.
Explain the law,
O thou most high of men !
I, thine eldest son,
beseech thee.
Here are thousands
of kotis of beings
who are to believe in the law
by thee revealed.

35.
And those beings
that in former births
so long and constantly
have by thee been brought
to full maturity
and now are all standing here

with joined hands, they, too,
are to believe in this law.

36.
Let the Sugata,
seeing the twelve hundred,
my equals,
and those who are striving
after superior enlightenment,
speak to them
and produce in them
an extreme joy.

When the Lord
for the third time
heard the entreaty
of the venerable Sâriputra,
he spoke to him as follows :
Now that thou entreatest
the Tathâgata a third time,
Sâriputra, I will answer thee.
Listen then, Sâriputra,
take well and duly to heart
what I am saying ;
I am going to speak.

Now it happened
that the five thousand
proud monks,
nuns and lay devotees
of both sexes
in the congregation
rose from their seats and,
after saluting
with their heads
the Lord's feet,
went to leave the assembly.
Owing
to the principle of good
which there is in pride
they imagined having

attained what they had not,
and having understood
what they had not.
Therefore,
thinking themselves
aggrieved, they went
to leave the assembly,
to which the Lord
by his silence showed assent.

Thereupon
the Lord addressed
the venerable Sâriputra :
My congregation, Sâriputra,
has been cleared
from the chaff,
freed from the trash ;
it is firmly established
in the strength of faith.
It is good, Sâriputra,
that those proud ones
are gone away.
Now I am going to expound
the matter, Sâriputra.
'Very well, Lord,' replied
the venerable Sâriputra.
The Lord
then began and said :

It is but now and then,
Sâriputra,
that the Tathâgata
preaches such a discourse
on the law as this.
Just as but now and then
is seen the blossom
of the glomerous fig-tree,
Sâriputra,
so does the Tathâgata
but now and then preach
such a discourse on the law.

Believe me, Sâriputra ;
I speak what is real,
I speak what is truthful,
I speak what is right.
It is difficult to understand
the exposition of the mystery
of the Tathâgata, Sâriputra ;
for in elucidating the law,
Sâriputra,
I use hundred thousands
of various skilful means, such
as different interpretations,
indications, explanations,
illustrations.
It is not by reasoning,
Sâriputra,
that the law is to be found :
it is beyond the pale
of reasoning,
and must be learnt
from the Tathâgata.
For, Sâriputra,
it is for a sole object,
a sole aim,
verily a lofty object,
a lofty aim that the Buddha,
the Tathâgata, &c.,
appears in the world.
And what is that sole object,
that sole aim,
that lofty object,
that lofty aim of the Buddha,
the Tathâgata, &c.,
appearing in the world ?
To show all creatures
the sight
of Tathâgata-knowledge
does the Buddha,
the Tathâgata, &c.,
appear in the world ;
to open the eyes of creatures

for the sight
of Tathâgata-knowledge
does the Buddha,
the Tathâgata, &c.,
appear in the world.
This, O Sâriputra,
is the sole object,
the sole aim,
the sole purpose
of his appearance
in the world.
Such then, Sâriputra,
is the sole object,
the sole aim,
the lofty object,
the lofty aim
of the Tathâgata.
And it is achieved
by the Tathâgata.
For, Sâriputra,
I do show all creatures
the sight
of Tathâgata-knowledge ;
I do open the eyes
of creatures for the sight
of Tathâgata-knowledge,
Sâriputra ;
I do firmly establish
the teaching
of Tathâgata-knowledge,
Sâriputra ;
I do lead the teaching
of Tathâgata-knowledge
on the right path, Sâriputra.
By means of one sole vehicle,
to wit, the Buddha-vehicle,
Sâriputra,
do I teach creatures the law ;
there is no second vehicle,
nor a third.
This is the nature of the law,
Sâriputra,
universally in the world,
in all directions.
For, Sâriputra,
all the Tathâgatas, &c.,
who in times past
existed in countless,
innumerable spheres
in all directions
for the weal of many,
the happiness of many,
out of pity to the world,
for the benefit, weal,
and happiness
of the great body of creatures,
and who preached the law
to gods and men
with able means,
such as several directions
and indications,
various arguments,
reasons, illustrations,
fundamental ideas,
interpretations,
paying regard to
the dispositions of creatures
whose inclinations
and temperaments
are so manifold,
all those Buddhas and Lords,
Sâriputra,
have preached the law
to creatures
by means of only one vehicle,
the Buddha-vehicle,
which finally
leads to omniscience ;
it is identical with showing
all creatures the sight
of Tathâgata-knowledge ;
with opening the eyes

of creatures for the sight
of Tathâgata-knowledge ;
with the awakening
or admonishing
by the display or sight
of Tathâgata-knowledge ;
with leading the teaching
of Tathâgata-knowledge
on the right path.
Such is the law
they have preached
to creatures.
And those creatures,
Sâriputra,
who have heard the law
from the past Tathâgatas, &c.,
have all of them
reached supreme,
perfect enlightenment.

And the Tathâgatas, &c.,
who shall exist in future,
Sâriputra,
in countless, innumerable
spheres in all directions
for the weal of many,
the happiness of many,
out of pity to the world,
for the benefit, weal,
and happiness
of the great body of creatures,
and who shall preach
the law to gods and men
the right path.
Such is the law they
shall preach to creatures.
And those creatures,
Sâriputra,
who shall hear the law from
the future Tathâgatas, &c.,
shall all of them
reach supreme,
perfect enlightenment.

And the Tathâgatas, &c.,
who now at present
are staying, living, existing,
Sâriputra,
in countless, innumerable
spheres in all directions, &c.,
and who are preaching
the law to gods and men
the right path.
Such is the law
they are preaching
to creatures.
And those creatures,
Sâriputra,
who are hearing the law from
the present Tathâgatas, &c.,
shall all of them
reach supreme,
perfect enlightenment.

I myself also, Sâriputra,
am at the present period
a Tathâgata, &c.,
for the weal of many &c.,
till manifold ;
I myself also,
Sâriputra,
am preaching the law
to creatures &c.,
till the right path.
Such is the law
I preach to creatures.
And those creatures,
Sâriputra,
who now are hearing
the law from me,
shall all of them
reach supreme,

perfect enlightenment.
In this sense, Sâriputra,
it must be understood
that nowhere in the world
a second vehicle is taught,
far less a third.

Yet, Sâriputra,
when the Tathâgatas, &c.,
happen to appear
at the decay of the epoch,
the decay of creatures,
the decay of besetting sins,
the decay of views,
or the decay of lifetime ;
when they appear
amid such signs of decay at
the disturbance of the epoch ;
when creatures
are much tainted, full of greed
and poor in roots of goodness ;
then, Sâriputra,
the Tathâgatas, &c.,
use, skilfully,
to designate that one
and sole Buddha-vehicle
by the appellation
of the threefold vehicle.
Now, Sâriputra,
such disciples, Arhats,
or Pratyekabuddhas
who do not hear
their actually being called
to the Buddha-vehicle
by the Tathâgata,
who do not perceive,
nor heed it, those, Sâriputra,
should not be acknowledged
as disciples of the Tathâgata,
nor as Arhats,
nor as Pratyekabuddhas.

Again, Sâriputra,
if there be some monk or nun
pretending to Arhatship
without an earnest vow
to reach supreme, perfect
enlightenment and saying,
'I am standing too high
for the Buddha-vehicle,
I am in my last appearance
in the body
before complete Nirvâna,'
then, Sâriputra,
consider such a one
to be conceited.
For, Sâriputra, it is unfit,
it is improper that a monk,
a faultless Arhat,
should not believe in the law
which he hears
from the Tathâgata
in his presence.
I leave out of question
when the Tathâgata
shall have reached
complete Nirvâna ;
for at that period,
that time, Sâriputra,
when the Tathâgata
shall be wholly extinct,
there shall be none
who either knows by heart
or preaches such Sûtras as this.
It will be under other
Tathâgatas, &c.,
that they are to be
freed from doubts.
In respect to these things
believe my words,
Sâriputra, value them,
take them to heart ;

for there is no falsehood
in the Tathâgatas, Sâriputra.
There is but one vehicle,
Sâriputra, and that
the Buddha-vehicle.

And on that occasion
to set forth this matter
more copiously
the Lord uttered
the following stanzas :

37.
No less than five thousand
monks, nuns, and lay
devotees of both sexes,
full of unbelief and conceit,

38.
Remarking this slight, went,
defective in training
and foolish as they were,
away in order
to beware of damage.

39.
The Lord,
who knew them
to be the dregs
of the congregation,
exclaimed :
They have no sufficient merit
to hear this law.

40.
My congregation
is now pure, freed from chaff ;
the trash is removed
and the pith only remains.

41.
Hear from me,
Sâriputra,
how this law
has been discovered
by the highest man,
and how the mighty Buddhas
are preaching it
with many hundred proofs
of skilfulness.

42.
I know the disposition
and conduct,
the various inclinations
of kotis of living beings
in this world ;
I know their various actions
and the good
they have done before.

43.
Those living beings
I initiate in this law
by the aid of manifold
interpretations
and reasons ;
and by hundreds
of arguments
and illustrations have I,
in one way or another,
gladdened all creatures.

44.
I utter both Sûtras
and stanzas ; legends,
Gâtakas, and prodigies,
besides
hundreds of introductions
and curious parables.

45.
I show Nirvâna to the ignorant
with low dispositions,
who have followed
no course of duty
under many kotis of Buddhas,
are bound to continued
existence and wretched.

46.
The self-born one
uses such means to manifest
Buddha-knowledge,
but he shall never say to them,
Ye also
are to become Buddhas.

47.
Why should not
the mighty one,
after having waited
for the right time, speak,
now that he perceives
the right moment is come ?
This is the fit opportunity,
met somehow,
of commencing the exposition
of what really is.

48.
Now the word
of my commandment,
as contained in nine divisions,
has been published according
to the varying degree
of strength of creatures.
Such is the device
I have shown in order
to introduce creatures
to the knowledge
of the giver of boons.

49.
And to those in the world
who have always been pure,
wise, good-minded,
compassionate sons of Buddha
and done their duty
under many kotis of Buddhas
will I make known
amplified Sûtras.

50.
For they are endowed
with such gifts
of mental disposition
and such advantages
of a blameless outward form
that I can announce to them :
in future ye shall become
Buddhas benevolent
and compassionate.

51.
Hearing which,
all of them will be pervaded
with delight at the thought :
We shall become Buddhas
pre-eminent in the world.
And I,
perceiving their conduct,
will again reveal
amplified Sûtras.

52.
And those are
the disciples of the Leader,
who have listened
to my word of command.
One single stanza learnt
or kept in memory suffices,
no doubt of it, to lead
all of them to enlightenment.

53.
There is, indeed,
but one vehicle;
there is no second,
nor a third anywhere
in the world,
apart from the case
of the Purushottamas
using an expedient
to show that there is
a diversity of vehicles.

54.
The Chief of the world
appears in the world
to reveal
the Buddha-knowledge.
He has but one aim,
indeed,
no second;
the Buddhas
do not bring over creatures
by an inferior vehicle.

55.
There where the self-born one
has established himself,
and where the object
of knowledge is,
of whatever form or kind;
where the powers,
the stages of meditation,
the emancipations,
the perfected faculties are;
there the beings
also shall be established.

56.
I should be guilty of envy,
should I,
after reaching
the spotless eminent state
of enlightenment,
establish any one
in the inferior vehicle.
That would not beseem me.

57.
There is no envy
whatever in me;
no jealousy,
no desire, nor passion.
Therefore I am the Buddha,
because the world
follows my teaching.

58.
When,
splendidly marked
with the thirty-two
characteristics,
I am illuminating
this whole world,
and, worshipped
by many hundreds of beings,
I show
the unmistakable stamp
of the nature of the law;

59.
Then, Sâriputra, I think thus:
How will all beings
by the thirty-two
characteristics
mark the self-born Seer,
who of his own accord
sheds his lustre
all over the world?

60.
And while I am thinking
and pondering,
when my wish
has been fulfilled
and my vow accomplished,
I no more reveal
Buddha-knowledge

61.
If, O son of Sâri,
I spoke to the creatures,
'Vivify in your minds
the wish for enlightenment,'
they would in their ignorance
all go astray
and never catch the meaning
of my good words.

62.
And
considering them to be such,
and that they have
not accomplished
their course of duty
in previous existences,
I see how they are attached
and devoted
to sensual pleasures,
infatuated by desire
and blind with delusion.

63.
From lust they run into distress;
they are tormented
in the six states of existence
and people the cemetery
again and again;
they are overwhelmed
with misfortune,
as they possess little virtue.

64.
They are continually
entangled in the thickets
of sectarian theories,
such as, 'It is and it is not;
it is thus and it is not thus.'
In trying to get
a decided opinion
on what is found
in the sixty-two
heretical theories they
come to embrace falsehood
and continue in it.

65.
They are hard to correct,
proud, hypocritical,
crooked, malignant,
ignorant, dull;
hence they do not hear
the good Buddha-call,
not once in kotis of births.

66.
To those, son of Sâri,
I show a device and say:
Put an end to your trouble.
When I perceive creatures
vexed with mishap
I make them see Nirvâna.

67.
And so do I reveal
all those laws
that are ever holy and correct
from the very first.
And the son of Buddha
who has completed his course
shall once be a Gina.

68.
It is but my skilfulness
which prompts me
to manifest three vehicles ;
for there is but one vehicle
and one track ;
there is also
but one instruction
by the leaders.

69.
Remove all doubt
and uncertainty ;
and should there be
any who feel doubts,
let them know that
the Lords of the world
speak the truth ;
this is the only vehicle,
a second there is not.

70.
The former Tathâgatas also,
living in the past
for innumerable Æons,
the many thousands
of Buddhas
who are gone to final rest,
whose number
can never be counted,

71.
Those highest of men
have all of them revealed
most holy laws
by means of illustrations,
reasons, and arguments,
with many hundred
proofs of skilfulness.

72.
And all of them have
manifested but one vehicle
and introduced
but one on earth ;
by one vehicle
have they led to full ripeness
inconceivably many
thousands of kotis of beings.

73.
Yet the Ginas possess
various and manifold means
through which the Tathâgata
reveals to the world,
including the gods,
superior enlightenment,
in consideration
of the inclinations
and dispositions
of the different beings.

74.
And all in the world who are
hearing or have heard the law
from the mouth
of the Tathâgatas, given alms,
followed the moral precepts,
and patiently accomplished
the whole
of their religious duties ;

75.
Who have acquitted
themselves in point of zeal
and meditation, with wisdom
reflected on those laws,
and performed
several meritorious actions,
have all of them
reached enlightenment.

76.
And such beings as were
living patient, subdued,
and disciplined,
under the rule of the Ginas
of those times,
have all of them
reached enlightenment.

77.
Others also,
who paid worship to the relics
of the departed Ginas,
erected many thousands
of Stûpas made of gems,
gold, silver, or crystal,

78.
Or built Stûpas of emerald,
cat's eye, pearls, egregious
lapis lazuli, or sapphire ;
they have all of them
reached enlightenment.

79.
And those who erected Stûpas
from marble, sandal-wood,
or eagle-wood ;
constructed Stûpas
from Deodar or a combination
of different sorts of timber ;

80.
And who in gladness of heart
built for the Ginas
Stûpas of bricks or clay ;
or caused mounds of earth
to be raised in forests
and wildernesses
in dedication to the Ginas ;

81.
The little boys even,
who in playing
erected here and there
heaps of sand
with the intention
of dedicating them
as Stûpas to the Ginas,
they have all of them
reached enlightenment.

82.
Likewise have all
who caused jewel images
to be made and dedicated,
adorned with the thirty-two
characteristic signs,
reached enlightenment.

83.
Others who had images
of Sugatas made of
the seven precious substances,
of copper or brass,
have all of them
reached enlightenment.

84.
Those who ordered
beautiful statues of Sugatas
to be made of lead, iron,
clay, or plaster have &c.

85.
Those who made images of
the Sugatas on painted walls,
with complete limbs
and the hundred holy signs,
whether they drew them
themselves or had them
drawn by others, have &c.

86.
Those even,
whether men or boys,
who during the lesson
or in play,
by way of amusement,
made upon the walls
such images with the nail
or a piece of wood,

87.
Have all of them
reached enlightenment;
they have become
compassionate,
and, by rousing
many Bodhisattvas,
have saved kotis of creatures.

88.
Those who offered
flowers and perfumes
to the relics of the Tathâgatas,
to Stûpas, a mound of earth,
images of clay
or drawn on a wall;

89.
Who caused
musical instruments, drums,
conch trumpets, and noisy
great drums to be played,
and raised the rattle
of tymbals at such places
in order to celebrate
the highest enlightenment;

90.
Who caused sweet lutes,
cymbals, tabors,
small drums, reed-pipes,
flutes of ekonnada
or sugar-cane to be made,
have all of them
reached enlightenment.

91.
Those who
to celebrate the Sugatas
made iron cymbals resound,
or small drums;
who sang a song
sweet and lovely;

92.
They have all of them
reached enlightenment.
By paying
various kinds of worship
to the relics of the Sugatas,
by doing but a little
for the relics, by
making resound were it but
a single musical instrument;

93.
Or by worshipping were it
but with a single flower,
by drawing on a wall
the images of the Sugatas,
by doing worship
were it even
with distracted thoughts,
one shall in course of time
see kotis of Buddhas.

94.
Those who,
when in presence of a Stûpa,
have offered
their reverential salutation,
be it in a complete form

or by merely
joining the hands ; who, were
it but for a single moment,
bent their head or body ;

95.
And who at Stûpas
containing relics
have one single time said :
Homage be to Buddha !
albeit they did it
with distracted thoughts,
all have attained
superior enlightenment.

96.
The creatures who in the days
of those Sugatas,
whether already extinct
or still in existence,
have heard no more
than the name of the law,
have all of them
reached enlightenment.

97.
Many kotis of future Buddhas
beyond imagination
and measure
shall likewise reveal
this device as Ginas
and supreme Lords.

98.
Endless shall be the skilfulness
of these leaders of the world,
by which they shall educate
kotis of beings
to that Buddha-knowledge
which is free
from imperfection.

99.
Never has there been
any being who,
after hearing the law
of those leaders,
shall not become Buddha ;
for this is the fixed vow
of the Tathâgatas :
Let me, by accomplishing
my course of duty,
lead others to enlightenment.

100.
They are to expound
in future days many thousand
kotis of heads of the law ;
in their Tathâgataship
they shall teach the law
by showing the sole
vehicle before-mentioned.

101.
The line of the law forms
an unbroken continuity
and the nature
of its properties
is always manifest.
Knowing this, the Buddhas,
the highest of men,
shall reveal this single vehicle.

102.
They shall reveal
the stability of the law,
its being subjected
to fixed rules,
its unshakeable
perpetuity in the world,
the awaking of the Buddhas
on the elevated terrace
of the earth, their skilfulness.

103.
In all directions of space
are standing Buddhas,
like sand of the Ganges,
honoured by gods and men ;
these also do, for the weal
of all beings in the world,
expound
superior enlightenment.

104.
Those Buddhas
while manifesting skilfulness
display various vehicles
though, at the same time,
indicating
the one single vehicle :
the supreme place
of blessed rest.

105.
Acquainted as they are
with the conduct
of all mortals, with their
peculiar dispositions
and previous actions ;
with due regard to their
strenuousness and vigour,
as well as their inclination,
the Buddhas impart
their lights to them.

106.
By dint of knowledge
the leaders produce
many illustrations,
arguments, and reasons ;
and considering how
the creatures have various
inclinations they
impart various directions.

107.
And myself also,
the leader of the chief Ginas,
am now manifesting,
for the weal of creatures
now living, this Buddha
enlightenment by thousands
of kotis of various directions.

108.
I reveal the law
in its multifariousness
with regard to the inclinations
and dispositions of creatures.
I use different means
to rouse each according
to his own character.
Such is the might
of my knowledge.

109.
I likewise see
the poor wretches,
deficient in wisdom
and conduct,
lapsed into
the mundane whirl
retained in dismal places,
plunged in affliction
incessantly renewed.

110.
Fettered
as they are by desire
like the yak by its tail,
continually blinded
by sensual pleasure,
they do not seek the Buddha,
the mighty one ;
they do not seek the law
that leads to the end of pain.

111.
Staying
in the six states of existence,
they are benumbed
in their senses,
stick unmoved
to the low views,
and suffer pain on pain.
For those I feel
a great compassion.

112.
On the terrace
of enlightenment
I have remained
three weeks in full,
searching and pondering
on such a matter,
steadily looking up
to the tree there standing.

113.
Keeping in view
that king of trees
with an unwavering gaze
I walked round
at its foot thinking : This law
is wonderful and lofty,
whereas creatures are blind
with dulness and ignorance.

114.
Then it was that Brahma
entreated me,
and so did Indra,
the four rulers
of the cardinal points,
Mahesvara, Îsvara,
and the hosts of Maruts
by thousands of kotis.

115.
All stood with joined
hands and respectful,
while myself
was revolving the matter
in my mind and thought :
What shall I do ?
At the very time
that I am uttering syllables,
beings are oppressed
with evils.

116.
In their ignorance
they will not heed the law
I announce,
and in consequence of it
they will incur some penalty.
It would be better were
I never to speak.
May my quiet extinction
take place this very day !

117.
But on remembering
the former Buddhas
and their skilfulness,
I thought :
Nay, I also will manifest
this tripartite
Buddha-enlightenment.

118.
When I was
thus meditating on the law,
the other Buddhas
in all the directions of space
appeared to me
in their own body and raised
their voice, crying 'Amen.

119.
'Amen, Solitary,
first Leader of the world !
now that thou hast come
to unsurpassed knowledge,
and art meditating on
the skilfulness of the leaders
of the world,
thou repeatest their teaching.

120.
'We also, being Buddhas,
will make clear
the highest word,
divided into three parts ;
for men occasionally
have low inclinations,
and might perchance
from ignorance
not believe us,
when we say,
Ye shall become Buddhas.

121.
'Hence we will rouse
many Bodhisattvas
by the display of skilfulness
and the encouraging of
the wish of obtaining fruits.'

122.
And I was delighted
to hear the sweet voice
of the leaders of men ;
in the exultation of my heart
I said to the blessed saints,
'The words of the eminent
sages are not spoken in vain.

123.
'I, too, will act according
to the indications of
the wise leaders of the world ;
having myself been born
in the midst of
the degradation of creatures,
I have known agitation
in this dreadful world.'

124.
When I had come
to that conviction,
O son of Sâri,
I instantly went to Benares,
where I skilfully preached
the law to the five Solitaries,
that law which is
the base of final beatitude.

125.
From that moment the wheel
of my law has been moving,
and the name of Nirvâna
made its appearance
in the world,
as well as the name of Arhat,
of Dharma, and Sangha.

126.
Many years
have I preached and pointed
to the stage of Nirvâna,
the end of wretchedness
and mundane existence.
Thus
I used to speak at all times.

127.
And when I saw, Sâriputra,
the children
of the highest of men
by many thousands of kotis,
numberless,
striving after the supreme,
the highest enlightenment;

128.
And when such as had
heard the law of the Ginas,
owing to the many-sidedness
of their skilfulness,
had approached me
and stood before my face,
all of them with joined hands,
and respectful;

129.
Then I conceived
the idea that the time
had come for me
to announce the excellent law
and to reveal
supreme enlightenment,
for which task
I had been born in the world.

130.
This event to-day
will be hard to be understood
by the ignorant who imagine
they see here a sign,
as they are proud and dull.
But the Bodhisattvas,
they will listen to me.

131.
And I felt free from hesitation
and highly cheered;
putting aside all timidity,
I began speaking
in the assembly
of the sons of Sugata,
and roused them
to enlightenment.

132.
On beholding such worthy
sons of Buddha I said:
Thy doubts
also will be removed,
and these twelve hundred
disciples of mine,
free from imperfections,
will all of them
become Buddhas.

133.
Even as the nature of the law
of the former mighty saints
and the future Ginas is,
so is my law
free from any doubtfulness,
and it is such as I to-day
preach it to thee.

134.
At certain times,
at certain places,
somehow do the leaders
appear in the world,
and after their appearance
will they,
whose view is boundless,
at one time or another
preach a similar law.

135.
It is most difficult to meet
with this superior law,
even in myriads
of kotis of Æons;
very rare are the beings
who will adhere
to the superior law which
they have heard from me.

136.
Just as the blossom of the
glomerous fig-tree is rare,
albeit sometimes,
at some places,
and somehow it is met with,
as something pleasant
to see for everybody,
as a wonder to the world
including the gods;

137.
So wonderful
and far more wonderful
is the law I proclaim.
Any one who, on hearing
a good exposition of it,
shall cheerfully accept it
and recite but one word of it,
will have done honour
to all Buddhas.

138.
Give up all doubt
and uncertainty
in this respect;
I declare that I am the king
of the law Dharmarâga;
I am urging others
to enlightenment, but
I am here without disciples.

139.
Let this mystery
be for thee, Sâriputra,
for all disciples of mine, and
for the eminent Bodhisattvas,
who are to keep this mystery.

140.
For the creatures,
when at the period
of the five depravities,
are vile and bad;
they are blinded
by sensual desires,
the fools,
and never turn their minds
to enlightenment.

141.
Some beings,
having heard this one
and sole vehicle
manifested by the Gina,
will in days to come
swerve from it,
reject the Sûtra,
and go down to hell.

142.
But those beings
who shall be modest and pure,
striving after the supreme
and the highest
enlightenment,
to them shall I unhesitatingly
set forth the endless forms
of this one and sole vehicle.

143.
Such is the mastership
of the leaders ; that is,
their skilfulness.
They have spoken
in many mysteries ;
hence it is difficult
to understand them.

144.
Therefore try to understand
the mystery of the Buddhas,
the holy masters of the world ;
forsake all doubt
and uncertainty :
you shall become Buddhas ;
rejoice !

Chapter III
A Parable

Then the venerable Sâriputra,
pleased, glad,
charmed, cheerful,
thrilling with delight and joy,
stretched his joined hands
towards the Lord, and,
looking up to the Lord
with a steady gaze,
addressed him in this strain :
I am astonished, amazed,
O Lord !
I am in ecstasy
to hear such a call
from the Lord.
For when,
before I had heard of this law
from the Lord,
I saw other Bodhisattvas,
and heard
that the Bodhisattvas
would in future
get the name of Buddhas,
I felt extremely sorry,
extremely vexed
to be deprived
from so grand a sight as
the Tathâgata-knowledge.
And whenever, O Lord,
for my daily recreation
I was visiting the caves
of rocks or mountains,
wood thickets,
lovely gardens, rivers,
and roots of trees,
I always was occupied
with the same
and ever-recurring thought :
'Whereas the entrance
into the fixed points
or elements of the law
is nominally equal,
we have been dismissed
by the Lord
with the inferior vehicle.'
Instantly, however, O Lord,
I felt that it was our own fault,
not the Lord's.
For had we regarded the Lord
at the time of his giving
the allsurpassing
demonstration of the law,
that is,
the exposition of supreme,
perfect enlightenment,
then, O Lord,
we should have
become adepts in those laws.
But because,
without understanding
the mystery of the Lord,
we, at the moment
of the Bodhisattvas
not being assembled,
heard only in a hurry,
caught, meditated, minded,
took to heart the first lessons
pronounced of the law,
therefore, O Lord,
I used to pass day
and night in self-reproach.
But to-day, O Lord,
I have reached complete
extinction ; to-day, O Lord,
I have become calm ;
to-day, O Lord,
I am wholly come to rest ;
to-day, O Lord,
I have reached Arhatship ;
to-day, O Lord,

I am the Lord's eldest son,
born from his law,
sprung into existence
by the law,
made by the law,
inheriting from the law,
accomplished by the law.
My burning has left me,
O Lord, now that I have
heard this wonderful law,
which I had not leant before,
announced by the voice
from the mouth of the Lord.

And on that occasion
the venerable Sâriputra
addressed the Lord
in the following stanzas :

1.
I am astonished,
great Leader,
I am charmed
to hear this voice ;
I feel no doubt any more ;
now am I fully ripe
for the superior vehicle.

2.
Wonderful
is the voice of the Sugatas ;
it dispels the doubt
and pain of living beings ;
my pain also is all gone
now that I,
freed from imperfections,
have heard that voice or, call.

3.
When I was taking
my daily recreation
or was walking
in woody thickets,
when betaking myself
to the roots of trees
or to mountain caves,
I indulged
in no other thought but this :

4.
'O how am I deluded
by vain thoughts !
whereas the faultless laws are,
nominally, equal,
shall I in future
not preach the superior law
in the world ?

5.
'The thirty-two characteristic
signs have failed me,
and the gold colour
of the skin has vanished ;
all the ten powers
and emancipations
have likewise been lost.
O how have I gone
astray at the equal laws !

6.
'The secondary signs
also of the great Seers,
the eighty excellent
specific signs,
and the eighteen
uncommon properties
have failed me.
O how am I deluded !'

7.
And when
I had perceived thee,
so benign
and merciful to the world,
and was lonely walking
to take my daily recreation,
I thought : 'I am excluded
from that inconceivable,
unbounded knowledge !'

8.
Days and nights, O Lord,
I passed always thinking
of the same subject ;
I would ask the Lord whether
I had lost my rank or not.

9.
In such reflections,
O Chief of Ginas,
I constantly passed
my days and nights ;
and on seeing many other
Bodhisattvas praised
by the Leader of the world,

10.
And on hearing
this Buddha-law, I thought :
'To be sure, this is
expounded mysteriously ;
it is an inscrutable, subtle,
and faultless science,
which is announced
by the Ginas
on the terrace
of enlightenment.'

11.
Formerly I was attached
to heretical theories,
being a wandering monk
and in high honour or,
of the same opinions
with the heretics ;
afterwards has the Lord,
regarding my disposition,
taught me Nirvâna,
to detach me
from perverted views.

12.
After having completely
freed myself
from all heretical views
and reached the laws of void,
I conceive that I have
become extinct ; yet this
is not deemed to be extinction.

13.
But when one becomes
Buddha, a superior being,
honoured by men,
gods, goblins, Titans,
and adorned with the
thirty-two characteristic signs,
then one
will be completely extinct.

14.
All those former cares
have now been dispelled,
since I have heard the voice.
Now am I extinct,
as thou announcest
my destination to Nirvâna
before the world
including the gods.

15.
When I first heard
the voice of the Lord,
I had a great terror
lest it might be Mâra,
the evil one,
who on this occasion
had adopted
the disguise of Buddha.

16.
But when the unsurpassed
Buddha-wisdom
had been displayed in
and established
with arguments, reasons,
and illustrations,
by myriads of kotis,
then I lost all doubt
about the law I heard.

17.
And when thou hadst
mentioned to me
the thousands
of kotis of Buddhas,
the past Ginas
who have come to final rest,
and how
they preached this law
by firmly establishing
it through skilfulness ;

18.
How the many
future Buddhas and those
who are now existing,
as knowers of the real truth,
shall expound
or are expounding this law
by hundreds of able devices ;

19.
And when thou
wert mentioning
thine own course
after leaving home,
how the idea
of the wheel of the law
presented itself to thy mind
and how thou decidedst
upon preaching the law ;

20.
Then I was convinced :
This is not Mâra ;
it is the Lord of the world,
who has shown
the true course ;
no Mâras can here abide.
So then my mind
for a moment
was overcome
with perplexity ;

21.
But when the sweet, deep,
and lovely voice of Buddha
gladdened me,
all doubts were scattered,
my perplexity vanished,
and I stood firm in knowledge.

22.
I shall become a Tathâgata,
undoubtedly,
worshipped in the world
including the gods ;
I shall manifest
Buddha-wisdom,
mysteriously rousing
many Bodhisattvas.

After this speech
of the venerable Sâriputra,
the Lord said to him :
I declare to thee,
Sâriputra,
I announce to thee,
in presence of this world
including the gods,
Mâras, and Brahmas,
in presence of this people,
including ascetics
and Brahmans,
that thou, Sâriputra,
hast been by me made ripe
for supreme,
perfect enlightenment,
in presence of twenty
hundred thousand
myriads of kotis of Buddhas,
and that thou, Sâriputra,
hast for a long time followed
my commandments.
Thou, Sâriputra,
art, by the counsel
of the Bodhisattva,
by the decree
of the Bodhisattva,
reborn here under my rule.
Owing to the mighty will
of the Bodhisattva thou,
Sâriputra,
hast no recollection
of thy former vow to observe
the religious course ;
of the counsel
of the Bodhisattva,
the decree of the Bodhisattva.
Thou thinkest that thou
hast reached final rest.
I, wishing to revive
and renew in thee
the knowledge
of thy former vow to observe
the religious course,
will reveal to the disciples
the Dharmaparyâya called
'the Lotus of the True Law,'
this Sûrânta, &c.

Again, Sâriputra,
at a future period,
after innumerable,
inconceivable,
immeasurable Æons,
when thou shalt have learnt
the true law
of hundred thousand
myriads of kotis
of Tathâgatas,
showed devotion
in various ways,
and achieved the present
Bodhisattva-course,
thou shalt become
in the world
a Tathâgata, &c.,
named Padmaprabha,
endowed with science
and conduct, a Sugata,
a knower of the world,
an unsurpassed tamer of men,
a master of gods and men,
a Lord Buddha.

At that time then, Sâriputra,
the Buddha-field of that Lord,
the Tathâgata Padmaprabha,
to be called Viraga,
will be level,
pleasant, delightful,
extremely beautiful to see,
pure, prosperous,

rich, quiet,
abounding with food,
replete
with many races of men;
it will consist of lapis lazuli,
and contain a checker-board
of eight compartments
distinguished by gold threads,
each compartment
having its jewel tree
always and perpetually
filled with blossoms and fruits
of seven precious substances.

Now that Tathâgata
Padmaprabha, &c.,
Sâriputra,
will preach the law
by the instrumentality
of three vehicles.
Further, Sâriputra,
that Tathâgata
will not appear
at the decay of the Æon,
but preach the law
by virtue of a vow.

That Æon, Sâriputra,
will be named
Mahâratnapratimandita
(i.e. ornamented with
magnificent jewels).
Knowest thou, Sâriputra,
why that Æon is named
Mahâratnapratimandita?
The Bodhisattvas
of a Buddha-field, Sâriputra,
are called ratnas,
and at that time
there will be
many Bodhisattvas
in that sphere called Viraga;
innumerable, incalculable,
beyond computation,
abstraction made from
their being computed
by the Tathâgatas.
On that account
is that Æon called
Mahâratnapratimandita.

Now, to proceed,
Sâriputra,
at that period the Bodhisattvas
of that field will in walking
step on jewel lotuses.
And these Bodhisattvas
will not be plying
their work for the first time,
they having accumulated
roots of goodness
and observed
the course of duty
under many hundred
thousand Buddhas;
they are praised
by the Tathâgatas
for their zealous application
to Buddha-knowledge;
are perfectioned
in the rites preparatory
to transcendent knowledge;
accomplished in
the direction of all true laws;
mild, thoughtful.
Generally, Sâriputra,
will that Buddha-region
teem with such Bodhisattvas.

As to the lifetime,
Sâriputra,
of that Tathâgata

Padmaprabha,
it will last twelve
intermediate kalpas,
if we leave out of account
the time of his being
a young prince.
And the lifetime
of the creatures
then living will measure
eight intermediate kalpas.
At the expiration of twelve
intermediate kalpas,
Sâriputra,
the Tathâgata Padmaprabha,
after announcing
the future destiny
of the Bodhisattva
called Dhritiparipûrna
to superior
perfect enlightenment,
is to enter complete Nirvâna.
'This Bodhisattva
Mahâsattva Dhritiparipûrna,
O monks, shall immediately
after me come to supreme,
perfect enlightenment.
He shall become in
the world a Tathâgata named
Padmavrishabhavikrâmin,
an Arhat, &c., endowed with
science and conduct, &c. &c.'

Now the Tathâgata
Padmavrishabhavikrâmin,
Sâriputra,
will have a Buddha-field
of quite the same description.
The true law, Sâriputra,
of that Tathâgata
Padmavrishabhavikrâmin
will, after his extinction,
last thirty-two intermediate
kalpas, and the counterfeit
of his true law will last
as many intermediate kalpas.

And on that occasion
the Lord uttered
the following stanzas :

23.
Thou also, son of Sâri,
shalt in future be a Gina,
a Tathâgata
named Padmaprabha,
of illimited sight ;
thou shalt educate thousands
of kotis of living beings.

24.
After paying honour
to many kotis of Buddhas,
making strenuous efforts
in the course of duty,
and after having produced
in thyself the ten powers,
thou shalt reach supreme,
perfect enlightenment.

25.
Within a period
inconceivable and immense
there shall be an Æon
rich in jewels,
and a sphere named Viraga,
the pure field
of the highest of men ;

26.
And its ground
will consist of lapis lazuli,
and be set off
with gold threads;
it will have
hundreds of jewel trees,
very beautiful, and covered
with blossoms and fruits.

27.
Bodhisattvas of good memory,
able in showing
the course of duty
which they have been taught
under hundreds of Buddhas,
will come to be born
in that field.

28.
And
the afore-mentioned Gina,
then
in his last bodily existence,
shall,
after passing the state
of prince royal,
renounce sensual pleasures,
leave home to become
a wandering ascetic,
and thereafter reach
the supreme and
the highest enlightenment.

29.
The lifetime of that Gina
will be precisely
twelve intermediate kalpas,
and the life of men
will then last
eight intermediate kalpas.

30.
After the extinction
of the Tathâgata
the true law will continue
thirty-two Æons in full,
for the benefit of the world,
including the gods.

31.
When the true law
shall have come to an end,
its counterfeit
will stand for thirty-two
intermediate kalpas.
The dispersed relics
of the holy one
will always be honoured
by men and gods.

32.
Such will be the fate
of that Lord.
Rejoice, O son of Sâri,
for it is thou who shalt
be that most excellent of men,
so unsurpassed.

The four classes
of the audience,
monks, nuns,
lay devotees male and female,
gods, Nâgas,
goblins, Gandharvas,
demons, Garudas,
Kinnaras, great serpents,
men and beings not human,
on hearing the announcement
of the venerable Sâriputra's
destiny to supreme,
perfect enlightenment,
were so pleased,

glad, charmed,
thrilling with delight and joy,
that they covered
the Lord severally
with their own robes,
while Indra the chief of gods,
Brahma Sahâmpati,
besides
hundred thousands of kotis
of other divine beings,
covered him
with heavenly garments
and bestrewed him
with flowers of heaven,
Mandâravas
and great Mandâravas.
High aloft they whirled
celestial clothes and struck
hundred thousands
of celestial musical
instruments and cymbals,
high in the sky;
and after pouring
a great rain of flowers
they uttered these words:
The wheel of the law
has been put in motion
by the Lord,
the first time at Benares
at Rishipatana
in the Deer-park;
to-day has the Lord
again put in motion
the supreme wheel of the law.

And on that occasion
those divine beings uttered
the following stanzas:

33.
The wheel of the law
was put in motion by thee,
O thou that art unrivalled
in the world, at Benares,
O great hero! that wheel
which is the rotation
of the rise and decay
of all aggregates.

34.
There it was put in motion
for the first time; now,
a second time, is it turned here,
O Lord. Today, O Master,
thou hast preached this law,
which is hard
to be received with faith.

35.
Many laws have we heard
near the Lord of the world,
but never before did we hear
a law like this.

36.
We receive with gratitude,
O great hero,
the mysterious speech
of the great Sages,
such as this prediction
regarding the self-possessed
Ârya Sâriputra.

37.
May we also become such
incomparable Buddhas
in the world,
who by mysterious speech
announce supreme
Buddha-enlightenment.

38.
May we also,
by the good we have done
in this world and in the next,
and by our having
propitiated the Buddha,
be allowed to make
a vow for Buddhaship.

Thereupon
the venerable Sâriputra
thus spoke to the Lord :
My doubt is gone, O Lord,
my uncertainty is at an end
on hearing from the mouth
of the Lord my destiny
to supreme enlightenment.
But these twelve hundred
self-controlled disciples,
O Lord,
who have been placed by thee
on the stage of Saikshas,
have been thus admonished
and instructed :
'My preaching of the law,
O monks, comes to this,
that deliverance from birth,
decrepitude, disease,
and death is inseparably
connected with Nirvâna ;'
and
these two thousand monks,
O Lord, thy disciples,
both those who are still
under training and adepts,
who all of them are free from
false views about the soul,
false views about existence,
false views about cessation
of existence, free, in short,
from all false views,
who are fancying themselves
to have reached
the stage of Nirvâna,
these have fallen
into uncertainty
by hearing from the mouth
of the Lord this law which
they had not heard before.
Therefore, O Lord,
please speak to these monks,
to dispel their uneasiness,
so that the four classes
of the audience,
O Lord,
may be relieved from
their doubt and perplexity.

On this speech
of the venerable Sâriputra
the Lord
said to him the following :
Have I not told thee before,
Sâriputra,
that the Tathâgata, &c.,
preaches the law
by able devices,
varying directions
and indications,
fundamental ideas,
interpretations,
with due regard
to the different dispositions
and inclinations of creatures
whose temperaments
are so various ?
All his preachings of the law
have no other end
but supreme
and perfect enlightenment,
for which he is rousing beings
to the Bodhisattva-course.

But, Sâriputra,
to elucidate this matter
more at large,
I will tell thee a parable,
for men
of good understanding
will generally readily enough
catch the meaning
of what is taught
under the shape of a parable.

Let us suppose
the following case, Sâriputra.
In a certain village, town,
borough, province, kingdom,
or capital, there was
a certain housekeeper,
old, aged, decrepit,
very advanced in years,
rich, wealthy, opulent ;
he had a great house,
high, spacious,
built a long time ago and old,
inhabited by some two,
three, four,
or five hundred living beings.
The house had but one door,
and a thatch ;
its terraces were tottering,
the bases of its pillars rotten,
the coverings and plaster
of the walls loose.
On a sudden the whole house
was from every side
put in conflagration
by a mass of fire.
Let us suppose that the man
had many little boys, say five,
or ten, or even twenty,
and that he himself
had come out of the house.

Now, Sâriputra,
that man, on seeing the house
from every side
wrapt in a blaze
by a great mass of fire,
got afraid, frightened,
anxious in his mind,
and made
the following reflection :
I myself am able to come out
from the burning house
through the door,
quickly and safely,
without being touched
or scorched
by that great mass of fire ;
but my children,
those young boys, are
staying in the burning house,
playing, amusing,
and diverting themselves
with all sorts of sports.
They do not perceive,
nor know, nor understand,
nor mind
that the house is on fire,
and do not get afraid.
Though scorched
by that great mass of fire,
and affected
with such a mass of pain,
they do not mind the pain,
nor do they conceive
the idea of escaping.

The man, Sâriputra,
is strong, has powerful arms,
and so he makes
this reflection : I am strong,
and have powerful arms ;

why,
let me gather all my little boys
and take them to my breast
to effect their escape
from the house.
A second reflection
then presented itself
to his mind : This house
has but one opening ;
the door is shut ;
and those boys,
fickle, unsteady,
and childlike as they are,
will, it is to be feared,
run hither and thither,
and come to grief and disaster
in this mass of fire.
Therefore I will warn them.
So resolved,
he calls to the boys :
Come, my children ;
the house is burning
with a mass of fire ;
come, lest ye be burnt
in that mass of fire,
and come to grief and disaster.
But the ignorant boys
do not heed the words of him
who is their well-wisher ;
they are not afraid,
not alarmed,
and feel no misgiving ;
they do not care, nor fly,
nor even know
nor understand the purport
of the word 'burning ;'
on the contrary,
they run hither and thither,
walk about, and repeatedly
look at their father ; all,
because they are so ignorant.

Then the man
is going to reflect thus :
The house is burning,
is blazing by a mass of fire.
It is to be feared that myself
as well as my children
will come to grief and disaster.
Let me therefore
by some skilful means
get the boys out of the house.
The man knows
the disposition of the boys,
and has a clear perception
of their inclinations.
Now these boys
happen to have
many and manifold toys
to play with,
pretty, nice, pleasant, dear,
amusing, and precious.
The man, knowing
the disposition of the boys,
says to them :
My children, your toys,
which are so pretty,
precious, and admirable,
which you are so loth to miss,
which are so various
and multifarious,
such as bullock-carts,
goat-carts, deer-carts,
which are so pretty, nice,
dear, and precious to you,
have all been put by me
outside the house-door
for you to play with.
Come, run out,
leave the house ;
to each of you
I shall give what he wants.

Come soon ; come out
for the sake of these toys.
And the boys, on hearing
the names mentioned
of such playthings
as they like and desire,
so agreeable to their taste,
so pretty, dear,
and delightful,
quickly rush out
from the burning house,
with eager effort
and great alacrity,
one having no time
to wait for the other,
and pushing each other on
with the cry of
'Who shall arrive first,
the very first ?'

The man,
seeing that his children
have safely
and happily escaped,
and knowing that they are
free from danger,
goes and sits down
in the open air
on the square of the village,
his heart filled
with joy and delight,
released from trouble
and hindrance, quite at ease.
The boys go up to the place
where their father is sitting,
and say : 'Father, give us
those toys to play with,
those bullock-carts,
goat-carts, and deer-carts.'
Then, Sâriputra,
the man gives to his sons,
who run swift as the wind,
bullock-carts only, made
of seven precious substances,
provided with benches,
hung with a multitude
of small bells, lofty,
adorned with rare
and wonderful jewels,
embellished
with jewel wreaths,
decorated
with garlands of flowers,
carpeted
with cotton mattresses
and woollen coverlets,
covered
with white cloth and silk,
having on both sides
rosy cushions,
yoked with white,
very fair and fleet bullocks,
led by a multitude of men.
To each of his children
he gives several bullockcarts
of one appearance
and one kind,
provided with flags,
and swift as the wind.
That man does so,
Sâriputra,
because being rich, wealthy,
and in possession of many
treasures and granaries,
he rightly thinks :
Why should I give these boys
inferior carts,
all these boys
being my own children,
dear and precious ?
I have got such great vehicles,
and ought to treat

all the boys equally
and without partiality.
As I own many treasures
and granaries,
I could give
such great vehicles
to all beings,
how much more then
to my own children.
Meanwhile
the boys are mounting
the vehicles with feelings
of astonishment and wonder.
Now, Sâriputra,
what is thy opinion?
Has that man
made himself guilty
of a falsehood
by first holding out
to his children
the prospect of three vehicles
and afterwards
giving to each of them
the greatest vehicles only,
the most magnificent vehicles?

Sâriputra answered:
By no means, Lord;
by no means, Sugata.
That is not sufficient,
O Lord,
to qualify the man
as a speaker of falsehood,
since
it only was a skilful device
to persuade his children
to go out
of the burning house
and save their lives.
Nay, besides
recovering their very body,
O Lord,
they have received
all those toys.
If that man, O Lord,
had given no single cart,
even then
he would not have been
a speaker of falsehood,
for he had previously
been meditating
on saving the little boys
from a great mass of pain
by some able device.
Even in this case, O Lord,
the man would not have
been guilty of falsehood,
and far less now that he,
considering his having
plenty of treasures
and prompted
by no other motive
but the love of his children,
gives to all, to coax them,
vehicles of one kind,
and those
the greatest vehicles.
That man, Lord,
is not guilty of falsehood.

The venerable Sâriputra
having thus spoken,
the Lord said to him:
Very well, very well,
Sâriputra, quite so;
it is even as thou sayest.
So, too, Sâriputra,
the Tathâgata, &c.,
is free from all dangers,
wholly exempt from all
misfortune, despondency,
calamity, pain, grief,

the thick enveloping
dark mists of ignorance.
He, the Tathâgata, endowed
with Buddha-knowledge,
forces, absence of hesitation,
uncommon properties, and
mighty by magical power,
is the father of the world,
who has reached
the highest perfection
in the knowledge
of skilful means,
who is most merciful,
long-suffering, benevolent,
compassionate.
He appears
in this triple world,
which is like a house
the roof and shelter
whereof are decayed,
a house burning
by a mass of misery,
in order
to deliver from affection,
hatred, and delusion
the beings subject to birth,
old age, disease, death,
grief, wailing, pain,
melancholy, despondency,
the dark enveloping mists
of ignorance,
in order to rouse them
to supreme
and perfect enlightenment.
Once born,
he sees how
the creatures are burnt,
tormented, vexed,
distressed by birth,
old age, disease, death, grief,
wailing, pain, melancholy,
despondency;
how for the sake
of enjoyments,
and prompted
by sensual desires,
they severally suffer
various pains.
In consequence
both of what in this world
they are seeking
and what they have acquired,
they will in a future state
suffer various pains, in hell,
in the brute creation,
in the realm of Yama;
suffer such pains as poverty
in the world of gods or men,
union with hateful persons
or things, and separation
from the beloved ones.
And whilst
incessantly whirling
in that mass of evils
they are sporting, playing,
diverting themselves;
they do not fear, nor dread,
nor are they
seized with terror;
they do not know, nor mind;
they are not startled,
do not try to escape,
but are enjoying themselves
in that triple world
which is like unto
a burning house,
and run hither and thither.
Though overwhelmed
by that mass of evil,
they do not conceive the idea
that they must beware of it.

Under such circumstances,
Sâriputra,
the Tathâgata reflects thus :
Verily,
I am the father
of these beings ;
I must save them
from this mass of evil,
and bestow on them
the immense,
inconceivable bliss
of Buddha-knowledge,
wherewith they shall sport,
play, and divert themselves,
wherein they shall
find their rest.

Then, Sâriputra,
the Tathâgata reflects thus :
If, in the conviction
of my possessing
the power of knowledge
and magical faculties,
I manifest to these beings
the knowledue, forces,
and absence of hesitation
of the Tathâgata,
without availing myself
of some device,
these beings will not escape.
For they are attached
to the pleasures
of the five senses,
to worldly pleasures ;
they will not be freed
from birth, old age,
disease, death,
grief, wailing, pain,
melancholy, despondency,
by which they are burnt,
tormented, vexed, distressed.

Unless they are forced
to leave the triple world
which is like a house
the shelter and roof
whereof is in a blaze,
how are they to get acquainted
with Buddha-knowledge ?

Now, Sâriputra,
even as that man
with powerful arms,
without using
the strength of his arms,
attracts his children
out of the burning
house by an able device,
and afterwards gives them
magnificent, great carts,
so, Sâriputra,
the Tathâgata,
the Arhat, &c.,
possessed of knowledge
and freedom
from all hesitation,
without using them,
in order to attract
the creatures out
of the triple world
which is like a burning house
with decayed roof and shelter,
shows,
by his knowledge
of able devices,
three vehicles,
namely the vehicle
of the disciples,
the vehicle
of the Pratyekabuddhas,
and the vehicle
of the Bodhisattvas.
By means

of these three vehicles
he attracts the creatures
and speaks to them thus :
Do not delight
in this triple world,
which is like a burning house,
in these miserable forms,
sounds, odours,
flavours, and contacts.
For in delighting
in this triple world
ye are burnt, heated,
inflamed with the thirst
inseparable from the
pleasures of the five senses.
Fly from this triple world ;
betake yourselves
to the three vehicles :
the vehicle of the disciples,
the vehicle
of the Pratyekabuddhas,
the vehicle
of the Bodhisattvas.
I give you my pledge for it,
that I shall give you
these three vehicles ;
make an effort to run out
of this triple world.
And to attract them I say :
These vehicles are grand,
praised by the Âryas,
and provided
with most pleasant things ;
with such you are to sport,
play, and divert yourselves
in a noble manner.
Ye will feel the great delight
of the faculties, powers,
constituents of Bodhi,
meditations,
the eight degrees
of emancipation,
self-concentration,
and the results
of self-concentration,
and ye will become
greatly happy and cheerful.

Now, Sâriputra,
the beings
who have become wise
have faith in the Tathâgata,
the father of the world,
and consequently
apply themselves
to his commandments.
Amongst them
there are some who,
wishing to follow the dictate
of an authoritative voice,
apply themselves
to the commandment
of the Tathâgata
to acquire the knowledge
of the four great truths,
for the sake of
their own complete Nirvâna.
These one may say
to be those who,
coveting the vehicle
of the disciples,
fly from the triple world,
just as some of the boys will
fly from that burning house,
prompted by a desire
of getting a cart
yoked with deer.
Other beings desirous
of the science
without a master,
of self-restraint
and tranquillity,

apply themselves
to the commandment
of the Tathâgata
to learn to understand
causes and effects,
for the sake of
their own complete Nirvâna.
These one may say to be
those who,
coveting the vehicle
of the Pratyekabuddhas,
fly from the triple world,
just as some of the boys
fly from the burning house,
prompted by the desire
of getting a cart
yoked with goats.
Others again desirous
of the knowledge
of the all-knowing,
the knowledge of Buddha,
the knowledge
of the self-born one,
the science without a master,
apply themselves
to the commandment
of the Tathâgata
to learn to understand
the knowledge, powers,
and freedom from hesitation
of the Tathâgata,
for the sake
of the common weal
and happiness,
out of compassion
to the world,
for the benefit,
weal, and happiness
of the world at large,
both gods and men,
for the sake
of the complete Nirvâna
of all beings.
These one may say
to be those who,
coveting the great vehicle,
fly from the triple world.
Therefore they are called
Bodhisattvas Mahâsattvas.
They may be likened
to those among the boys
who have fled
from the burning house
prompted by the desire
of getting a cart
yoked with bullocks.

In the same manner,
Sâriputra, as that man,
on seeing his children
escaped
from the burning house
and knowing them safely
and happily rescued
and out of danger,
in the consciousness
of his great wealth,
gives the boys
one single grand cart;
so, too, Sâriputra,
the Tathâgata, the Arhat, &c.,
on seeing many kotis of beings
recovered from
the triple world,
released from sorrow, fear,
terror, and calamity,
having escaped owing
to the command
of the Tathâgata,
delivered from all fears,
calamities, and difficulties,
and having reached the bliss

of Nirvâna, so, too, Sâriputra,
the Tathâgata, the Arhat, &c.,
considering that
he possesses great wealth
of knowledge, power,
and absence of hesitation,
and that all beings
are his children,
leads them by no other vehicle
but the Buddha-vehicle
to full development.
But he does not teach
a particular Nirvâna
for each being ;
he causes all beings
to reach complete Nirvâna
by means
of the complete Nirvâna
of the Tathâgata.
And those beings, Sâriputra,
who are delivered
from the triple world,
to them the Tathâgata
gives as toys
to amuse themselves
with the lofty pleasures
of the Âryas,
the pleasures of meditation,
emancipation,
self-concentration,
and its results ;
toys all of the same kind.
Even as that man, Sâriputra,
cannot be said
to have told a falsehood
for having held out
to those boys
the prospect of three vehicles
and given to all of them
but one great vehicle,
a magnificent vehicle made
of seven precious substances,
decorated
with all sorts of ornaments,
a vehicle of one kind,
the most egregious of all, so,
too, Sâriputra, the Tathâgata,
the Arhat, &c.,
tells no falsehood
when by an able device
he first holds forth
three vehicles and afterwards
leads all to complete Nirvâna
by the one great vehicle.
For the Tathâgata, Sâriputra,
who is rich in treasures
and storehouses
of abundant knowledge,
powers,
and absence of hesitation,
is able to teach all beings
the law which is connected
with the knowledge
of the all-knowing.
In this way, Sâriputra,
one has to understand
how the Tathâgata
by an able device
and direction
shows but one vehicle,
the great vehicle.

And on that occasion
the Lord uttered
the following stanzas :

39.
A man has an old house,
large, but very infirm ;
its terraces are decaying
and the columns rotten
at their bases.

40.
The windows and balconies
are partly ruined,
the wall
as well as its coverings
and plaster decaying;
the coping
shows rents from age;
the thatch is everywhere
pierced with holes.

41.
It is inhabited by no less
than five hundred beings;
containing many cells
and closets filled with
excrements and disgusting.

42.
Its roof-rafters
are wholly ruined;
the walls and partitions
crumbling away;
kotis of vultures nestle in it,
as well as doves, owls,
and other birds.

43.
There are in every corner
dreadful snakes,
most venomous and horrible;
scorpions
and mice of all sorts;
it is the abode
of very wicked creatures
of every description.

44.
Further, one may meet in it
here and there
beings not belonging
to the human race.
It is defiled
with excrement and urine,
and teeming with worms,
insects, and fire-flies;
it resounds from the
howling of dogs and jackals.

45.
In it are horrible hyenas
that are wont
to devour human carcasses;
many dogs and jackals
greedily seeking
the matter of corpses.

46.
Those animals weak
from perpetual hunger
go about in several places
to feed upon their prey,
and quarrelling
fill the spot with their cries.
Such
is that most horrible house.

47.
There are also
very malign goblins,
who violate human corpses;
in several spots
there are centipedes,
huge snakes, and vipers.

48.
Those animals creep
into all corners,
where they make nests
to deposit their brood,
which is often devoured
by the goblins.

49.
And when those cruel-minded
goblins are satiated
with feeding upon
the flesh of other creatures,
so that their bodies are big,
then they commence sharply
fighting on the spot.

50.
In the wasted retreats
are dreadful, malign urchins,
some of them
measuring one span,
others one cubit or two cubits,
all nimble
in their movements.

51.
They are in the habit
of seizing dogs by the feet,
throwing them
upside down upon the floor,
pinching their necks
and using them ill.

52.
There also live
yelling ghosts naked,
black, wan, tall, and high,
who,
hungry and in quest of food,
are here and there
emitting cries of distress.

53.
Some have a mouth
like a needle,
others have a face like a cow's;
they are of the size
of men or dogs,
go with entangled hair,
and utter plaintive cries
from want of food.

54.
Those goblins, ghosts,
imps, like vultures,
are always looking out
through the windows
and loopholes,
in all directions
in search of food.

55.
Such is that dreadful house,
spacious and high,
but very infirm,
full of holes,
frail and dreary.
Let us suppose
that it is the property
of a certain man,

56.
And that while
he is out of doors
the house is reached
by a conflagration,
so that on a sudden
it is wrapt
in a blazing mass of fire
on every side.

57.
The beams and rafters
consumed by the fire,
the columns and partitions
in flame are crackling
most dreadfully,
whilst goblins
and ghosts are yelling.

58.
Vultures are driven out
by hundreds ;
urchins withdraw
with parched faces ;
hundreds of mischievous
beasts of prey run,
scorched,
on every side,
crying and shouting.

59.
Many poor devils move about,
burnt by the fire ;
while burning
they tear one another
with the teeth,
and bespatter
each other with their blood.

60.
Hyenas also perish there,
in the act
of eating one another.
The excrements burn,
and a loathsome stench
spreads in all directions.

61.
The centipedes,
trying to fly,
are devoured by the urchins.
The ghosts, with burning hair,
hover about, equally vexed
with hunger and heat.

62.
In such a state
is that awful house,
where thousands of flames
are breaking out on every side.

But the man
who is the master
of the house
looks on from without.

63.
And he hears
his own children,
whose minds are engaged
in playing with their toys,
in their fondness of which
they amuse themselves,
as fools do in their ignorance.

64.
And as he hears them
he quickly steps in
to save his children,
lest his ignorant children
might perish in the flames.

65.
He tells them
the defect of the house,
and says : This,
young man of good family,
is a miserable house,
a dreadful one ;
the various creatures in it,
and this fire to boot,
form a series of evils.

66.
In it are snakes,
mischievous goblins, urchins,
and ghosts in great number ;
hyenas,
troops of dogs and jackals,
as well as vultures,
seeking their prey.

67.
Such beings live in this house,
which, apart from the fire,
is extremely dreadful,
and miserable enough;
and now comes to it
this fire blazing on all sides.

68.
The foolish boys, however,
though admonished,
do not mind
their father's words,
deluded as they are
by their toys; they
do not even understand him.

69.
Then the man thinks:
I am now in anxiety
on account of my children.
What is the use
of my having sons
if I lose them? No, they
shall not perish by this fire.

70.
Instantly a device
occurred to his mind:
These young
and ignorant children
are fond of toys,
and have none just now
to play with.
Oh, they are so foolish!

71.
He then says to them:
Listen, my sons,
I have carts of different sorts,
yoked with deer, goats,
and excellent bullocks,
lofty, great,
and completely furnished.

72.
They are outside the house;
run out,
do with them what you like;
for your sake have I
caused them to be made.
Run out all together,
and rejoice to have them.

73.
All the boys,
on hearing of such carts,
exert themselves,
immediately rush out hastily,
and reach, free from harm,
the open air.

74.
On seeing that
the children have come out,
the man betakes himself
to the square
in the centre of the village,
and there from the throne
he is sitting on he says:
Good people,
now I feel at ease.

75.
These poor sons of mine,
whom I have recovered
with difficulty,
my own dear
twenty young children,
were in a dreadful,
wretched, horrible house,
full of many animals.

76.
As it was burning and wrapt
in thousands of flames, they
were amusing themselves
in it with playing, but now
I have rescued them all.
Therefore
I now feel most happy.

77.
The children,
seeing their father happy,
approached him, and said :
Dear father, give us,
as you have promised,
those nice vehicles
of three kinds ;

78.
And make true
all that you promised us
in the house when saying,
'I will give you
three sorts of vehicles.'
Do give them ;
it is now the right time.

79.
Now the man
as we have supposed
had a mighty treasure of gold,
silver, precious stones,
and pearls ;
he possessed bullion,
numerous slaves, domestics,
and vehicles of various kinds ;

80.
Carts
made of precious substances,
yoked with bullocks,
most excellent, with benches
and a row of tinkling bells,
decorated
with umbrellas and flags,
and adorned with
a network of gems and pearls.

81.
They are
embellished with gold,
and artificial wreaths
hanging down here and there ;
covered all around
with excellent cloth
and fine white muslin.

82.
Those carts are moreover
furnished with
choice mattresses of fine silk,
serving for cushions, and
covered with choice carpets
showing the images
of cranes and swans,
and worth thousands of kotis.

83.
The carts are yoked
with white bullocks,
well fed, strong,
of great size, very fine,
who are tended
by numerous persons.

84.
Such excellent carts
that man gives to all his sons,
who,
overjoyed and charmed,
go and play with them
in all directions.

85.
In the same manner,
Sâriputra,
I, the great Seer,
am the protector
and father of all beings,
and all creatures who,
childlike, are captivated
by the pleasures
of the triple world,
are my sons.

86.
This triple world
is as dreadful as that house,
overwhelmed
with a number of evils,
entirely inflamed
on every side
by a hundred different sorts
of birth, old age, and disease.

87.
But I, who am detached from
the triple world and serene,
am living in absolute
retirement in a wood. This
triple world is my domain,
and those who in it are
suffering from burning heat
are my sons.

88.
And I told its evils
because I had resolved
upon saving them, but
they would not listen to me,
because
all of them were ignorant
and their hearts attached
to the pleasures of sense.

89.
Then I employ an able device,
and tell them
of the three vehicles,
so showing them
the means of evading
the numerous evils
of the triple world
which are known to me.

90.
And those of my sons
who adhere to me,
who are mighty in the six
transcendent faculties
and the triple science,
the Pratyekabuddhas,
as well as the Bodhisattvas
unable to slide back;

91.
And those others
who equally are my sons,
to them
I just now am showing,
by means of this
excellent allegory,
the single Buddha-vehicle.
Receive it;
ye shall all become Ginas.

92.
It is most excellent and sweet,
the most exalted in the world,
that knowledge
of the Buddhas,
the most high among men;
it is something
sublime and adorable.

93.
The powers, meditations,
degrees of emancipation
and self-concentration
by many hundreds of kotis,
that is the exalted vehicle
in which the sons of Buddha
take a never-ending delight.

94.
In playing with it they pass
days and nights, fortnights,
months, seasons, years,
intermediate kalpas, nay,
thousands of kotis of kalpas.

95.
This
is the lofty vehicle of jewels
which sundry Bodhisattvas
and the disciples
listening to the Sugata
employ to go and sport on
the terrace of enlightenment.

96.
Know then, Tishya,
that there is no second
vehicle in this world
anywhere to be found,
in whatever direction
thou shalt search,
apart from the device shown
by the most high among men.

97.
Ye are my children,
I am your father,
who has removed
you from pain,
from the triple world,
from fear and danger,
when you had been burning
for many kotis of Æons.

98.
And I am teaching
blessed rest Nirvâna,
in so far as,
though you have
not yet reached final rest,
you are delivered
from the trouble
of the mundane whirl,
provided you seek
the vehicle of the Buddhas.

99.
Any Bodhisattvas here present
obey my Buddha-rules.
Such is
the skilfulness of the Gina
that he disciplines
many Bodhisattvas.

100.
When the creatures
in this world delight in low
and contemptible pleasures,
then the Chief of the world,
who always speaks the truth,
indicates pain
as the first great truth.

101.
And to those
who are ignorant
and too simple-minded
to discover the root
of that pain
I lay open the way :
'Awaking

of full consciousness,
strong desire
is the origin of pain.'

102.
Always try, unattached,
to suppress desire.
This is my third truth,
that of suppression.
It is an infallible
means of deliverance ;
for by practising this method
one shall
become emancipated.

103.
And from what
are they emancipated,
Sâriputra ?
They are emancipated
from chimeras.
Yet they are not wholly freed ;
the Chief declares
that they have not yet
reached final
and complete rest in this world.

104.
Why is it that I do not
pronounce one to be delivered
before one's having
reached the highest,
supreme enlightenment ?
Because such is my will ;
I am the ruler of the law,
who is born in this world
to lead to beatitude.

105.
This, Sâriputra,
is the closing word of my law
which now at the last time
I pronounce
for the weal of the world
including the gods.
Preach it in all quarters.

106.
And if some one
speaks to you these words,
'I joyfully accept,'
and with signs
of utmost reverence
receives this Sûtra,
thou mayst consider that man
to be unable to slide back.

107.
To believe in this Sûtra
one must have seen
former Tathâgatas,
paid honour to them, and
heard a law similar to this.

108.
To believe in
my supreme word
one must have seen me ;
thou and the assembly
of monks have seen
all these Bodhisattvas.

109.
This Sûtra
is apt to puzzle the ignorant,
and I do not pronounce it
before having penetrated
to superior knowledge.
Indeed, it is not within
the range of the disciples,
nor do the
Pratyekabuddhas come to it.

110.
But thou, Sâriputra,
hast good will, not to speak
of my other disciples here.
They will walk in my faith,
though each cannot have
his individual knowledge.

111.
But do not speak of this matter
to haughty persons,
nor to conceited ones,
nor to Yogins
who are not self-restrained ;
for the fools,
always revelling
in sensual pleasures,
might in their blindness
scorn the law manifested.

112.
Now hear the dire results
when one scorns
my skilfulness
and the Buddha-rules
for ever fixed in the world ;
when one, with sullen brow,
scorns the vehicle.

113.
Hear the destiny
of those who have scorned
such a Sûtra like this,
whether during my lifetime
or after my Nirvâna,
or who
have wronged the monks.

114.
After having disappeared
from amongst men,
they shall dwell
in the lowest hell Avîki
during a whole kalpa,
and thereafter they shall fall
lower and lower, the fools,
passing through
repeated births
for many intermediate kalpas.

115.
And when they have
vanished from amongst
the inhabitants of hell,
they shall further descend
to the condition of brutes,
be even as dogs and jackals,
and become a sport to others.

116.
Under such circumstances
they shall grow blackish
of colour, spotted,
covered with sores, itchy ;
moreover, they shall be
hairless and feeble,
all those who have an aversion
to my supreme enlightenment.

117.
They are ever despised
amongst animals ;
hit by clods
or weapons they yell ;
everywhere they are
threatened with sticks,
and their bodies
are emaciated
from hunger and thirst.

118.
Sometimes they become
camels or asses,
carrying loads,
and are beaten
with whips and sticks ;
they are constantly occupied
with thoughts of eating,
the fools who have
scorned the Buddha-rule.

119.
At other times
they become ugly jackals,
half blind and crippled ;
the helpless creatures
are vexed by the village boys,
who throw clods
and weapons at them.

120.
Again shooting off
from that place,
those fools become animals
with bodies
of five hundred yoganas,
whirling round,
dull and lazy.

121.
They have no feet,
and creep on the belly ;
to be devoured
by many kotis of animals
is the dreadful punishment
they have to suffer
for having scorned
a Sûtra like this.

122.
And whenever they assume
a human shape,
they are born crippled,
maimed, crooked, one-eyed,
blind, dull, and low, they
having no faith in my Sûtra.

123.
Nobody keeps their side ;
a putrid smell is continually
issuing from their mouths ;
an evil spirit has entered
the body of those
who do not believe in
this supreme enlightenment.

124.
Needy,
obliged to do menial labour,
always in another's service,
feeble,
and subject to many diseases
they go about in the world,
unprotected.

125.
The man whom
they happen to serve is
unwilling to give them much,
and what he gives is soon lost.
Such is the fruit of sinfulness.

126.
Even the
best-prepared medicaments,
administered to them
by able men, do,
under those circumstances,
but increase their illness,
and the disease has no end.

127.
Some commit thefts, affrays,
assaults, or acts of hostility,
whereas others
commit robberies of goods;
all this befalls the sinner.

128.
Never does he behold
the Lord of the world,
the King of kings
ruling the earth,
for he is doomed
to live at a wrong time, he
who scorns my Buddha-rule.

129.
Nor does that foolish
person listen to the law;
he is deaf and senseless;
he never finds rest,
because he has scorned
this enlightenment.

130.
During many hundred
thousand myriads of kotis
of Æons equal
to the sand of the Ganges
he shall be dull and defective;
that is the evil result
from scorning this Sûtra.

131.
Hell is his garden
or monastery, a place
of misfortune his abode;
he is continually living
amongst asses, hogs,
jackals, and dogs.

132.
And when he has assumed
a human shape
he is to be blind,
deaf, and stupid,
the servant of another,
and always poor.

133.
Diseases, myriads of kotis
of wounds on the body,
scab, itch, scurf, leprosy,
blotch, a foul smell are,
in that condition,
his covering and apparel.

134.
His sight is dim
to distinguish the real.
His anger
appears mighty in him,
and his passion
is most violent;
he always delights
in animal wombs.

135.
Were I to go on,
Sâriputra,
for a whole Æon,
enumerating the evils of him
who shall scorn my Sûtra,
I should not come to an end.

136.
And
since I am fully aware of it,
I command thee, Sâriputra,
that thou shalt not expound
a Sûtra like this
before foolish people.

137.
But those who are sensible,
instructed, thoughtful,
clever, and learned,
who strive after the highest
supreme enlightenment,
to them expound
its real meaning.

138.
Those who have seen
many kotis of Buddhas,
planted immeasurably
many roots of goodness,
and undertaken
a strong vow,
to them expound
its real meaning.

139.
Those who,
full of energy
and ever kindhearted,
have a long time
been developing
the feeling of kindness,
have given up body and life,
in their presence
thou mayst preach this Sûtra.

140.
Those who show
mutual love and respect,
keep no intercourse
with ignorant people,
and are content to live
in mountain caverns,
to them expound
this hallowed Sûtra.

141.
If thou see sons of Buddha
who attach themselves
to virtuous friends
and avoid bad friends,
then reveal to them this Sûtra.

142.
Those sons of Buddha
who have not broken
the moral vows,
are pure like gems and jewels,
and devoted to the study
of the great Sûtras,
before those thou mayst
propound this Sûtra.

143.
Those who are not irascible,
ever sincere,
full of compassion
for all living beings,
and respectful
towards the Sugata,
before those thou mayst
propound this Sûtra.

144.
To one who
in the congregation,
without any hesitation
and distraction of mind,
speaks to expound the law,
with many myriads
of kotis of illustrations,
thou mayst
manifest this Sûtra.

145.
And he who, desirous
of acquiring all-knowingness,
respectfully lifts
his joined hands to his head,
or who seeks in all directions
to find some monk
of sacred eloquence ;

146.
And he who keeps in memory
the great Sûtras,
while he never shows
any liking for other books,
nor even knows
a single stanza
from another work ;
to all of them
thou mayst expound
this sublime Sûtra.

147.
He who seeks such
an excellent Sûtra as this,
and after obtaining it
devoutly worships it,
is like the man
who wears a relic
of the Tathâgata
he has eagerly sought for.

148.
Never mind other Sûtras
nor other books in which
a profane philosophy
is taught ;
such books are
fit for the foolish ;
avoid them
and preach this Sûtra.

149.
During a full Æon,
Sâriputra,
I could speak
of thousands of kotis
of connected points,
but this suffices ;
thou mayst reveal this Sûtra
to all who are
striving after the highest
supreme enlightenment.

Chapter IV
Disposition

As the venerable Subhûti,
the venerable
Mahâ-Kâtyâyana,
the venerable Mahâ-Kâsyapa,
and the venerable
Mahâ-Maudgalyâyana
heard this law
unheard of before,
and as from the mouth
of the Lord they heard
the future destiny of Sâriputra
to superior perfect
enlightenment,
they were struck
with wonder,
amazement,
and rapture.
They instantly
rose from their seats
and went up
to the place
where the Lord was sitting ;
after throwing their cloak
over one shoulder,
fixing the right knee
on the ground
and lifting up
their joined hands
before the Lord,
looking up to him,
their bodies bent,
bent down and inclined,
they addressed the Lord
in this strain :

Lord, we are old, aged,
advanced in years ;
honoured as seniors
in this assemblage of monks.
Worn out by old age
we fancy that we
have attained Nirvâna ;
we make no efforts,
O Lord,
for supreme perfect
enlightenment ;
our force and exertion
are inadequate to it.
Though the Lord
preaches the law
and has long
continued sitting,
and though we have attended
to that preaching of the law,
yet, O Lord,
as we have so long
been sitting and so long
attended the Lord's service,
our greater
and minor members,
as well as the joints
and articulations,
begin to ache.
Hence, O Lord,
we are unable, in spite
of the Lord's preaching,
to realise the fact
that all is vanity or void,
purposeless or causeless,
or unconditioned,
and unfixed ;
we have conceived
no longing after
the Buddha-laws,
the divisions
of the Buddha-fields,
the sports of the Bodhisattvas
or Tathâgatas.
For by having fled

out of the triple world,
O Lord, we imagined
having attained Nirvâna,
and we are decrepit
from old age.
Hence, O Lord,
though we have exhorted
other Bodhisattvas
and instructed them
in supreme
perfect enlightenment,
we have in doing so
never conceived
a single thought of longing.
And just now,
O Lord,
we are hearing from the Lord
that disciples also may
be predestined to supreme
perfect enlightenment. We
are astonished and amazed,
and deem it a great gain,
O Lord,
that to-day, on a sudden,
we have heard
from the Lord a voice such
as we never heard before.
We have acquired
a magnificent jewel,
O Lord,
an incomparable jewel.
We had not sought,
nor searched,
nor expected,
nor required
so magnificent a jewel.
It has become clear to us,
O Lord ;
it has become clear to us,
O Sugata.

It is a case, O Lord,
as if a certain man
went away from his father
and betook himself
to some other place.
He lives there in foreign parts
for many years,
twenty or thirty
or forty or fifty.
In course of time
the one the father
becomes a great man ;
the other the son is poor ;
in seeking a livelihood
for the sake of food
and clothing he roams
in all directions
and goes to some place,
whereas his father
removes to another country.
The latter has much wealth,
gold, corn, treasures,
and granaries ;
possesses much wrought
gold and silver,
many gems, pearls,
lapis lazuli, conch shells,
and stones, corals,
gold and silver ;
many slaves male and female,
servants for menial work.
and journeymen ;
is rich in elephants, horses,
carriages, cows, and sheep.
He keeps a large retinue ;
has his money invested
in great territories,
and does great things
in business, money-lending,
agriculture, and commerce.

In course of time, Lord,
that poor man,
in quest of food and clothing,
roaming through villages,
towns, boroughs, provinces,
kingdoms, and royal capitals,
reaches the place
where his father, the owner
of much wealth and gold,
treasures and granaries,
is residing.
Now the poor man's father,
Lord,
the owner of much wealth
and gold, treasures
and granaries,
who was residing
in that town,
had always and ever been
thinking of the son
he had lost fifty years ago,
but he gave no utterance
to his thoughts before others,
and was only pining
in himself and thinking :
I am old, aged,
advanced in years,
and possess abundance
of bullion, gold,
money and corn,
treasures and granaries,
but have no son.
It is to be feared
lest death shall overtake me
and all this perish unused.
Repeatedly
he was thinking of that son :
O how happy should I be,
were my son to enjoy
this mass of wealth !

Meanwhile, Lord,
the poor man
in search of food and clothing
was gradually approaching
the house of the rich man,
the owner
of abundant bullion,
gold, money and corn,
treasures and granaries.
And the father
of the poor man
happened to sit
at the door of his house,
surrounded and waited upon
by a great crowd
of Brahmans, Kshatriyas,
Vaisyas, and Sûdras ;
he was sitting
on a magnificent throne
with a footstool decorated
with gold and silver,
while dealing
with hundred thousands
of kotis of gold-pieces,
and fanned with a chowrie,
on a spot
under an extended awning
inlaid with pearls and flowers
and adorned with hanging
garlands of jewels ;
sitting in great pomp.
The poor man, Lord,
saw his own father
in such pomp sitting
at the door of the house,
surrounded with a great
crowd of people and doing
a householder's business.
The poor man frightened,
terrified, alarmed,
seized with a feeling

Disposition 85

of horripilation
all over the body,
and agitated in mind,
reflects thus :
Unexpectedly
have I here fallen in
with a king or grandee.
People like me have
nothing to do here ;
let me go ;
in the street of the poor
I am likely to find food
and clothing
without much difficulty.
Let me no longer
tarry at this place,
lest I be taken
to do forced labour
or incur some other injury.

Thereupon, Lord,
the poor man
quickly departs, runs off,
does not tarry from fear of
a series of supposed dangers.
But the rich man,
sitting on the throne
at the door of his mansion,
has recognised
his son at first sight,
in consequence whereof
he is content, in high spirits,
charmed, delighted, filled
with joy and cheerfulness.
He thinks : Wonderful !
he who is to enjoy
this plenty of bullion, gold,
money and corn,
treasures and granaries,
has been found !
He of whom

I have been thinking
again and again,
is here now that I am old,
aged, advanced in years.

At the same time, moment,
and instant, Lord,
he despatches couriers,
to whom he says : Go, sirs,
and quickly fetch me that man.
The fellows thereon
all run forth in full speed
and overtake the poor man,
who, frightened,
terrified, alarmed,
seized with a feeling
of horripilation
all over his body,
agitated in mind,
utters a lamentable
cry of distress,
screams, and exclaims :
I have given you no offence.
But the fellows
drag the poor man,
however lamenting,
violently with them.
He, frightened, terrified,
alarmed, seized
with a feeling of horripilation
all over his body,
and agitated in mind,
thinks by himself :
I fear lest I shall be punished
with capital punishment ;
I am lost.
He faints away,
and falls on the earth.
His father dismayed
and near despondency
says to those fellows :

Do not carry the man
in that manner.
With these words
he sprinkles him
with cold water
without addressing him
any further.
For that householder
knows the poor man's
humble disposition and
his own elevated position;
yet he feels that
the man is his son.

The householder, Lord,
skilfully conceals from
every one that it is his son.
He calls one of his servants
and says to him:
Go, sirrah,
and tell that poor man:
Go, sirrah,
whither thou likest;
thou art free.
The servant obeys,
approaches the poor man
and tells him:
Go, sirrah,
whither thou likest;
thou art free,
The poor man is astonished
and amazed
at hearing these words;
he leaves that spot
and wanders
to the street of the poor
in search of food and clothing.
In order to attract him
the householder
practises an able device.
He employs for it

two men ill-favoured
and of little splendour.
Go, says he,
go to the man
you saw in this place;
hire him in your own name
for a double daily fee,
and order him to do work
here in my house.
And if he asks:
What work shall I have to do?
tell him:
Help us in clearing
the heap of dirt.
The two fellows go
and seek the poor man
and engage him
for such work as mentioned.
Thereupon
the two fellows conjointly
with the poor man
clear the heap of dirt
in the house
for the daily pay
they receive
from the rich man,
while they take up their abode
in a hovel of straw
in the neighbourhood
of the rich man's dwelling.
And that rich man
beholds through a window
his own son
clearing the heap of dirt,
at which sight he is anew
struck with wonder
and astonishment.

Then the householder
descends from his mansion,
lays off his wreath

and ornaments,
parts with his soft, clean,
and gorgeous attire,
puts on dirty raiment,
takes a basket
in his right hand,
smears his body with dust,
and goes to his son,
whom he greets from afar,
and thus addresses :
Please, take the baskets
and without delay
remove the dust.
By this device he manages
to speak to his son,
to have a talk with him
and say :
Do, sirrah,
remain here in my service ;
do not go again
to another place ;
I will give thee extra pay,
and whatever thou wantest
thou mayst
confidently ask me,
be it the price of a pot,
a smaller pot,
a boiler or wood,
or be it the price of salt,
food, or clothing.
I have got an old cloak, man ;
if thou shouldst want it,
ask me for it, I will give it.
Any utensil of such sort,
when thou wantest to have it,
I will give thee.
Be at ease, fellow ;
look upon me
as if I were thy father,
for I am older
and thou art younger,

and thou hast rendered me
much service
by clearing this heap of dirt,
and as long as thou hast been
in my service
thou hast never shown
nor art showing wickedness,
crookedness, arrogance,
or hypocrisy ;
I have discovered in thee
no vice at all of such as are
commonly seen
in other man-servants.
From henceforward
thou art to me
like my own son.

From that time, Lord,
the householder,
addresses the poor man
by the name of son,
and the latter feels
in presence of the householder
as a son to his father.
In this manner, Lord,
the householder
affected with longing
for his son
employs him
for the clearing of the heap
of dirt during twenty years,
at the end of which
the poor man feels
quite at ease in the mansion
to go in and out,
though he continues
taking his abode
in the hovel of straw.

After a while, Lord,
the householder falls sick,

and feels that the time
of his death is near at hand.
He says to the poor man :
Come hither, man,
I possess abundant bullion,
gold, money and corn,
treasures and granaries.
I am very sick,
and wish to have one upon
whom to bestow my wealth ;
by whom it is to be received,
and with whom
it is to be deposited.
Accept it.
For in the same manner
as I am the owner of it,
so art thou,
but thou shalt not
suffer anything of it
to be wasted.

And so, Lord,
the poor man accepts
the abundant bullion,
gold, money and corn,
treasures and granaries
of the rich man,
but for himself
he is quite indifferent to it,
and requires nothing from it,
not even so much as
the price of a prastha of flour ;
he continues living
in the same hovel of straw
and considers himself
as poor as before.

After a while, Lord,
the householder perceives
that his son is able to save,
mature

and mentally developed ;
that in the consciousness
of his nobility
he feels abashed,
ashamed, disousted,
when thinking
of his former poverty.
The time
of his death approaching,
he sends for the poor man,
presents him to a gathering
of his relations,
and before the king
or king's peer
and in the presence of citizens
and country-people
makes the following speech :
Hear, gentlemen !
this is my own son,
by me begotten.
It is now fifty years
that he disappeared
from such and such a town.
He is called so and so,
and myself
am called so and so.
In searching after him
I have from that town
come hither.
He is my son,
I am his father.
To him I leave
all my revenues,
and all my personal
or private wealth shall he
acknowledge his own.

The poor man, Lord,
hearing this speech
was astonished and amazed ;
he thought by himself :

Disposition 89

Unexpectedly
have I obtained this bullion,
gold, money and corn,
treasures and granaries.

Even so, O Lord,
do we represent
the sons of the Tathâgata,
and the Tathâgata says to us :
Ye are my sons,
as the householder did.
We were oppressed, O Lord,
with three difficulties,
namely the difficulty of pain,
the difficulty of conceptions,
the difficulty
of transition or evolution ;
and in the worldly whirl
we were disposed
to what is low.
Then have we been
prompted by the Lord
to ponder on the numerous
inferior laws or conditions,
things that
are similar to a heap of dirt.
Once directed to them
we have been practising,
making efforts,
and seeking for nothing
but Nirvâna as our fee.
We were content, O Lord,
with the Nirvâna obtained,
and thought to have gained
much at the hands
of the Tathâgata
because of our having
applied ourselves
to these laws, practised,
and made efforts.
But the Lord
takes no notice of us,
does not mix with us,
nor tell us that this treasure
of the Tathâgata's
knowledge shall belong to us,
though the Lord skilfully
appoints us as heirs
to this treasure
of the knowledge
of the Tathâgata.
And we, O Lord,
are not impatiently longing
to enjoy it,
because we deem it
a great gain already
to receive from the Lord
Nirvâna as our fee.
We preach to the
Bodhisattvas Mahâsattvas
a sublime sermon about the
knowledge of the Tathâgata ;
we explain, show,
demonstrate the knowledge
of the Tathâgata, O Lord,
without longing.
For the Tathâgata
by his skilfulness
knows our disposition,
whereas we ourselves
do not know,
nor apprehend.
It is for this very reason
that the Lord just now
tells us that we are
to him as sons,
and that he reminds us
of being heirs
to the Tathâgata.
For the case stands thus :
we are as sons
to the Tathâgata, but low

or humble of disposition ;
the Lord perceives the
strength of our disposition
and applies to us
the denomination
of Bodhisattvas ; we are,
however, charged with
a double office in so far as
in presence of Bodhisattvas
we are called persons
of low disposition
and at the same time
have to rouse them
to Buddha-enlightenment.
Knowing the strength
of our disposition
the Lord has thus spoken,
and in this way, O Lord,
do we say that we have
obtained unexpectedly
and without longing
the jewel of omniscience,
which we did not desire,
nor seek, nor search after,
nor expect, nor require ;
and that inasmuch as we are
the sons of the Tathâgata.

On that occasion the
venerable Mahâ-Kâsyapa
uttered the following stanzas :

1.
We are stricken with wonder,
amazement, and rapture
at hearing a Voice ;
it is the lovely voice,
the leader's voice,
that so unexpectedly
we hear to-day.

2.
In a short moment
we have acquired a great heap
of precious jewels such as
we were not thinking of,
nor requiring.
All of us are astonished
to hear it.

3.
It is like the history
of a young person who,
seduced by foolish people,
went away from his father
and wandered
to another country far distant.

4.
The father was sorry
to perceive that his son
had run away
and in his sorrow roamed
the country in all directions
during no less than fifty years.

5.
In search of his son
he came to some great city,
where he built a house
and dwelt,
blessed with all that can
gratify the five senses.

6.
He had plenty of bullion
and gold, money and corn,
conch shells, stones,
and coral ; elephants,
horses, and footboys ;
cows, cattle, and sheep ;

7.
Interests, revenues,
landed properties ;
male and female slaves
and a great number
of servants ;
was highly honoured
by thousands of kotis
and a constant favourite
of the king's.

8.
The citizens bow to him
with joined hands,
as well as the villagers
in the rural districts ;
many merchants
come to him,
and persons charged
with numerous affairs.

9.
In such way the man
becomes wealthy,
but he gets old, aged,
advanced in years,
and he passes days
and nights always
sorrowful in mind
on account of his son.

10.
'It is fifty years
since that foolish son
has run away.
I have got plenty of wealth
and the hour of my death
draws near.'

11.
Meanwhile that foolish
son is wandering
from village to village,
poor and miserable,
seeking food and clothing.

12.
When begging,
he at one time gets something,
another time he does not.
He grows lean in his travels,
the unwise boy,
while his body is vitiated
with scabs and itch.

13.
In course of time
he in his rovings
reaches the town
where his father is living,
and comes
to his father's mansion
to beg for food and raiment.

14.
And the wealthy,
rich man happens to sit
at the door on a throne
under a canopy
expanded in the sky
and surrounded with many
hundreds of living beings.

15.
His trustees stand round him,
some of them counting
money and bullion,
some writing bills,
some lending money
on interest.

16.
The poor man,
seeing the splendid mansion
of the householder,
thinks within himself:
Where am I here?
This man must be a king
or a grandee.

17.
Let me not incur some injury
and be caught
to do forced labour.
With these reflections
he hurried away inquiring
after the road to the street
of the poor.

18.
The rich man on the throne
is glad to see his own son,
and despatches messengers
with the order
to fetch that poor man.

19.
The messengers
immediately seize the man,
but he is no sooner caught
than he faints away
as he thinks:
These
are certainly executioners
who have approached me;
what do I want
clothing or food?

20.
On seeing it,
the rich,
sagacious man thinks:
This ignorant
and stupid person
is of low disposition
and will have no faith
in my magnificence,
nor believe
that I am his father.

21.
Under those circumstances
he orders persons
of low character,
crooked, one-eyed,
maimed, ill-clad,
and blackish,
to go and search that man
who shall do menial work.

22.
'Enter my service
and cleanse
the putrid heap of dirt,
replete with faeces and urine;
I will give thee
a double salary'
are the words of the message.

23.
On hearing this call
the poor man comes
and cleanses the said spot;
be takes up his abode there
in a hovel near the mansion.

24.
The rich man
continually observes him
through the windows
and thinks :
There is my son engaged
in a low occupation,
cleansing the heap of dirt.

25.
Then he descends,
takes a basket,
puts on dirty garments,
and goes near the man.
He chides him, saying :
Thou dost not perform
thy work.

26.
I will give thee
double salary
and twice more ointment
for the feet ;
I will give thee food with salt,
potherbs, and, besides,
a cloak.

27.
So he chides him
at the time,
but afterwards
he wisely conciliates him
by saying :
Thou dost thy work
very well, indeed ;
thou art my son, surely ;
there is no doubt of it.

28.
Little by little
he makes the man
enter the house,
and employs him in his service
for fully twenty years,
in the course of which time
he succeeds in inspiring him
with confidence.

29.
At the same time he lays up
in the house gold, pearls,
and crystal,
draws up the sum total,
and is always occupied
in his mind
with all that property.

30.
The ignorant man,
who is living
outside the mansion,
alone in a hovel,
cherishes no other ideas
but of poverty,
and thinks to himself :
Mine are no such possessions !

31.
The rich man
perceiving this of him thinks :
My son has arrived
at the consciousness
of being noble.
He calls together
a gathering of his friends
and relatives and says :
I will give all my property
to this man.

32.
In the midst of the assembly
where the king,
burghers, citizens,
and many merchantmen
were present,
he speaks thus :
This is my son
whom I lost a long time ago.

33.
It is now fully fifty years-
and twenty years more
during which I have seen him-
that he disappeared
from such and such a place
and that in his search
I came to this place.

34.
He is owner
of all my property ;
to him I leave it all
and entirely ;
let him do with it
what he wants ;
I give him
my whole family property.

35.
And the poor man
is struck with surprise ;
remembering
his former poverty,
his low disposition,
and as he receives those
good things of his father's
and the family property,
he thinks :
Now am I a happy man.

36.
In like manner
has the leader,
who knows
our low disposition
or position,
not declared to us :
'Ye shall become Buddhas,'
but, 'Ye are, certainly,
my disciples and sons.'

37.
And the Lord of the world
enjoins us : Teach, Kâsyapa,
the superior path
to those that strive to attain
the highest summit
of enlightenment,
the path by following which
they are to become Buddhas.

38.
Being thus ordered
by the Sugata,
we show the path
to many Bodhisattvas
of great might,
by means of myriads of kotis
of illustrations and proofs.

39.
And by hearing us
the sons of Gina
realise that eminent path
to attain enlightenment,
and in that case receive
the prediction
that they are to become
Buddhas in this world.

40.
Such is the work we are
doing strenuously,
preserving this law-treasure
and revealing it
to the sons of Gina,
in the manner of that man
who had deserved
the confidence
of that other man.

41.
Yet, though we diffuse
the Buddha-treasure
we feel ourselves to be poor ;
we do not require
the knowledge of the Gina,
and yet, at the same time,
we reveal it.

42.
We fancy an individual,
separate, Nirvâna ; so far,
no further does
our knowledge reach ;
nor do we ever rejoice
at hearing of the divisions
of Buddha-fields.

43.
All these laws are faultless,
unshaken,
exempt from destruction
and commencement ;
but there is no law in them.
When we hear this,
however, we cannot believe.

44.
We have put aside
all aspiration
to superior
Buddha-knowledge
a long time ago ;
never have we
devoted ourselves to it.
This is the last and decisive
word spoken by the Gina.

45.
In this bodily existence,
closing with Nirvâna,
we have continually
accustomed our thoughts
to the void ;
we have been released from
the evils of the triple world
we were suffering from,
and have accomplished
the command of the Gina.

46.
To whomsoever
among the sons of Gina
who in this world
are on the road
to superior enlightenment
we revealed the law,
and whatever law we taught,
we never
had any predilection for it.

47.
And the Master of the world,
the Self-born one,
takes no notice of us,
waiting his time ;
he does not explain
the real connection
of the things,
as he is testing
our disposition.

48.
Able in applying devices
at the right time,
like that rich man he says :
'Be constant in subduing
your low disposition,'
and to those
who are subdued
he gives his wealth.

49.
It is a very difficult task
which the Lord of the world
is performing,
a task in which he displays
his skilfulness,
when he tames
his sons of low disposition
and thereupon
imparts to them
his knowledge.

50.
On a sudden have we to-day
been seized with surprise,
just as the poor man
who acquired riches ;
now for the first time
have we obtained the fruit
under the rule of Buddha,
a fruit as excellent as faultless.

51.
As we have always observed
the moral precepts
under the rule
of the Knower of the world,
we now receive the fruit
of that morality which
we have formerly practised.

52.
Now have we obtained
the egregious, hallowed,
exalted, and perfect fruit
of our having observed
an excellent
and pure spiritual life
under the rule of the Leader.

53.
Now, O Lord,
are we disciples,
and we shall proclaim
supreme
enlightenment everywhere,
reveal
the word of enlightenment,
by which
we are formidable disciples.

54.
Now have we become
Arhats, O Lord ;
and deserving
of the worship of the world,
including the gods,
Mâras and Brahmas,
in short, of all beings.

55.
Who is there,
even were he to exert himself
during kotis of Æons,
able to thwart thee,
who accomplishes
in this world of mortals
such difficult things as those,
and others
even more difficult ?

56.
It would be difficult
to offer resistance
with hands, feet, head,
shoulder, or breast,
even were one to try during
as many complete Æons
as there are grains of sand
in the Ganges.

57.
One may charitably
give food, soft and solid,
clothing, drink,
a place for sleeping
and sitting,
with clean coverlets ;
one may build monasteries
of sandal-wood,
and after furnishing them
with double pieces
of fine white muslin,
present them ;

58.
One may be assiduous
in giving medicines
of various kinds to the sick,
in honour of the Sugata ;
one may spend alms
during as many Æons
as there are grains of sand
in the Ganges - even then
one will not be able
to offer resistance.

59.
Of sublime nature,
unequalled power,
miraculous might,
firm in the strength
of patience is the Buddha ;
a great ruler is the Gina,
free from imperfections.
The ignorant cannot bear
or understand
such things as these.

60.
Always returning,
he preaches the law
to those whose course of life
is conditioned,
he, the Lord of the law,
the Lord of all the world,
the great Lord,
the Chief among
the leaders of the world.

61.
Fully aware
of the circumstances
or places of all beings
he indicates their duties,
so multifarious,
and considering the variety
of their dispositions
he inculcates the law
with thousands
of arguments.

62.
He, the Tathâgata,
who is fully aware
of the course of all beings
and individuals,
preaches a multifarious law,
while pointing to this
superior enlightenment.

Chapter V
On Plants

Thereupon the Lord
addressed the venerable
Mahâ-Kâsyapa and the other
senior great disciples,
and said : Very well,
very well, Kâsyapa ;
you have done very well
to proclaim the real qualities
of the Tathâgata.
They are the real qualities
of the Tathâgata, Kâsyapa,
but he has many more,
innumerable, incalculable,
the end of which
it would be difficult to reach,
even were one to continue
enumerating them
for immeasurable Æons.
The Tathâgata, Kâsyapa,
is the master of the law,
the king, lord,
and master of all laws.
And whatever law
for any case
has been instituted
by the Tathâgata,
remains unchanged.
All laws, Kâsyapa,
have been aptly instituted
by the Tathâgata.
In his Tathâgata-wisdom
he has instituted them
in such a manner
that all those laws
finally lead to the stage
of those who know all.
The Tathâgata
also distinctly knows
the meaning of all laws.
The Tathâgata,
the Arhat, &c.
is possessed of the faculty
of penetrating all laws,
possessed of the highest
perfection of knowledge,
so that he is able
to decide all laws,
able to display the knowledge
of the all-knowing,
impart the knowledge
of the all-knowing,
and lay down the rules
of the knowledge
of the all-knowing.

It is a case, Kâsyapa,
similar to that
of a great cloud
big with rain,
coming up
in this wide universe
over all grasses,
shrubs, herbs,
trees of various species
and kind,
families of plants
of different names
growing on earth,
on hills,
or in mountain caves,
a cloud covering
the wide universe
to pour down
its rain everywhere
and at the same time.
Then, Kâsyapa,
the grasses, shrubs,
herbs, and wild trees
in this universe,

such as have young
and tender stalks, twigs,
leaves, and foliage,
and such as have
middle-sized stalks,
twigs, leaves, and foliage,
and such as have
the same fully developed,
all those grasses, shrubs,
herbs, and wild trees,
smaller and greater
other trees will each,
according
to its faculty and power,
suck the humid element
from the water
emitted by that great cloud,
and by that water which,
all of one essence,
has been abundantly
poured down by the cloud,
they will each,
according to its germ,
acquire
a regular development,
growth, shooting up,
and bigness;
and so they will produce
blossoms and fruits,
and will receive,
each severally, their names.
Rooted in one
and the same soil,
all those families of plants
and germs are drenched
and vivified by water
of one essence throughout.

In the same manner, Kâsyapa,
does the Tathâgata,
the Arhat, &c.

appear in the world.
Like unto a great cloud
coming up,
the Tathâgata appears
and sends forth his call
to the whole world,
including gods, men,
and demons.
And even as a great cloud,
Kâsyapa,
extending over
the whole universe,
in like manner, Kâsyapa,
the Tathâgata, the Arhat, &c.,
before the face of the world,
including gods, men,
and demons,
lifts his voice
and utters these words:
I am the Tathâgata,
O ye gods and men!
the Arhat,
the perfectly enlightened one;
having reached
the shore myself,
I carry others to the shore;
being free, I make free;
being comforted, I comfort;
being perfectly at rest,
I lead others to rest.
By my perfect wisdom I know
both this world and the next,
such as they really are.
I am all-knowing, all-seeing.
Come to me,
ye gods and men!
hear the law.
I am he
who indicates the path;
who shows the path,
as knowing the path,

being acquainted
with the path.
Then, Kâsyapa,
many hundred thousand
myriads of kotis of beings
come to hear
the law of the Tathâgata ;
and the Tathâgata,
who knows the difference
as to the faculties and
the energy of those beings,
produces various
Dharmaparyâyas,
tells many tales,
amusing, agreeable,
both instructive and pleasant,
tales by means of which
all beings not only
become pleased with the law
in this present life,
but also after death
will reach happy states,
where they are to enjoy
many pleasures
and hear the law.
By listening to the law
they will be freed
from hindrances
and in due course
apply themselves to the law
of the all-knowing,
according to their faculty,
power, and strength.

Even as the great cloud,
Kâsyapa, after expanding
over the whole universe,
pours out the same water
and recreates by it all grasses,
shrubs, herbs, and trees ;
even as all these grasses,
shrubs, herbs, and trees,
according to their faculty,
power, and strength,
suck in the water and thereby
attain the full development
assigned to their kind ;
in like manner, Kâsyapa,
is the law preached
by the Tathâgata,
the Arhat, &c.,
of one and the same essence,
that is to say,
the essence of it
is deliverance,
the final aim being
absence of passion,
annihilation,
knowledge of the all-knowing.
As to that, Kâsyapa,
it must be understood that
the beings who hear the law
when it is preached
by the Tathâgata,
who keep it in their memory
and apply themselves to it,
do not know, nor perceive,
nor understand their own self.
For, Kâsyapa,
the Tathâgata
only really knows who,
how, and of what kind
those beings are ;
what, how, and whereby
they are meditating ;
what, how, and whereby
they are contemplating ;
what, why, and whereby
they are attaining.
No one but the Tathâgata,
Kâsyapa,
is there present,

seeing all intuitively,
and seeing
the state of those beings
in different stages,
as of the lowest, highest,
and mean grasses, shrubs,
herbs, and trees.
I am he, Kâsyapa, who,
knowing the law
which is of but one essence,
namely
the essence of deliverance,
the law ever peaceful,
ending in Nirvâna,
the law of eternal rest,
having but one stage
and placed in voidness,
who knowing this
do not on a sudden
reveal to all the knowledge
of the all-knowing,
since I pay regard to
the dispositions of all beings.

You are astonished, Kâsyapa,
that you cannot fathom
the mystery expounded
by the Tathâgata.
It is, Kâsyapa,
because the mystery
expounded by the Tathâgatas,
the Arhats, &c.
is difficult to be understood.

And on that occasion,
the more fully to explain
the same subject,
the Lord uttered
the following stanzas :

1.
I am the Dharmarâga,
born in the world
as the destroyer of existence.
I declare the law to all beings
after discriminating
their dispositions.

2.
Superior men
of wise understanding
guard the word,
guard the mystery,
and do not reveal it
to living beings.

3.
That science is difficult
to be understood ;
the simple,
if hearing it on a sudden,
would be perplexed ;
they would in their ignorance
fall out of the way
and go astray.

4.
I speak according
to their reach and faculty ;
by means of various meanings
I accommodate
my view or the theory.

5.
It is, Kâsyapa,
as if a cloud
rising above the horizon
shrouds all space in darkness
and covers the earth.

6.
That great rain-cloud
big with water, is wreathed
with flashes of lightning
and rouses
with its thundering call
all creatures.

7.
By warding off the sunbeams,
it cools the region;
and gradually lowering
so as to come
in reach of hands,
it begins pouring down
its water all around.

8.
And so,
flashing on every side,
it pours out
an abundant mass
of water equally,
and refreshes this earth.

9.
And all herbs
which have sprung up
on the face of the earth,
all grasses, shrubs,
forest trees,
other trees small and great;

10.
The various field fruits
and whatever is green;
all plants on hills,
in caves and thickets;

11.
All those grasses, shrubs,
and trees are vivified
by the cloud that both
refreshes the thirsty earth
and waters the herbs.

12.
Grasses and shrubs
absorb the water
of one essence which issues
from the cloud according
to their faculty and reach.

13.
And all trees, great,
small, and mean,
drink that water
according to their growth
and faculty, and grow lustily.

14.
The great plants whose trunk,
stalk, bark, twigs, pith,
and leaves are moistened
by the water from the cloud
develop
their blossoms and fruits.

15.
They yield their products,
each according
to its own faculty, reach,
and the particular
nature of the germ;
still the water
emitted from the cloud
is of but one essence.

16.
In the same way, Kâsyapa,
the Buddha comes
into the world
like a rain-cloud,
and, once born,
he, the world's Lord,
speaks and shows
the real course of life.

17.
And the great Seer,
honoured in the world,
including the gods,
speaks thus :
I am the Tathâgata,
the highest of men, the Gina ;
I have appeared in this world
like a cloud.

18.
I shall refresh all beings
whose bodies are withered,
who are clogged
to the triple world.
I shall bring to felicity
those that are pining away
with toils,
give them pleasures
and final rest.

19.
Hearken to me,
ye hosts of gods and men ;
approach to behold me :
I am the Tathâgata,
the Lord,
who has no superior,
who appears
in this world to save.

20.
To thousands of kotis
of living beings I preach
a pure and most bright law
that has but one scope,
to wit, deliverance and rest.

21.
I preach with ever
the same voice,
constantly taking
enlightenment as my text.
For this is equal for all ;
no partiality is in it,
neither hatred nor affection.

22.
I am inexorable,
bear no love nor hatred
towards any one,
and proclaim the law to all
creatures without distinction,
to the one as well as the other.

23.
Whether walking, standing,
or sitting, I am exclusively
occupied with this task
of proclaiming the law.
I never get tired of sitting
on the chair I have ascended.

24.
I recreate the whole world
like a cloud shedding
its water without distinction ;
I have the same feelings
for respectable people
as for the low ;
for moral persons
as for the immoral ;

25.
For the depraved
as for those who observe
the rules of good conduct ;
for those who hold
sectarian views
and unsound tenets
as for those whose views
are sound and correct.

26.
I preach the law to the inferior
in mental culture
as well as to persons
of superior understanding
and extraordinary faculties ;
inaccessible to weariness,
I spread in season
the rain of the law.

27.
After hearing me,
each according to his faculty,
the several beings
find their determined place
in various situations,
amongst gods, men,
beautiful beings,
amongst Indras,
Brahmas,
or the monarchs,
rulers of the universe.

28.
Hear, now,
I am going to explain
what is meant by those plants
of different size,
some of them
being low in the world,
others middle-sized and great.

29.
Small plants
are called the men who walk
in the knowledge of the law,
which is free from evil
after the attaining
of Nirvâna,
who possess the six
transcendent faculties
and the triple science.

30.
Mean plants
are called the men who,
dwelling
in mountain caverns,
covet the state
of a Pratyekabuddha,
and whose intelligence
is moderately purified.

31.
Those who aspire
to become leading men
thinking,
I will become a Buddha,
a chief of gods and men,
and who practise exertion
and meditation,
are called the highest plants.

32.
But the sons of Sugata,
who sedulously
practise benevolence
and a peaceful conduct,
who
have arrived at certainty
about their being
leading men,
these are called trees.

On Plants 105

33.
Those who
move forward the wheel
that never rolls back,
and with manly strength
stand firm in the exercise
of miraculous power,
releasing many kotis of beings,
those are called great trees.

34.
Yet it is one and the same law
which is preached by the Gina,
like the water
emitted by the cloud
is one and the same ;
different only
are the faculties as described,
just as the plants
on the face of the earth.

35.
By this parable thou mayst
understand the skilfulness
of the Tathâgata,
how he preaches one law,
the various developments
whereof may be likened
to drops of rain.

36.
I also pour out rain :
the rain of the law
by which this whole world
is refreshed ;
and each according
to his faculty takes to heart
this well-spoken law
that is one in its essence.

37.
Even as all grasses and shrubs,
as well as
plants of middle size,
trees and great trees
at the time of rain
look bright in all quarters ;

38.
So
it is the very nature of the law
to promote the everlasting
weal of the world ;
by the law
the whole world is recreated,
and as the plants
when refreshed
expand their blossoms,
the world does the same
when refreshed.

39.
The plants that in their growth
remain middle-sized,
are Arhats
saints stopping when
they have overcome frailties,
and the Pratyekabuddhas who,
living in woody thickets,
accomplish
this well-spoken law.

40.
But the many Bodhisattvas
who, thoughtful and wise,
go their way
all over the triple world,
striving after
supreme enlightenment,
they continue increasing
in growth like trees.

41.
Those who,
endowed
with magical powers
and being adepts
in the four degrees
of meditation,
feel delight at hearing
of complete voidness
and emit thousands of rays,
they are called
the great trees on earth.

42.
So then, Kâsyapa,
is the preaching of the law,
like the water poured out by
the cloud everywhere alike ;
by which plants and men
thrive, endless and eternal
blossoms are produced.

43.
I reveal the law
which has its cause in itself ;
at due time I show
Buddha-enlightenment ;
this is my supreme skilfulness
and that of all leaders
of the world.

44.
What I here say is true
in the highest sense
of the word ;
all my disciples
attain Nirvâna ;
by following the sublime path
of enlightenment
all my disciples
shall become Buddhas.

And further, Kâsyapa,
the Tathâgata,
in his educating creatures,
is equal, (i.e. impartial) and
not unequal, (i.e. partial).
As the light
of the sun and moon,
Kâsyapa,
shines upon all the world,
upon the virtuous
and the wicked,
upon high and low,
upon the fragrant
and the ill-smelling ;
as their beams are sent down
upon everything equally,
without inequality (partiality) ;
so, too, Kâsyapa,
the intellectual light
of the knowledge
of the omniscient,
the Tathâgatas,
the Arhats, &c.,
the preaching of the true law
proceeds equally
in respect to all beings
in the five states of existence,
to all who according to
their particular disposition are
devoted to the great vehicle,
or to the vehicle
of the Pratyekabuddhas,
or to the vehicle
of the disciples.
Nor is there any deficiency
or excess in the brightness
of the Tathâgata knowledge
up to one's becoming fully
acquainted with the law.
There are not three vehicles,

Kâsyapa;
there are but beings
who act differently;
therefore it is declared
that there are three vehicles.

When the Lord
had thus spoken,
the venerable Mahâ-Kâsyapa
said to him : Lord,
if there are not three vehicles,
for what reason then
is the designation
of disciples,
Buddhas, and Bodhisattvas
kept up in the present times ?

On this speech the Lord
answered the venerable
Mahâ-Kâsyapa as follows :
It is, Kâsyapa,
as if a potter
made different vessels
out of the same clay.
Some of those pots
are to contain sugar,
others ghee,
others curds and milk ;
others, of inferior quality,
are vessels of impurity.
There is no diversity
in the clay used ; no,
the diversity of the pots
is only due to the substances
which are put
into each of them.
In like manner, Kâsyapa,
is there but one vehicle,
namely the Buddha-vehicle ;
there is no second vehicle,
no third.

The Lord having thus spoken,
the venerable
Mahâ-Kâsyapa said :
Lord, if the beings
are of different disposition,
will there be for those
who have left the triple world
one Nirvâna,
or two, or three ?
The Lord replied :
Nirvâna, Kâsyapa,
is a consequence
of understanding
that all laws are equal.
Hence there is but one
Nirvâna, not two, not three.
Therefore, Kâsyapa,
I will tell thee a parable, for
men of good understanding
will generally readily enough
catch the meaning
of what is taught
under the shape of a parable.

It is a case, Kâsyapa,
similar to that
of a certain blind-born man,
who says : There are no
handsome or ugly shapes ;
there are no men
able to see handsome
or ugly shapes ;
there exists no sun nor moon ;
there are no asterisms
nor planets ;
there are no men
able to see planets.
But other persons
say to the blind-born :
There are handsome

and ugly shapes ;
there are men able to see
handsome and ugly shapes ;
there is a sun and moon ;
there are asterisms
and planets ;
there are men
able to see planets.
But the blind-born
does not believe them,
nor accept what they say.
Now there is a physician
who knows all diseases.
He sees that blind-born man
and makes to himself
this reflection :
The disease of this man
originates in his sinful actions
in former times.
All diseases possible
to arise are fourfold :
rheumatical, cholerical,
phlegmatical,
and caused by a complication
of the corrupted humours.
The physician,
after thinking again and again
on a means
to cure the disease,
makes to himself
this reflection :
Surely,
with the drugs in common use
it is impossible
to cure this disease,
but there are in the Himâlaya,
the king of mountains,
four herbs, to wit :
first, one called
Possessed-of-all-sorts-
of-colours-and-flavours ;
second,
Delivering-from-all-diseases ;
third,
Delivering-from-all-poisons ;
fourth,
Procuring-happiness-
to those-standing-
in-the-right-place.
As the physician
feels compassion
for the blind-born man
he contrives some device
to get to the Himâlaya,
the king of mountains.
There he goes up and down
and across to search.
In doing so
he finds the four herbs.
One he gives after
chewing it with the teeth ;
another after pounding ;
another after having it
mixed with another drug
and boiled ;
another after having it
mixed with a raw drug ;
another after piercing
with a lancet
somewhere a vein ; another
after singeing it in fire ;
another after combining it
with various other substances
so as to enter in
a compound potion, food, &c.
Owing to these means
being applied the blind-born
recovers his eyesight,
and in consequence of that
recovery he sees outwardly
and inwardly, far and near,
the shine of sun and moon,

On Plants 109

the asterisms, planets,
and all phenomena.
Then he says :
O how foolish was I
that I did not believe
what they told me,
nor accepted
what they affirmed.
Now I see all ;
I am delivered
from my blindness and have
recovered my eyesight ;
there is none in the world
who could surpass me.
And at the same moment
Seers of the five
transcendent faculties,
strong in the divine sight
and hearing,
in the knowledge
of others' minds,
in the memory
of former abodes,
in magical science
and intuition,
speak to the man thus :
Good man,
thou hast just recovered
thine eyesight,
nothing more,
and dost not know
yet anything.
Whence comes
this conceitedness to thee ?
Thou hast no wisdom,
nor art thou a clever man.
Further they say to him :
Good man, when sitting
in the interior of thy room,
thou canst not see
nor distinguish forms outside,
nor discern which beings
are animated
with kind feelings and which
with hostile feelings ;
thou canst not distinguish
nor hear at the distance
of five yoganas
the voice of a man
or the sound of a drum,
conch trumpet, and the like ;
thou canst not even walk
as far as a kos
without lifting up thy feet ;
thou hast been produced
and developed
in thy mother's womb
without remembering the fact ;
how then wouldst
thou be clever,
and how canst thou say :
I see all ?
Good man,
thou takest darkness for light,
and takest light for darkness.

Whereupon the Seers
are asked by the man :
By what means
and by what good work
shall I acquire such wisdom
and with your favour
acquire those good qualities
or virtues ?
And the Seers say to that man :
If that be thy wish,
go and live in the wilderness
or take thine abode
in mountain caves,
to meditate on the law
and cast off evil passions.
So shalt thou become

endowed with the virtues
of an ascetic and acquire
the transcendent faculties.
The man catches
their meaning
and becomes an ascetic.
Living in the wilderness,
the mind intent upon
one sole object,
he shakes off worldly desires,
and acquires
the five transcendent faculties.
After that acquisition
he reflects thus:
Formerly I did not do
the right thing;
hence no good accrued to me.
Now, however,
I can go whither
my mind prompts me;
formerly I was ignorant,
of little understanding,
in fact, a blind man.

Such, Kâsyapa,
is the parable I have invented
to make thee understand
my meaning.
The moral to be drawn
from it is as follows.
The word 'blind-born,'
Kâsyapa,
is a designation
for the creatures
staying in the whirl
of the world
with its six states;
the creatures
who do not know the true law
and are heaping up
the thick darkness

of evil passions.
Those are blind
from ignorance,
and in consequence of it
they build up conceptions;
in consequence of the latter
name-and-form, and so forth,
up to the genesis of this
whole huge mass of evils.

So the creatures
blind from ignorance
remain in the whirl of life,
but the Tathâgata,
who is out of the triple world,
feels compassion,
prompted by which,
like a father for his dear
and only son,
he appears in the triple world
and sees
with his eye of wisdom
that the creatures
are revolving in the circle
of the mundane whirl,
and are toiling
without finding
the right means to escape
from the rotation.
And on seeing this he comes
to the conclusion:
Yon beings,
according to the good works
they have done
in former states,
have feeble aversions
and strong attachments;
or feeble attachments
and strong aversions;
some have little wisdom,
others are clever;

some have soundly
developed views,
others have unsound views.
To all of them the Tathâgata
skilfully shows three vehicles.

The Seers in the parable,
those possessing
the five transcendent faculties
and clear-sight,
are the Bodhisattvas
who produce
enlightened thought,
and by the acquirement
of acquiescence
in the eternal law
awake us to supreme,
perfect enlightenment.

The great physician
in the parable
is the Tathâgata.
To the blind-born
may be likened
the creatures blind
with infatuation.
Attachment, aversion,
and infatuation are likened
to rheum, bile, and phlegm.
The sixty-two false theories
also must be
looked upon as such.
The four herbs
are like vanity or voidness,
causelessness
or purposelessness,
unfixedness,
and reaching Nirvâna.
Just as by using
different drugs
different diseases are healed,

so by developing
the idea of vanity or voidness,
purposelessness,
unfixedness,
which are the principles
of emancipation,
is ignorance suppressed ;
the suppression of ignorance
is succeeded
by the suppression
of conceptions or fancies ;
and so forth,
up to the suppression of
the whole huge mass of evils.
And thus one's mind
will dwell no more
on good nor on evil.

To the man
who recovers his eyesight
is likened the votary
of the vehicle of the disciples
and of Pratyekabuddhas.
He rends the ties
of evil passion
in the whirl of the world ;
freed from those ties
he is released
from the triple world
with its six states of existence.
Therefore the votary
of the vehicle of the disciples
may think and speak thus :
There are no more laws
to be penetrated ;
I have reached Nirvâna.
Then the Tathâgata
preaches to him :
How can he who has
not penetrated all laws
have reached Nirvâna ?

The Lord rouses him
to enlightenment,
and the disciple,
when the consciousness
of enlightenment
has been awakened in him,
no longer stays
in the mundane whirl,
but at the same time
has not yet reached Nirvâna.
As he has arrived
at true insight,
he looks upon
this triple world
in every direction as void,
resembling
the produce of magic,
similar to a dream,
a mirage, an echo.
He sees that all laws
and phenomena
are unborn and undestroyed,
not bound and not loose,
not dark and not bright.
He who views
the profound laws
in such a light,
sees, as if he were not seeing,
the whole triple world
full of beings of contrary
and omnifarious fancies
and dispositions.

And on that occasion,
in order to more amply
explain the same subject,
the Lord uttered
the following stanzas :

45.
As the rays
of the sun and moon
descend alike on all men,
good and bad,
without deficiency in one case
or surplus in the other ;

46.
So the wisdom
of the Tathâgata
shines like the sun and moon,
leading all beings
without partiality.

47.
As the potter,
making clay vessels,
produces from
the same clay pots for sugar,
milk, ghee, or water ;

48.
Some for impurities,
others for curdled milk,
the clay used
by the artificer for the vessels
being of but one sort ;

49.
As a vessel
is made to receive
all its distinguishing qualities
according to the quality
of the substance laid into it,
so the Tathâgatas,
on account
of the diversity of taste,

50.
Mention a diversity
of vehicles,
though the Buddha-vehicle
be the only indisputable one.
He who ignores the rotation
of mundane existence,
has no perception
of blessed rest ;

51.
But he who understands
that all laws are void
and without reality and
without individual character
penetrates the enlightenment
of the perfectly enlightened
Lords in its very essence.

52.
One who occupies
a middle position of wisdom
is called a Pratyekagina,
that is, Pratyekabuddha ;
one lacking
the insight of voidness
is termed a disciple.

53.
But after
understanding all laws
one is called
a perfectly-enlightened one ;
such a one is assiduous
in preaching the law
to living beings by means
of hundreds of devices.

54.
It is as if
some blind-born man,
because he sees no sun,
moon, planets, and stars,
in his blind ignorance
should say : There are
no visible things at all.

55.
But a great physician
taking compassion
on the blind man,
goes to the Himâlaya,
where seeking across,
up and down,

56.
He fetches from
the mountain four plants ;
the herb Of-all-colours-
flavours-and-cases,
and others.
These he intends to apply.

57.
He applies them
in this manner :
one he gives to the blind man
after chewing it,
another after pounding,
again another
by introducing it
with the point of a needle
into the man's body.

58.
The man
having got his eyesight,
sees the sun, moon,
planets, and stars, and
arrives at the conclusion that
it was from sheer ignorance
that he spoke thus
as he had formerly done.

59.
In the same way do people
of great ignorance,
blind from their birth, move
in the turmoil of the world,
because they do not know
the wheel
of causes and effects,
the path of toils.

60.
In the world
so blinded by ignorance
appears the highest
of those who know all,
the Tathâgata,
the great physician,
of compassionate nature.

61.
As an able teacher
he shows the true law;
he reveals supreme
Buddha-enlightenment to him
who is most advanced.

62.
To those of middling wisdom
the Leader preaches
a middling enlightenment;
again another enlightenment
he recommends
to him who is afraid
of the mundane whirl.

63.
The disciple who
by his discrimination
has escaped
from the triple world
thinks he has reached pure,
blest Nirvâna,
but it is only
by knowing all laws
and the universal laws
that the immortal
Nirvâna is reached.

64.
In that case
it is as if the great Seers,
moved by compassion,
said to him:
Thou art mistaken; do not
be proud of thy knowledge.

65.
When thou art
in the interior of thy room,
thou canst not perceive
what is going on without,
fool as thou art.

66.
Thou who,
when staying within,
dost not perceive even now
what people outside
are doing or not doing,
how wouldst thou be wise,
fool as thou art?

67.
Thou art not able to hear
a sound at a distance
of but five yoganas,
far less at a greater distance.

68.
Thou canst not discern
who are malevolent
or benevolent towards thee.
Whence then comes
that pride to thee ?

69.
If thou hast to walk
so far as a kos,
thou canst not go
without a beaten track ; and
what happened to thee when
in thy mother's womb thou
hast immediately forgotten.

70.
In this world he is called
all-knowing who possesses
the five transcendent faculties,
but when thou
who knowest nothing
pretendest to be all-knowing,
it is an effect of infatuation.

71.
If thou art desirous
of omniscience,
direct thy attention
to transcendent wisdom ;
then betake thy self
to the wilderness
and meditate on the pure law ;
by it thou shalt acquire
the transcendent faculties.

72.
The man catches the meaning,
goes to the wilderness,
meditates
with the greatest attention,
and, as he is endowed
with good qualities,
ere long acquires
the five transcendent faculties.

73.
Similarly all disciples fancy
having reached Nirvâna,
but the Gina instructs them
by saying : This is a temporary
repose, no final rest.

74.
It is an artifice of the Buddhas
to enunciate this dogma.
There is no real Nirvâna
without all-knowingness ;
try to reach this.

75.
The boundless knowledge
of the three paths of time,
the six utmost perfections,
voidness, the absence
of purpose or object,
the absence of finiteness ;

76.
The idea of enlightenment
and the other laws
leading to Nirvâna,
both such as are mixed
with imperfection
and such as are exempt from it,
such as are tranquil and
comparable to ethereal space ;

77.
The four Brahmavihâras
and the four Sangrahas,
as well as the laws sanctioned
by eminent sages
for the education of creatures ;

78.
He who knows these things
and that all phenomena
have the nature
of illusion and dreams,
that they are pithless
as the stem of the plantain,
and similar to an echo ;

79.
And who knows
that the triple world
throughout is of that nature,
not fast and not loose,
he knows rest.

80.
He who considers all laws
to be alike, void,
devoid of particularity
and individuality,
not derived
from an intelligent cause ;
nay, who discerns
that nothingness is law ;

81.
Such a one
has great wisdom and sees
the whole of the law entirely.
There are no three vehicles
by any means ;
there is but one vehicle
in this world.

82.
All laws
or the laws of all are alike,
equal, for all, and ever alike.
Knowing this,
one understands
immortal, blest Nirvâna.

Chapter VI
Announcement of Future Destiny

After pronouncing
these stanzas
the Lord addressed
the complete assembly
of monks :
I announce to you, monks,
I make known to you
that the monk Kâsyapa,
my disciple,
here present,
shall do homage
to thirty thousand
kotis of Buddhas ;
shall respect, honour,
and worship them ;
and shall keep the true law
of those Lords and Buddhas.
In his last bodily existence
in the world Avabhâsa,
(i.e. lustre),
in the age Æon Mahâvyûha
(i.e. great division)
he shall be a Tathâgata,
an Arhat, &c. &c.,
by the name
of Rasmiprabhâsa
(i.e. beaming with rays).
His lifetime shall last
twelve intermediate kalpas,
and his true law
twenty intermediate kalpas ;
the counterfeit of his true law
shall last as many
intermediate kalpas.
His Buddha-field
will be pure, clean,
devoid of stones, grit, gravel ;
of pits and precipices ;
devoid of gutters
and dirty pools ;
even, pretty, beautiful,
and pleasant to see ;
consisting of lapis lazuli,
adorned with jewel-trees,
and looking
like a checker-board
with eight compartments
set off with gold threads.
It will be strewed
with flowers,
and many hundred thousand
Bodhisattvas
are to appear in it.
As to disciples,
there will be innumerable
hundred thousands
of myriads of kotis of them.
Neither Mâra the evil one,
nor his host
will be discoverable in it,
though Mâra
and his followers
shall afterwards be there ;
for they will apply
themselves to receive
the true law
under the command
of that very Lord
Rasmiprabhâsa.
And on that occasion
the Lord uttered
the following stanzas :

1.
With my Buddha-eye, monks,
I see that
the senior Kâsyapa here
shall become a Buddha
at a future epoch,
in an incalculable Æon, after
he shall have paid homage
to the most high of men.

2.
This Kâsyapa shall see
fully thirty thousand
kotis of Ginas,
under whom he shall lead
a spiritual life for the sake
of Buddha-knowledge.

3.
After having paid homage
to those highest of men
and acquired
that supreme knowledge,
he shall
in his last bodily existence
be a Lord of the world,
a matchless, great Seer.

4.
And his field
will be magnificent,
excellent, pure,
goodly, beautiful,
pretty, nice,
ever delightful,
and set off with gold threads.

5.
That field, monks,
appearing
like a board divided
into eight compartments,
will have several jewel-trees,
one in each compartment,
from which issues
a delicious odour.

6.
It will be adorned
with plenty of flowers,
and embellished
with variegated blossoms ;
in it are no pits
nor precipices ;
it is even, goodly, beautiful.

7.
There will be found
hundreds of kotis
of Bodhisattvas,
subdued of mind
and of great magical power,
mighty keepers of Sûtrântas
of great extension.

8.
As to disciples, faultless,
princes of the law,
standing
in their last period of life,
their number
can never be known,
even if one should
go on counting for Æons,
and that with
the aid of divine knowledge.

9.
He himself shall stay
twelve intermediate kalpas,
and his true law
twenty complete Æons ;

the counterfeit is to continue
as many Æons,
in the domain
of Rasmiprabhâsa.

Thereupon
the venerable senior
Mahâ-Maudgalyâyana,
the venerable Subhûti,
and the venerable
Mahâ-Kâtyâyana,
their bodies trembling,
gazed up to the Lord
with unblenching eyes,
and at the same moment
severally uttered,
in mental concert,
the following stanzas :

10.
O hallowed one,
great hero, Sâkya lion,
most high of men !
out of compassion to us
speak the Buddha-word.

11.
The highest of men, the Gina,
he who knows the fatal term,
will, as it were,
sprinkle us with nectar
by predicting our destiny also.

12.
It is as if a certain man,
in time of famine,
comes and gets good food,
but to whom,
when the food
is already in his hands,
they say that he should wait.

13.
Similarly it was with us,
who after minding
the lower vehicle,
at the calamitous
conjuncture of a bad time,
were longing
for Buddha-knowledge.

14.
But the perfectly-enlightened
great Seer
has not yet favoured us
with a prediction
of our destiny,
as if he would say :
Do not eat the food that has
been put into your hand.

15.
Quite so, O hero,
we were longing
as we heard the exalted voice
and thought :
Then shall we be at rest,
when we shall have
received a prediction.

16.
Utter a prediction,
O great hero,
so benevolent and merciful !
let there be an end
of our feeling of poverty !

And the Lord,
who in his mind
apprehended the thoughts
arising in the minds
of those great senior disciples,
again addressed

the complete
assembly of monks :
This great disciple of mine,
monks, the senior Subhûti,
shall likewise pay homage
to thirty hundred thousand
myriads of kotis of Buddhas ;
shall show them respect,
honour,
reverence,
veneration,
and worship.
Under them
shall he lead a spiritual life
and achieve enlightenment.
After the performance
of such duties shall he,
in his last bodily existence,
become a Tathâgata
in the world,
an Arhat, &c. &c.,
by the name of Sasiketu.

His Buddha-field
will be called Ratnasambhava
and his epoch Ratnaprabhâsa.
And that Buddha-field
will be even,
beautiful,
crystalline,
variegated with jewel-trees,
devoid of pits and precipices,
devoid of sewers, nice,
covered with flowers.
And there will men
have their abode
in palaces or towers
given them for their use.
In it will be many disciples,
innumerable,
so that it would be impossible
to terminate the calculation.
Many hundred thousand
myriads of kotis
of Bodhisattvas
also will be there.
The lifetime
of that Lord is to last
twelve intermediate kalpas ;
his true law is to continue
twenty intermediate kalpas,
and its counterfeit as many.
That Lord will,
while standing
poised in the firmament,
preach the law to the monks,
and educate many thousands
of Bodhisattvas and disciples.

And on that occasion
the Lord uttered
the following stanzas :

17.
I have something
to announce monks,
something to make known ;
listen then to me :
The senior Subhûti,
my disciple,
shall in days to come
be a Buddha.

18.
After having seen
of most mighty Buddhas
thirty myriads of kotis in full,
he shall enter upon
the straight course
to obtain this knowledge.

19.
In his last bodily
existence shall the hero,
possessed of the
thirty-two distinctive signs,
become a great Seer,
similar to a column of gold,
beneficial and bounteous
to the world.

20.
The field where
that friend of the world
shall save myriads of kotis
of living beings
will be most beautiful,
pretty, and delightful
to people at large.

21.
In it will be
many Bodhisattvas
to turn the wheel
that never rolls back ;
endowed with keen faculties
they will, under that Gina,
be the ornaments
of the Buddha-field.

22.
His disciples
are so numerous
as to pass calculation
and measure ;
gifted with
the six transcendent faculties,
the triple science
and magic power ;
firm
in the eight emancipations.

23.
His magic power,
while he reveals
supreme enlightenment,
is inconceivable.
Gods and men,
as numerous
as the sands of the Ganges,
will always
reverentially salute him
with joined hands.

24.
He shall stay
twelve intermediate kalpas ;
the true law
of that most high of men
is to last twenty
intermediate kalpas and
the counterfeit of it as many.

Again the Lord addressed
the complete assembly
of monks :
I announce to you, monks,
I make known that
the senior Mahâ-Katyâyana
here present, my disciple,
shall pay homage to eight
thousand kotis of Buddhas ;
shall show them respect,
honour, reverence,
veneration, and worship ;
at the expiration
of those Tathâgatas
he shall build Stûpas,
a thousand yoganas in height,
fifty yoganas
in circumference,
and consisting
of seven precious substances,

to wit, gold, silver,
lapis lazuli, crystal,
red pearl, emerald,
and, seventhly, coral.
Those Stûpas he shall
worship with flowers,
incense, perfumed wreaths,
ointments, powder, robes,
umbrellas, banners, flags,
triumphal streamers.
Afterwards he shall again
pay a similar homage
to twenty kotis of Buddhas ;
show them respect, honour,
reverence, veneration,
and worship.
Then in his last
bodily existence,
his last corporeal appearance,
he shall be
a Tathâgata in the world,
an Arhat, &c. &c., named
Gâmbûnada-prabhâsa
(i.e. gold-shine),
endowed with science
and conduct, &c.
His Buddha-field
will be thoroughly pure,
even, nice, pretty,
beautiful, crystalline,
variegated with jewel-trees,
interlaced with gold threads,
strewed with flowers,
free from beings
of the brute creation, hell,
and the host of demons,
replete with
numerous men and gods,
adorned with many
hundred thousand disciples
and many hundred thousand
Bodhisattvas.
The measure of his lifetime
shall be twelve
intermediate kalpas ;
his true law shall continue
twenty intermediate kalpas
and its counterfeit as many.

And on that occasion
the Lord uttered
the following stanzas :

25.
Listen all to me, ye monks,
since I am going to utter
an infallible word.
Kâtyâyana here, the senior,
my disciple,
shall render worship
to the Leaders.

26.
He shall show veneration
of various kinds
and in many ways
to the Leaders,
after whose expiration
he shall build Stûpas,
worshipping them
with flowers and perfumes.

27.
In his last bodily existence
he shall be a Gina,
in a thoroughly pure field,
and after acquiring
full knowledge
he shall preach
to a thousand kotis
of living beings.

28.
He shall be a mighty Buddha
and illuminator,
highly honoured
in this world,
including the gods,
under the name
of Gâmbûnada-prabhâsa,
and save kotis
of gods and men.

29.
Many Bodhisattvas
as well as disciples,
beyond measure
and calculation,
will in that field adorn
the reign of that Buddha,
all of them
freed from existence
and exempt from existence.

Again the Lord addressed the complete assembly of monks: I announce to you, monks, I make known, that the senior Mahâ-Maudgalyâyana here present, my disciple, shall propitiate twenty-eight thousand Buddhas and pay those Lords homage of various kinds; he shall show them respect, &c., and after their expiration build Stûpas consisting of seven precious substances, to wit, gold, silver, lapis lazuli, crystal, red pearl, emerald, and, seventhly, coral; Stûpas a thousand yoganas in height and five hundred yoganas in circumference, which Stûpas he shall worship in different ways, with flowers, incense, perfumed wreaths, ointments, powder, robes, umbrellas, banners, flags, and triumphal streamers. Afterwards he shall again pay a similar worship to twenty hundred thousand kotis of Buddhas; he shall show respect, &c., and in his last bodily existence become in the world a Tathâgata, &c., named Tamâlapatrakandanagandha, endowed with science and conduct, &c. The field of that Buddha will be called Manobhirâma; his period Ratipratipûrna. And that Buddha-field will be even, nice, pretty, beautiful, crystalline, variegated with jewel-trees, strewn with detached flowers, replete with gods and men, frequented by hundred thousands of Seers, that is to say, disciples and Bodhisattvas. The measure of his lifetime shall be twenty-four intermediate kalpas; his true law is to last forty intermediate kalpas and its counterfeit as many.

And on that occasion
the Lord uttered
the following stanzas :

30.
The scion of the Mudgala-race,
my disciple here,
after leaving human existence
shall see twenty thousand
mighty Ginas
and eight thousand more
of these faultless beings.

31.
Under them he shall
follow a course of duty,
trying to reach
Buddha-knowledge ;
he shall pay homage
in various ways
to those Leaders
and to the most high of men.

32.
After keeping their true law,
of wide reach and sublime,
for thousands
of kotis of Æons,
he shall
at the expiration
of those Sugatas
worship their Stûpas.

33.
In honour
of those most high Ginas,
those mighty beings
so beneficial to the world,
he shall erect Stûpas
consisting
of precious substances,
and decorated
with triumphal streamers,
worshipping them
with flowers, perfumes,
and the sounds of music.

34.
At the period
of his last bodily existence
he shall,
in a nice and beautiful field,
be a Buddha bounteous
and compassionate
to the world,
under the name of
Tamâlapatrakandanagandha.

35.
The measure
of that Sugata's life
shall be fully twenty-four
intermediate kalpas,
during which
he shall be assiduous
in declaring the Buddha-rule
to men and gods.

36.
That Gina shall have
many thousands
of kotis of disciples,
innumerable as the sands
of the Ganges,
gifted with
the six transcendent faculties
and the triple science,
and possessed
of magic power,
under the command
of that Sugata.

37.
Under the reign of that Sugata
there shall also appear
numerous Bodhisattvas,
many thousands of them,
unable to slide back
or to deviate,
developing zeal,
of extensive knowledge
and studious habits.

38.
After that Gina's expiration
his true law shall measure
in time twenty-four
intermediate kalpas in full ;
its counterfeit shall have
the same measure.

39.
These
are my five mighty disciples
whom I have destined
to supreme enlightenment
and to become in future
self-born Ginas ;
now hear from me
their course.

Chapter VII
Ancient Devotion

Of yore, monks,
in the past, incalculable,
more than incalculable,
inconceivable, immense,
measureless Æons since,
nay, at a period,
an epoch far beyond,
there appeared in the world
a Tathâgata, &c., named
Mahâbhigñâgñanâbhibhû,
endowed with science
and conduct,
a Sugata, &c. &c.,
in the sphere Sambhava
(i.e. origin, genesis),
in the period Mahârûpa.
You ask, monks,
how long ago is it that
the Tathâgata was born?
Well,
suppose some man
was to reduce to powder
the whole mass
of the earth element
as much as is to be found
in this whole universe;
that after taking one atom
of dust from this world
he is to walk
a thousand worlds
farther in easterly direction
to deposit that single atom;
that after taking a second
atom of dust and walking
a thousand worlds farther
he deposits that second atom,
and proceeding in this way
at last gets the whole
of the earth element
deposited in eastern direction.
Now, monks,
what do you think of it,
is it possible by calculation
to find the end or limit
of these worlds?
They answered:
Certainly not, Lord;
certainly not, Sugata.
The Lord said:
On the contrary, monks,
some arithmetician
or master of arithmetic might,
indeed,
be able by calculation to find
the end or limit of the worlds,
both those where the atoms
have been deposited
and where they have not,
but it is impossible
by applying
the rules of arithmetic
to find the limit
of those hundred thousands
of myriads of Æons,
so long,
so inconceivable,
so immense is the number
of Æons which have elapsed
since the expiration
of that Lord,
the Tathâgata
Mahâbhigñâgñanâbhibhû.
Yet, monks,
I perfectly remember
that Tathâgata
who has been extinct
for so long a time,
as if he had reached
extinction to-day or yesterday,

because of my possessing
the mighty knowledge
and sight of the Tathâgata.

And on that occasion
the Lord pronounced
the following stanzas :

1.
I remember the great Seer
Abhigñâgñânâbhibhû,
the most high of men,
who existed
many kotis of Æons ago
as the superior Gina
of the period.

2.
If, for example, some men
after reducing this universe
to atoms of dust
took one atom to deposit it
a thousand regions farther on ;

3.
If he deposited a second,
a third atom,
and so proceeded
until he had done with
the whole mass of dust,
so that this world were empty
and the mass of dust
exhausted ;

4.
To that immense mass
of the dust of these worlds,
entirely reduced to atoms,
I liken the number
of Æons past.

5.
So immense is the number
of kotis of Æons past
since that extinct Sugata ;
the whole of existing atoms
is no adequate
expression of it ;
so many are the Æons
which have expired since.

6.
That Leader
who has expired so long ago,
those disciples
and Bodhisattvas,
I remember all of them
as if it were to-day
or yesterday.
Such is the knowledge
of the Tathâgatas.

7.
So endless, monks,
is the knowledge
of the Tathâgata ;
I know what has taken place
many hundreds of Æons ago,
by my precise
and faultless memory.

To proceed, monks,
the measure of the lifetime
of the Tathâgata
Mahâbhigñâgñanâbhibhû,
the Arhat, &c.
was fifty-four hundred
thousand myriads
of kotis of Æons.

In the beginning
when the Lord

had not yet reached supreme,
perfect enlightenment
and had just occupied
the summit of the terrace
of enlightenment,
he discomfited and defeated
the whole host of Mâra,
after which he thought :
I am to reach
perfect enlightenment.
But those laws
of perfect enlightenment
had not yet
dawned upon him.
He stayed on the terrace
of enlightenment
at the foot of the tree
of enlightenment during
one intermediate kalpa.
He stayed there a second,
a third intermediate kalpa,
but did not yet attain
supreme,
perfect enlightenment.
He remained a fourth,
a fifth, a sixth, a seventh,
an eighth, a ninth,
a tenth intermediate kalpa on
the terrace of enlightenment
at the foot of the tree
of enlightenment,
continuing sitting
cross-legged without
in the meanwhile rising.
He stayed,
the mind motionless,
the body unstirring
and untrembling,
but those laws had not yet
dawned upon him.

Now, monks,
while the Lord was just
on the summit of the terrace
of enlightenment,
the gods of Paradise
prepared him
a magnificent royal throne,
a hundred yoganas high,
on occupying which
the Lord attained supreme,
perfect enlightenment ;
and no sooner
had the Lord occupied
the seat of enlightenment
than the Brahmakâyika gods
scattered a rain of flowers
all around
the seat of enlightenment
over a distance
of a hundred yoganas ;
in the sky they let loose storms
by which the flowers,
withered, were swept away.
From the beginning
of the rain of flowers,
while the Lord was sitting
on the seat of enlightenment,
it poured without interruption
during fully
ten intermediate kalpas,
covering the Lord.
That rain of flowers
having once begun falling
continued to the moment of
the Lord's complete Nirvâna.
The angels belonging
to the division
of the four guardians
of the cardinal points
made the celestial drums
of the gods resound ;

they made them resound
without interruption
in honour of the Lord
who had attained
the summit of the terrace
of enlightenment.
Thereafter, during
fully ten intermediate kalpas,
they made uninterruptedly
resound those celestial
musical instruments
up to the moment
of the complete extinction
of the Lord.

Again, monks,
after the lapse
of ten intermediate kalpas
the Lord
Mahâbhigñâgñanâbhibhû,
the Tathâgata, &c.,
reached supreme,
perfect enlightenment.
Immediately on knowing
his having
become enlightened
the sixteen sons
born to that Lord
when a prince royal,
the eldest of whom
was named Gñânâkara -
which sixteen young princes,
monks,
had severally toys
to play with,
variegated and pretty -
those sixteen princes,
I repeat, monks,
left their toys,
their amusements,
and since they knew
that the Lord
Mahâbhigñâgñanâbhibhû,
the Tathâgata, &c.,
had attained supreme,
perfect knowledge, went,
surrounded and attended
by their weeping mothers
and nurses,
along with the noble,
rich king Kakravartin,
many ministers,
and hundred thousands
of myriads of kotis
of living beings,
to the place where the Lord
Mahâbhigñâgñanâbhibhû,
the Tathâgata, &c.,
was seated on the summit of
the terrace of enlightenment.
They went up to the Lord
in order to honour, respect,
worship, revere,
and venerate him,
saluted his feet
with their heads,
made three turns round him
keeping him to the right,
lifted up their joined hands,
and praised the Lord,
face to face,
with the following stanzas :

8.
Thou art the great physician,
having no superior,
rendered perfect
in endless Æons.
Thy benign wish of saving
all mortals from darkness
has to-day been fulfilled.

9.
Most difficult things
hast thou achieved
during the ten intermediate
kalpas now past;
thou hast been
sitting all that time
without once moving
thy body, hand, foot,
or any other part.

10.
Thy mind also was tranquil
and steady, motionless,
never to be shaken;
thou knewest no distraction;
thou art completely
quiet and faultless.

11.
Joy with thee!
that thou so happily
and safely,
without any hurt,
hast reached
supreme enlightenment.
How great a fortune is ours!
we congratulate ourselves,
O Lion amongst kings!

12.
These unhappy creatures,
vexed in all ways,
deprived of eyes,
as it were, and joyless,
do not find the road
leading to the end of toils,
nor develop energy
for the sake of deliverance.

13.
Dangers are for a long time
on the increase
and the laws,
are deprived
of the possession
of a celestial body;
the word of the Gina
is not being heard;
the whole world
is plunged in thick darkness.

14.
But to-day hast thou,
Majesty of the world,
reached this hallowed,
high, and faultless spot;
we as well as the world
are obliged to thee,
and approach
to seek our refuge with thee,
O Protector!

When, O monks,
those sixteen princes
in the condition of boys,
childlike and young,
had with such stanzas
celebrated the Lord
Mahâbhigñâgñanâbhibhû,
the Tathâgata, &c.,
they urged the Lord to move
on the wheel of the law:
Preach the law, O Lord;
preach the law, O Sugata,
for the weal of the public,
the happiness of the public,
out of compassion
for the world;
for the benefit,
weal, and happiness

Ancient Devotion 133

of the people generally,
both of gods and men.
And on that occasion
they uttered
the following stanzas :

15.
Preach the law,
O thou who art marked with
a hundred auspicious signs,
O Leader,
O incomparable great Seer !
thou hast attained exalted,
sublime knowledge ;
let it shine in the world,
including the gods.

16.
Release us as well
as these creatures ;
display the knowledge
of the Tathâgatas,
that we also and, further,
these beings may obtain
this supreme enlightenment.

17.
Thou knowest every course
of duty and knowledge ;
thou knowest the mental
and moral disposition
and the good works
done in a former state ;
the natural bent
of all living beings.
Move on the most exalted,
sublime wheel !

Then, monks, as the Lord
Mahâbhigñâgñanâbhibhû,
the Tathâgata, &c.,

reached supreme,
perfect enlightenment,
fifty hundred thousand
myriads of kotis of spheres
in each of the ten directions
of space were shaken
in six different ways
and became illumined
with a great lustre.
And in the intervals
between all those spheres,
in the dreary places
of dark gloom,
where even the sun and moon,
so powerful,
mighty, and splendid,
have no advantage
of the shining power
they are endowed with,
have no advantage
of the colour
and brightness they possess,
even in those places
a great lustre arose instantly.
And the beings who appeared
in those intervals
behold each other,
acknowledge each other,
and exclaim :
Lo, there are other beings
also here appearing !
lo, there are other beings
also here appearing !
The palaces
and aerial cars of the gods
in all those spheres
up to the Brahma-world
shook in six different ways
and became illumined
with a great lustre,
surpassing the divine majesty

of the gods.
So then, monks,
a great earthquake and a great,
sublime lustre
arose simultaneously.
And the aerial cars
of the Brahma-angels
to the east,
in these fifty hundred
thousand myriads
of kotis of spheres,
began excessively to glitter,
glow, and sparkle
in splendour and glory.
And those Brahma-angels
made this reflection :
What may be foreboded
by these aerial cars
so excessively glittering,
glowing, and sparkling
in splendour and glory ?
Thereupon, monks,
the Brahma-angels
in the fifty hundred thousand
myriads of kotis of spheres
went all to each other's abodes
and communicated
the matter to one another.
After that, monks,
the great Brahma-angel,
named Sarvasattvatrâtri
(i.e. Saviour of all beings),
addressed the numerous
host of Brahma-angels
in the following stanzas :

18.
Our aerial cars to-day
are all bristling with rays
in an extraordinary degree,
and blazing
in beautiful splendour
and brilliancy.
What may be the cause of it ?

19.
Come,
let us investigate the matter,
what divine being has to-day
sprung into existence,
whose power,
such as was
never seen before,
here now appears ?

20.
Or should it be the Buddha,
the king of kings,
who to-day has been born
somewhere in the world,
and whose birth is announced
by such a token that all
the points of the horizon
are now blazing
in splendour ?

Thereupon, monks,
the great Brahma-angels
in the fifty hundred thousand
myriads of kotis of spheres
mounted all together
their own divine aerial cars,
took with them divine bags,
as large as Mount Sumeru,
with celestial flowers,
and went through
the four quarters successively
until they arrived
at the western quarter, where
those great Brahma-angels,
O monks, stationed
in the western quarter,

saw the Lord
Mahâbhigñâgñanâbhibhû,
the Tathâgata, &c.,
on the summit of the exalted
terrace of enlightenment,
seated on the royal throne
at the foot of the tree
of enlightenment,
surrounded and attended
by gods, Nâgas, goblins,
Gandharvas, demons,
Garudas, Kinnaras,
great serpents, men,
and beings not human,
while his sons,
the sixteen young princes,
were urging him
to move forward
the wheel of the law.
On seeing which
the Brahma-angels
came up to the Lord,
saluted his feet
with their heads,
walked many hundred
thousand times round him
from left to right,
strewing flowers
and overwhelming both him
and the tree of enlightenment,
over a distance of ten yoganas,
with those flower-bags
as large as Mount Sumeru.
After that they presented
to the Lord their aerial cars
with the words :
Accept, O Lord,
these aerial cars
out of compassion to us ;
use, O Sugata, those cars
out of compassion to us.

On that occasion, monks,
after presenting
their own cars to the Lord,
the Brahma-angels
celebrated the Lord,
face to face,
with the following
seasonable stanzas :

21.
A wonderful,
matchless Gina,
so beneficial and merciful,
has arisen in the world.
Thou art born a protector,
a ruler and teacher, a master ;
to-day all quarters are blessed.

22.
We have come as far
as fully fifty thousand
kotis of worlds from here
to humbly salute the Gina
by surrendering our lofty
aerial cars all together.

23.
We possess these variegated
and bright cars,
owing to previous works ;
accept them to oblige us,
and make use of them
to thine heart's content,
O Knower of the world !

After the great
Brahma-angels, monks,
had celebrated the Lord
Mahâbhigñâgñanâbhibhû,
the Tathâgata, &c., face to face,

with these seasonable stanzas,
they besought him, saying :
May the Lord move forward
the wheel of the law !
May the Lord
preach final rest !
May the Lord
release all beings !
Be favourable, O Lord,
to this world !
Preach the law, O Lord,
to this world,
including gods, Mâras,
and Brahma-angels ;
to all people,
including ascetics
and Brahmans,
gods, men, and demons !
It will tend to the weal
of the public,
to the happiness of the public ;
out of mercy to the world,
for the benefit and happiness
of the people at large,
both gods and men.
Thereupon, monks,
those fifty hundred thousand
myriads of kotis
of Brahma-angels
addressed the Lord,
with one voice,
in common chorus,
with the following stanza :

24.
Show the law, O Lord ;
show it, O most high of men !
Show the power
of thy kindness ;
save the tormented beings.

25.
Rare is the light of the world
like the blossom
of the glomerated fig-tree.
Thou hast arisen,
O great Hero ; we pray to thee,
the Tathâgata.

And the Lord, O monks,
silently intimated his assent
to the Brahma-angels.
Somewhat later, monks,
the aerial cars
of the Brahma-angels
in the south-eastern quarter
in the fifty hundred thousand
myriads of spheres
began excessively to glitter,
glow, and sparkle
in splendour and glory.
And those Brahma-angels
made this reflection :
What may be foreboded
by these aerial cars
so excessively glittering,
glowing, and sparkling
in splendour and glory ?
Thereupon, monks,
the Brahma-angels
in the fifty hundred thousand
myriads of kotis of spheres
went all to each other's abodes
and communicated
the matter to one another.
After that, monks,
the great Brahma-angel,
named Adhimâtrakârunika
(i.e. exceedingly compassionate),
addressed the numerous host
of Brahma-angels
with the following stanzas :

26.
What foretoken is it
we see to-day, friends ?
Who or what is foreboded
by the celestial cars shining
with such uncommon glory ?

27.
May, perhaps,
some blessed divine being
have come hither,
by whose power
all these aerial cars
are illumined ?

28.
Or may the Buddha,
the most high of men,
have appeared in this world,
that by his power
these celestial cars
are in such a condition
as we see them ?

29.
Let us all together
go and search ;
no trifle can be the cause of it ;
such a foretoken, indeed,
was never seen before.

30.
Come, let us go
and visit kotis of fields,
along the four quarters ;
a Buddha
will certainly now have made
his appearance in this world.

Thereupon, monks,
the great Brahma-angels
in the fifty hundred thousand
myriads of kotis of spheres
mounted all together
their own divine aerial cars,
took with them divine bags,
as large as Mount Sumeru,
with celestial flowers,
and went through
the four quarters successively
until they arrived
at the north-western quarter,
where those great
Brahma-angels, stationed
in the north-western quarter,
saw the Lord
Mahâbhigñâgñanâbhibhû.

On that occasion, monks,
after presenting their own cars
to the Lord the Brahma-angels
celebrated the Lord,
face to face,
with the following
seasonable stanzas :

31.
Homage to thee,
matchless great Seer,
chief god of gods,
whose voice is sweet
as the lark's.
Leader in the world,
including the gods,
I salute thee,
who art so benign
and bounteous to the world.

32.
How wonderful, O Lord,
is it that after so long a time
thou appearest in the world.

Eighty hundred
complete Æons
this world of the living
was without Buddha.

33.
It was deprived
of the most high of men ;
hell was prevailing
and the celestial bodies
constantly went on waning
during eighty hundred
complete Æons.

34.
But now he has appeared,
owing to our good works,
who is our eye, refuge,
resting-place, protection,
father, and kinsman ; he, the
benign and bounteous one,
the King of the law.

After
the great Brahma-angels,
monks,
had celebrated the Lord
Mahâbhigñâgñanâbhibhû,
the Tathâgata, &c.,
face to face,
with these seasonable stanzas :
they besought him :
May the Lord move forward
the wheel of the law !

Thereupon, monks,
those fifty hundred
thousand myriads
of kotis of Brahma-angels
addressed the Lord,
with one voice,

in common chorus,
with the following stanzas :

35.
Move forward
the exalted wheel,
O great ascetic !
reveal the law
in all directions ;
deliver all beings
oppressed with suffering ;
produce amongst mortals
gladness and joy !

36.
Let them by hearing the law
partake of enlightenment
and reach divine places.
Let all shake off
their demon body
and be peaceful,
meek, and at ease.

And the Lord, O monks,
silently intimated his assent
to these Brahma-angels also.

Somewhat later, monks,
the aerial cars
of the Brahma-angels
in the southern quarter.
After that, monks,
the great Brahma-angel,
named Sudharma,
addressed the numerous host
of Brahma-angels in stanzas :

37.
It cannot be
without cause or reason,
friends, that to-day or now

Ancient Devotion 139

all these celestial cars
are so brilliant;
this bespeaks some portent
somewhere in the world.
Come, let us go
and investigate the matter.

38.
No such portent has appeared
in hundreds of Æons past.
Either some god has been born
or a Buddha
has arisen in this world.

Thereupon, monks,
the great Brahma-angels
in the fifty hundred thousand
myriads of kotis
of spheres mounted.

On that occasion, monks,
after presenting
their own cars to the Lord,
the Brahma-angels
celebrated the Lord,
face to face,
with the following
seasonable stanzas:

39.
Most rare and precious
is the sight of the Leaders.
Be welcome,
thou dispeller
of worldly defilement.
It is after a long time that thou
now appearest in the world;
after hundreds
of complete Æons
one now beholds thee.

40.
Refresh the thirsty creatures,
O Lord of the world!
Now first thou art seen;
it is not easy to behold thee.
As rare or precious
as the flowers
of the glomerated fig-tree
is thine appearance, O Lord.

41.
By thy power these aerial cars
of ours are so uncommonly
illumined now, O Leader.
To show us
thy favour accept them,
O thou whose look
pierces everywhere!

After
the great Brahma-angels,
monks,
had celebrated the Lord
Mahâbhigñâgñanâbhibhû,
the Tathâgata, &c.,
face to face,
with these seasonable stanzas,
they besought him:
May the Lord move forward
the wheel of the law!

Thereupon, monks,
those fifty hundred thousand
myriads of kotis
of Brahma-angels
addressed the Lord,
with one voice,
in common chorus,
with the following stanzas:

42.
Preach the law,
O Lord and Leader !
move forward
the wheel of the law,
make the drum
of the law resound,
and blow the conch-trumpet
of the law.

43.
Shed the rain of the true law
over this world and proclaim
the sweet-sounding,
good word ;
manifest the law required,
save myriads of kotis
of beings.

And the Lord, monks,
silently intimated his assent
to the Brahma-angels.

Repetition ;
the same occurred
in the south-west,
in the west,
in the north-west,
in the north,
in the north-east,
in the nadir.

Then, monks,
the aerial cars
of the Brahma-angels
in the nadir,
in those fifty hundred
thousand myriads
of kotis of spheres.
After that, monks,
the great Brahma-angel,
named Sikhin,
addressed the numerous host
of Brahma-angels
with the following stanzas :

44.
What may be the cause,
O friends,
that our cars are so bright
with splendour,
colour, and light ?
What may be the reason
of their being
so exceedingly glorious ?

45.
We have seen
nothing like this before
nor heard of it from others.
These cars are now bright
with splendour
and exceedingly glorious ;
what may be the cause of it ?

46.
Should it be some god
who has been bestowed
upon the world
in recompense of good works,
and whose grandeur
thus comes to light ?
Or is perhaps a Buddha
born in the world ?

Thereupon, monks,
the great Brahma-angels
in the fifty hundred thousand
myriads of kotis of spheres
mounted all together
their own divine aerial cars,
took with them divine bags,

as large as Mount Sumeru,
with celestial flowers,
and went through
the four quarters successively
until they arrived
at the zenith,
where those great
Brahma-angels,
stationed at the zenith,
saw the Lord
Mahâbhigñâgñanâbhibhû.

On that occasion, monks,
after presenting
their own cars to the Lord,
the Brahma-angels
celebrated the Lord,
face to face,
with the following
seasonable stanzas :

47.
How goodly
is the sight of the Buddhas,
the mighty Lords
of the world ;
those Buddhas
who are to deliver all beings
in this triple world.

48.
The all-seeing Masters
of the world send their looks
in all directions of the horizon,
and by opening
the gate of immortality
they make people
reach the safe shore.

49.
An inconceivable number
of Æons now past were void,
and all quarters
wrapt in darkness, as
the chief Ginas did not appear.

50.
The dreary hells,
the brute creation and demons
were on the increase ;
thousands of kotis
of living beings
fell into the state of ghosts.

51.
The heavenly bodies
were on the wane ;
after their disappearance
they entered upon evil ways ;
their course became wrong
because they did not hear
the law of the Buddhas.

52.
All creatures
lacked dutiful behaviour,
purity, good state,
and understanding ;
their happiness was lost,
and the consciousness
of happiness was gone.

53.
They did not observe
the rules of morality ;
were firmly rooted
in the false law ; not being led
by the Lord of the world,
they were precipitated
into a false course.

54.
Hail! thou art come at last,
O Light of the world!
thou, born to be bounteous
towards all beings.

55.
Hail!
thou hast safely arrived at
supreme Buddha-knowledge;
we feel thankful before thee,
and so does the world,
including the gods.

56.
By thy power, O mighty Lord,
our aerial cars are glittering;
to thee we present them,
great Hero;
deign to accept them,
great Solitary.

57.
Out of grace to us,
O Leader, make use of them,
so that we,
as well as all other beings,
may attain
supreme enlightenment.

After
the great Brahma-angels,
O monks,
had celebrated the Lord
Mahâbhigñâgñanâbhibhû,
the Tathâgata, &c.,
face to face,
with seasonable stanzas,
they besought him:
May the Lord move forward
the wheel of the law!

Thereupon, monks,
those fifty hundred
thousand myriads
of kotis of Brahma-angels
addressed the Lord,
with one voice,
in common chorus,
with the following
two stanzas:

58.
Move forward the exalted,
unsurpassed wheel!
beat the drum of immortality!
release all beings
from hundreds of evils,
and show
the path of Nirvâna.

59.
Expound the law we pray for;
show thy favour to us
and this world.
Let us hear thy sweet
and lovely voice
which thou hast exercised
during thousands
of kotis of Æons.

Now, monks,
the Lord
Mahâbhigñâgñanâbhibhû
the Tathâgata, &c.,
being acquainted with
the prayer of the hundred
thousand myriads of kotis
of Brahma-angels
and of the sixteen princes,
his sons,
commenced at that juncture

to turn the wheel
that has three turns
and twelve parts,
the wheel never moved
by any ascetic,
Brahman, god, demon,
nor by any one else.
His preaching
consisted in this :
This is pain ;
this is the origin of pain ;
this is the suppression of pain ;
this is the treatment leading
to suppression of pain.
He moreover extensively
set forth how the series of
causes and effects is evolved,
and said : It is thus, monks.
From ignorance proceed
conceptions or fancies ;
from conceptions or fancies
proceeds understanding ;
from understanding
name and form ;
from name and form
the six senses ;
from the six senses
proceeds contact ;
from contact sensation ;
from sensation
proceeds longing ;
from longing
proceeds striving ;
from striving as cause
issues existence ;
from existence birth ;
from birth old age,
death, mourning,
lamentation, sorrow,
dismay, and despondency.
So originates
this whole mass of misery.
From the suppression
of ignorance results
the suppression
of conceptions ;
from the suppression
of conceptions results
that of understanding ;
from the suppression
of understanding results
that of name and form ;
from the suppression
of name and form results
that of the six senses ;
from the suppression
of the six senses results
that of contact ;
from the suppression
of contact results
that of sensation ;
from the suppression
of sensation results
that of longing ;
from the suppression
of longing results
that of striving ;
from the suppression
of striving results
that of existence ;
from the suppression
of existence
results that of birth ;
from the suppression of birth
results that of old age,
death, mourning,
lamentation, sorrow,
dismay, and despondency.
In this manner
the whole mass of misery
is suppressed.

And while
this wheel of the law, monks,
was being moved onward
by the Lord
Mahâbhigñâgñanâbhibhû,
the Tathâgata, &c.,
in presence of the world,
including the gods, demons,
and Brahma-angels;
of the assemblage,
including ascetics
and Brahmans;
then, at that time,
on that occasion,
the minds of sixty hundred
thousand myriads of kotis
of living beings
were without effort
freed from imperfections
and became all possessed
of the triple science,
of the sixfold
transcendent wisdom,
of the emancipations
and meditations.
In due course, monks,
the Lord
Mahâbhigñâgñanâbhibhû,
the Tathâgata, &c.,
again gave a second
exposition of the law;
likewise a third
and a fourth exposition.
And at each exposition,
monks,
the minds of hundred
thousands of myriads
of kotis of beings,
like the sands
of the river Ganges,
were without effort
freed from imperfections.
Afterwards, monks,
the congregation
of disciples of that Lord
was so numerous
as to surpass all calculation.

Meanwhile, monks,
the sixteen princes,
the youths, had, full of faith,
left home to lead
the vagrant life of mendicants,
and had all of them
become novices, clever,
bright, intelligent, pious,
followers
of the course of duty
under many
hundred thousand Buddhas,
and striving after supreme,
perfect enlightenment.
These sixteen novices,
monks, said to the Lord
Mahâbhigñâgñanâbhibhû,
the Tathâgata, &c.,
the following: O Lord,
these many hundred
thousand myriads of kotis
of disciples of the Tathâgata
have become very mighty,
very powerful,
very potent,
owing to
the Lord's teaching of the law.
Deign, O Lord,
to teach us also,
for mercy's sake, the law
with a view to supreme,
perfect enlightenment,
so that we also may follow
the teaching of the Tathâgata.

We want, O Lord,
to see the knowledge
of the Tathâgata ;
the Lord can himself
testify to this, for thou,
O Lord, who knowest
the disposition of all beings,
also knowest ours.

Then, monks,
on seeing that those princes,
the youths, had chosen
the vagrant life of mendicants
and become novices,
the half of the whole retinue
of the king Kakravartin,
to the number
of eighty hundred thousand
myriads of kotis
of living beings,
chose the vagrant life
of mendicants.

Subsequently, monks,
the Lord
Mahâbhigñâgñanâbhibhû,
the Tathâgata, &c.,
viewing the prayer
of those novices at the lapse
of twenty thousand Æons,
amply
and completely revealed
the Dharmaparyâya called
'the Lotus of the True Law, '
a text of great extent,
serving to instruct
Bodhisattvas
and proper for all Buddhas,
in presence of all
the four classes of auditors.

In course of time, monks,
those sixteen novices
grasped, kept,
and fully penetrated
the Lord's teaching.

Subsequently, monks,
the Lord
Mahâbhigñâgñanâbhibhû,
the Tathâgata, &c., foretold
those sixteen novices
their future destiny
to supreme,
perfect enlightenment.
And while the Lord
Mahâbhigñâgñanâbhibhû,
the Tathâgata, &c.,
was propounding
the Dharmaparyâya
of the Lotus of the True Law,
the disciples
as well as the sixteen novices
were full of faith,
and many hundred thousand
myriads of kotis of beings
acquired perfect certainty.

Thereupon, monks,
after propounding
the Dharmaparyâya
of the Lotus of the True Law
during eight thousand Æons
without interruption,
the Lord
Mahâbhigñâgñanâbhibhû,
the Tathâgata, &c.,
entered the monastery
to retire for
the purpose of meditation,
and in that retirement, monks,
the Tathâgata

continued in the monastery
during eighty-four thousand
kotis of Æons.

Now, monks,
when the sixteen novices
perceived that the Lord
was absorbed,
they sat down on the seats,
the royal thrones
which had been prepared
for each of them,
and amply expounded,
during eighty-four hundred
thousand myriads of kotis,
the Dharmaparyâya
of the Lotus of the True Law
to the four classes.
By doing this, monks,
each of those novices,
as Bodhisattvas
fully developed, instructed,
excited, stimulated, edified,
confirmed
in respect to supreme,
perfect enlightenment 60 x 60
hundred thousand myriads
of kotis of living beings,
equal to the sands
of the river Ganges.

Now, monks, at the lapse of
eighty-four thousand Æons
the Lord
Mahâbhigñâgñanâbhibhû,
the Tathâgata, &c.,
rose from his meditation,
in possession of memory
and consciousness,
whereafter he went up
to the seat of the law,
designed for him,
in order to occupy it.

As soon as the Lord had
occupied the seat of the law,
monks,
he cast his looks
over the whole circle
of the audience and addressed
the congregation of monks :
They are wonderfully gifted,
monks,
they are prodigiously gifted,
these sixteen novices, wise,
servitors to many
hundred thousand
myriads of kotis of Buddhas,
observers
of the course of duty,
who have received
Buddha-knowledge,
transmitted
Buddha-knowledge,
expounded
Buddha-knowledge.
Honour these sixteen novices,
monks, again and again ;
and all, be they devoted to
the vehicle of the disciples,
the vehicle
of the Pratyekabuddhas,
or the vehicle
of the Bodhisattvas,
who shall not reject
nor repudiate the preaching
of these young men
of good family, O monks,
shall quickly gain supreme,
perfect enlightenment,
and obtain
Tathâgata-knowledge.

Ancient Devotion

In the sequel also, monks,
have these young men
of good family
repeatedly revealed
this Dharmaparyâya
of the Lotus of the True Law
under the mastership
of that Lord.
And the 60 x 60
hundred thousand myriads
of kotis of living beings,
equal to the sands
of the river Ganges,
who by each
of the sixteen novices,
the Bodhisattvas Mahâsattvas,
in the quality of Bodhisattva,
had been roused
to enlightenment,
all those beings
followed the example
of the sixteen novices
in choosing along with them
the vagrant life of mendicants,
in their several existences ;
they enjoyed their sight
and heard the law
from their mouth.
They propitiated
forty kotis of Buddhas,
and some
are doing so up to this day.

I announce to you, monks,
I declare to you :
Those sixteen princes,
the youths,
who as novices under
the mastership of the Lord
were interpreters of the law,
have all reached supreme,
perfect enlightenment,
and all of them are staying,
existing, living even now, in
the several directions of space,
in different Buddha-fields,
preaching the law
to many hundred thousand
myriads of kotis of disciples
and Bodhisattvas, to wit :
In the east, monks,
in the world Abhirati
the Tathâgata named
Akshobhya, the Arhat, &c.,
and the Tathâgata Merukûta,
the Arhat, &c.
In the south-east, monks,
is the Tathâgata
Simhaghosha, &c.,
and the Tathâgata
Simhadhvaga, &c.
In the south, monks,
is the Tathâgata named
Âkâsapratishthita, &c.,
and the Tathâgata named
Nityaparinirvrita, &c.
In the southwest, monks,
is the Tathâgata named
Indradhvaga, &c.,
and the Tathâgata named
Brahmadhvaga, &c.
In the west, monks,
is the Tathâgata named
Amitâyus, &c.,
and the Tathâgata named
Sarvalokadhâtûpadravod-
vegapratyuttîrna, &c.
In the north-west, monks,
is the Tathâgata named
Tamâlapatrakandana-
gandhâbhigña, &c.,

and the Tathâgata
Merukalpa, &c.
In the north, monks,
is the Tathâgata named
Meghasvarapradîpa, &c.,
and the Tathâgata named
Meghasvararâga, &c.
In the north-east, monks,
is the Tathâgata named
Sarvalokabhayâgitakkham-
bhitatvavidhvamsanakara,
the Arhat, &c.,
and, the sixteenth, myself,
Sâkyamuni, the Tathâgata,
the Arhat, &c.,
who have attained supreme,
perfect enlightenment in
the centre of this Saha-world.

Further, monks,
those beings who have heard
the law from us
when we were novices,
those many hundred
thousand myriads
of kotis of beings,
numerous as the sands
of the river Ganges,
whom we have severally
initiated in supreme,
perfect enlightenment,
they are up to this day
standing on the stage
of disciples
and matured for supreme,
perfect enlightenment.
In regular turn
they are to attain supreme,
perfect enlightenment,
for it is difficult, monks,
to penetrate the knowledge
of the Tathâgatas.
And which are those beings,
monks, who, innumerable,
incalculable like
the sands of the Ganges,
those hundred thousands
of myriads of kotis
of living beings, whom I,
when I was a Bodhisattva
under the mastership
of that Lord,
have taught the law
of omniscience ?
Yourselves, monks,
were at that time those beings.

And those who shall be
my disciples in future,
when I shall have
attained complete Nirvâna,
shall learn the course of duty
of Bodhisattvas,
without conceiving the idea
of their being Bodhisattvas.
And, monks, all who shall
have the idea of complete
Nirvâna, shall reach it.
It should be added, monks,
as I stay under different names
in other worlds,
they shall there be born again
seeking after the knowledge
of the Tathâgatas,
and there they shall
anew hear this dogma :
The complete Nirvâna
of the Tathâgatas is but one ;
there is no other,
no second Nirvâna
of the Tathâgatas.
Herein, monks,

one has to see a device
of the Tathâgatas
and a direction
for the preaching of the law.
When the Tathâgata, monks,
knows that the moment
of his complete extinction
has arrived,
and sees that the assemblage
is pure, strong in faith,
penetrated
with the law of voidness,
devoted to meditation,
devoted to great meditation,
then, monks, the Tathâgata,
because the time has arrived,
calls together all Bodhisattvas
and all disciples
to teach them thus :
There is, O monks,
in this world
no second vehicle at all,
no second Nirvâna,
far less a third.
It is an able device
of the Tathâgata, monks,
that on seeing
creatures far advanced
on the path of perdition,
delighting in the low
and plunged
in the mud of sensual desires,
the Tathâgata
teaches them that Nirvâna
to which they are attached.

By way of example, monks,
suppose there is
some dense forest
five hundred yoganas
in extent

which has been reached
by a great company of men.
They have a guide
to lead them on their journey
to the Isle of Jewels,
which guide, being able,
clever, sagacious,
well acquainted
with the difficult passages
of the forest,
is to bring the whole company
out of the forest.
Meanwhile that great
troop of men, tired, weary,
afraid, and anxious, say :
'Verily, Master,
guide, and leader,
know that we are tired,
weary, afraid, and anxious ;
let us return ;
this dense forest
stretches so far.'
The guide,
who is a man of able devices,
on seeing those people
desirous of returning,
thinks within himself :
It ought not to be
that these poor creatures
should not reach
that great Isle of Jewels.
Therefore out of pity for them
he makes use of an artifice.
In the middle of that forest
he produces a magic city
more than a hundred
or two hundred yoganas
in extent.
Thereafter
he says to those men :
'Be not afraid, sirs,

do not return ;
there you see
a populous place where
you may take repose and
perform all you have to do ;
there stay in the enjoyment
of happy rest.
Let him who after reposing
there wants to do so,
proceed
to the great Isle of Jewels.'

Then, monks,
the men who are in the forest
are struck with astonishment,
and think :
We are out of the forest ;
we have reached
the place of happy rest ;
let us stay here.
They enter that magic city,
in the meaning that they have
arrived at the place
of their destination,
that they are saved
and in the enjoyment of rest.
They think : We are at rest,
we are refreshed.
After awhile,
when the guide perceives
that their fatigue is gone,
he causes
the magic city to disappear,
and says to them : 'Come, sirs,
there you see the great
Isle of Jewels quite near ;
as to this great city,
it has been produced by me
for no other purpose
but to give you some repose.'

In the same manner, monks,
is the Tathâgata,
the Arhat, &c.,
your guide, and
the guide of all other beings.
Indeed, monks,
the Tathâgata, &c.,
reflects thus :
Great is this forest of evils
which must be crossed,
left, shunned.
It ought not to be
that these beings,
after hearing
the Buddha-knowledge,
should suddenly turn back
and not proceed to the end
because they think :
This Buddha-knowledge
is attended
with too many difficulties
to be gone through to the end.
Under those circumstances
the Tathâgata,
knowing the creatures
to be feeble of character,
does as the guide
who produces the magic city
in order that those people
may have repose, and after
their having taken repose,
he tells them that the city
is one produced by magic.
In the same manner, monks,
the Tathâgata, &c., to give
a repose to the creatures,
very skilfully teaches
and proclaims two stages
of Nirvâna,
namely the stage
of the disciples and that

of the Pratyekabuddhas.
And, monks,
when the creatures
are there halting,
then the Tathâgata, &c.,
himself,
pronounces these words :
'You have not accomplished
your task, monks ;
you have not finished
what you had to do.
But behold, monks ! the
Buddha-knowledge is near ;
behold and be convinced :
what to you seems Nirvâna,
that is not Nirvâna.
Nay, monks,
it is an able device
of the Tathâgatas, &c.,
that they expound
three vehicles.'

And in order to explain
this same subject
more in detail,
the Lord on that occasion
uttered the following stanzas :

60.
The Leader of the world,
Abhigñâgñânâbhibhû,
having occupied
the terrace of enlightenment,
continued ten complete
intermediate kalpas
without gaining
enlightenment,
though he saw the things
in their very essence.

61.
Then the gods, Nâgas,
demons, and goblins,
zealous to honour the Gina,
sent down a rain of flowers
on the spot where the Leader
awakened to enlightenment.

62.
And high in the sky
they beat the cymbals
to worship
and honour the Gina,
and they were vexed
that the Gina
delayed so long in coming
to the highest place.

63.
After the lapse
of ten intermediate kalpas
the Lord Anâbhibhû
attained enlightenment ;
then all gods, men,
serpents, and demons
were glad and overjoyed.

64.
The sixteen sons
of the Leader of men,
those heroes,
being at the time
young princes,
rich in virtues,
came along
with thousands of kotis
of living beings to honour
the eminent chiefs of men.

65.
And after saluting
the feet of the Leader
they prayed :
Reveal the law and refresh us
as well as this world
with thy good word,
O Lion amongst kings.

66.
After a long time
thou art seen again
in the ten points
of this world ;
thou appearest,
great Leader,
while the aerial cars
of the Brahma-angels
are stirring to reveal
a token to living beings.

67.
In the eastern quarter
fifty thousand kotis of fields
have been shaken,
and the lofty angelic cars
in them have become
excessively brilliant.

68.
The Brahma-angels
on perceiving this foretoken
went and approached
the Chief of the Leaders
of the world, and,
covering him with flowers,
presented all of them
their cars to him.

69.
They prayed him
to move forward
the wheel of the law,
and celebrated him
with stanzas and songs.
But the king of kings
was silent, for he thought :
The time has not yet arrived
for me to proclaim the law.

70.
Likewise in the south, west,
north, the nadir, zenith,
and in the intermediate
points of the compass
there were thousands
of kotis of Brahma-angels.

71.
Unremittingly covering
the Lord with flowers
they saluted the feet
of the Leader,
presented all their aerial cars,
celebrated him,
and again prayed :

72.
Move forward the wheel,
O thou whose sight is infinite !
Rarely art thou met
in the course
of many kotis of Æons.
Display the benevolence
thou hast observed in so many
former generations ;
open the gate of immortality.

73.
On hearing their prayer,
he whose sight is infinite
exposed the multifarious law
and the four Truths,
extensively.
All existences said he
spring successively
from their antecedents.

74.
Starting from Ignorance,
the Seer proceeded
to speak of death,
endless woe;
all those evils
spring from birth.
Know likewise that death
is the lot of mankind.

75.
No sooner had he
expounded the multifarious,
different, endless laws,
than eighty myriads
of kotis of creatures
who had heard them
quickly attained
the stage of disciples.

76.
On a second occasion the Gina
expounded many laws,
and beings
like the sands of the Ganges
became instantly purified
and disciples.

77.
From that moment
the assembly of that Leader
of the world
was innumerable;
no man would be able to reach
the term of its number,
even were he to go on
counting for myriads
of kotis of Æons.

78.
Those sixteen princes also,
his own dear sons,
who had become
mendicants and novices,
said to the Gina:
'Expound, O Chief,
the superior law;

79.
'That we may become sages,
knowers of the world,
such as thyself art,
O supreme of all Ginas,
and that all these beings
may become
such as thyself art, O hero,
O clear-sighted one.'

80.
And the Gina,
considering the wish
of his sons,
the young princes,
explained the highest
superior enlightenment
by means of many myriads
of kotis of illustrations.

81.
Demonstrating with
thousands of arguments and
elucidating the knowledge
of transcendent wisdom,
the Lord of the world
indicated the veritable
course of duty
such as was followed
by the wise Bodhisattvas.

82.
This very Sûtra
of great extension, this
good Lotus of the True Law,
was by the Lord delivered
in many thousands of stanzas,
so numerous as to equal
the sands of the Ganges.

83.
After delivering this Sûtra,
the Gina entered
the monastery for the purpose
of becoming absorbed
in meditation ; during
eighty-four complete Æons
the Lord of the world
continued meditating,
sitting on the same seat.

84.
Those novices, perceiving
that the Chief remained
in the monastery
without coming out of it,
imparted to many kotis
of creatures
that Buddha-knowledge,
which is free from
imperfections and blissful.

85.
On the seats which they had
made to be prepared,
one for each,
they expounded
this very Sûtra
under the mastership
of the Sugata of that period.
A service of the same kind
they render to me.

86.
Innumerable as the sands
of sixty thousand rivers
like the Ganges
were the beings then taught ;
each of the sons of the Sugata
converted or trained
endless beings.

87.
After the Gina's
complete Nirvâna
they commenced
a wandering life
and saw kotis of Buddhas ;
along with those pupils
they rendered homage
to the most exalted
amongst men.

88.
Having observed
the extensive and sublime
course of duty
and reached enlightenment
in the ten points of space,
those sixteen sons of the Gina
became themselves Ginas,
two by two,
in each point of the horizon.

Ancient Devotion 155

89.
And all those
who had been their pupils
became disciples
of those Ginas,
and gradually obtained
possession of enlightenment
by various means.

90.
I myself
was one of their number,
and you
have all been taught by me.
Therefore you
are my disciples now also,
and I lead you all
to enlightenment
by my devices.

91.
This is the cause
dating from old,
this is the motive
of my expounding the law,
that I lead you
to superior enlightenment.
This being the case, monks,
you need not be afraid.

92.
It is as if
there were a forest dreadful,
terrific, barren,
without a place of refuge
or shelter,
replete with wild beasts,
deprived of water,
frightful for persons
of no experience.

93.
Suppose further
that many thousand men
have come to the forest,
that waste track of wilderness
which is fully five hundred
yoganas in extent.

94.
And he who is to act
as their guide
through that rough
and horrible forest
is a rich man,
thoughtful, intelligent,
wise, well instructed,
and undaunted.

95.
And those beings,
numbering many kotis,
feel tired,
and say to the guide :
'We are tired, Master ;
we are not able to go on ;
we should like now to return.'

96.
But he, the dexterous
and clever guide,
is searching in his mind
for some apt device.
Alas ! he thinks,
by going back
these foolish men
will be deprived
of the possession
of the jewels.

97.
Therefore let me
by dint of magic power
now produce a great city
adorned with thousands
of kotis of buildings
and embellished
by monasteries and parks.

98.
Let me produce
ponds and canals ;
a city adorned
with gardens and flowers,
provided
with walls and gates,
and inhabited
by an infinite number
of men and women.

99.
After creating that city
he speaks to them
in this manner :
'Do not fear,
and be cheerful ;
you have reached
a most excellent city ;
enter it and do your business,
speedily.

100.
'Be joyful and at ease ;
you have reached the limit
of the whole forest.'
It is to give them
a time for repose
that he speaks these words,
and, in fact, they recover
from their weariness.

101.
As he perceives that they
have sufficiently reposed,
he collects them
and addresses them again :
'Come,
hear what I have to tell you :
this city
have I produced by magic.

102.
'On seeing you fatigued,
I have,
lest you should go back,
made use of this device ;
now strain your energy
to reach the Isle.'

103.
In the same manner, monks,
I am the guide,
the conductor of thousands
of kotis of living beings ;
in the same manner
I see creatures toiling
and unable to break
the shell of the egg of evils.

104.
Then I reflect on this matter :
These beings have
enjoyed repose,
have been tranquillised ;
now I will remind them
of the misery
of all things and I say :
'At the stage of Arhat
you shall reach your aim.'

105.
At that time,
when you shall
have attained that state,
and when I see all of you
have become Arhats,
then will I call you
all together
and explain to you
how the law really is.

106.
It is an artifice of the Leaders,
when they,
the great Seers,
show three vehicles,
for there is but one vehicle,
no second ;
it is only to help creatures
that two vehicles
are spoken of.

107.
Therefore I now tell you,
monks : Rouse to the utmost
your lofty energy
for the sake of the knowledge
of the all-knowing ; as yet,
you have not come so far
as to possess complete Nirvâna.

108.
But when you shall have
attained the knowledge
of the all-knowing
and the ten powers
proper to Ginas,
you shall become Buddhas
marked by the thirty-two
characteristic signs
and have rest for ever.

109.
Such is the teaching
of the Leaders :
in order to give quiet
they speak of repose,
but when they see
that the creatures
have had a repose,
they, knowing this to be
no final resting-place,
initiate them
in the knowledge
of the all-knowing.

Chapter VIII
Announcement of the Future Destiny of Five Hundred Monks

On hearing from the Lord
that display of skilfulness
and the instruction by means
of mysterious speech ;
on hearing the announcement
of the future destiny
of the great Disciples,
as well as the foregoing tale
concerning ancient devotion
and the leadership
of the Lord,
the venerable Pûrna,
son of Maitrâyanî,
was filled with wonder
and amazement,
thrilled with
pure-heartedness,
a feeling of delight and joy.
He rose from his seat,
full of delight and joy,
full of great respect
for the law,
and while prostrating himself
before the Lord's feet,
made within himself
the following reflection :
Wonderful, O Lord ;
wonderful, O Sugata ;
it is an extremely difficult
thing that the Tathâgatas, &c.,
perform,
the conforming to this world,
composed
of so many elements,
and preaching
the law to all creatures
with many proofs
of their skilfulness,
and skilfully releasing them
when attached to this or that.
What could we do, O Lord,
in such a case ?
None but the Tathâgata
knows our inclination
and our ancient course.
Then, after saluting
with his head the Lord's feet,
Pûrna went and stood apart,
gazing up to the Lord
with unmoved eyes and
so showing his veneration.

And the Lord, regarding
the mental disposition
of the venerable Pûrna,
son of Maitrâyanî,
addressed the entire assembly
of monks in this strain :
Ye monks,
see this disciple, Pûrna,
son of Maitrâyanî,
whom I have designated
as the foremost of preachers
in this assembly,
praised for his many virtues,
and who has applied himself
in various ways
to comprehend the true law.
He is the man to excite,
arouse, and stimulate the
four classes of the audience ;
unwearied
in the preaching of the law ;
as capable to preach
the law as to oblige
his fellow-followers

of the course of duty.
The Tathâgata excepted,
monks, there is none
able to equal Pûrna,
son of Maitrâyanî,
either essentially
or in accessories.
Now, monks,
do you suppose that
he keeps my true law only ?
No, monks,
you must not think so.
For I remember, monks,
that in the past,
in the times
of the ninety-nine Buddhas,
the same Pûrna
kept the true law
under the mastership
of those Buddhas.
Even as he is now with me,
so he has, in all periods,
been the foremost
of the preachers of the law ;
has in all periods
been a consummate
knower of Voidness ;
has in all periods
acquired the four distinctive
qualifications of an Arhat ;
has in all periods
reached mastership
in the transcendent wisdom
of the Bodhisattvas.
He has been a strongly
convinced preacher of the law,
exempt from doubt,
and quite pure.
Under the mastership
of those Buddhas he has
during his whole existence
observed a spiritual life, and
everywhere they termed him
'the Disciple.'
By this means
he has promoted
the interest of innumerable,
incalculable
hundred thousands
of myriads of kotis of beings,
and brought innumerable
and incalculable beings
to full ripeness for supreme
and perfect enlightenment.
In all periods
he has assisted the creatures
in the function of a Buddha,
and in all periods
he has purified
his own Buddha-field,
always striving to bring
creatures to ripeness.
He was also, monks,
the foremost among
the preachers of the law
under the seven Tathâgatas,
the first of whom is Vipasyin
and the seventh myself.

And as to the Buddhas,
monks,
who have in future to appear
in this Bhadra-kalpa,
to the number
of a thousand less four,
under the mastership of them
also shall this same Pûrna,
son of Maitrâyanî,
be the foremost among
the preachers of the law
and the keeper of the true law.
Thus he shall keep

the true law of innumerable
and incalculable Lords
and Buddhas in future,
promote the interest
of innumerable
and incalculable beings,
and bring innumerable
and incalculable beings
to full ripeness for supreme
and perfect enlightenment.
Constantly and assiduously
he shall be instant
in purifying
his own Buddha-field
and bringing
creatures to ripeness.
After completing
such a Bodhisattva-course,
at the end of innumerable,
incalculable Æons,
he shall reach supreme
and perfect enlightenment ;
he shall in the world
be the Tathâgata
called Dharmaprabhâsa,
an Arhat, &c.,
endowed with science
and conduct, a Sugata, &c.
He shall appear
in this very Buddha-field.

Further, monks,
at that time
the Buddha-field spoken of
will look as if formed
by thousands of spheres
similar to the sands
of the river Ganges.
It will be even,
like the palm of the hand,
consist of seven
precious substances,
be without hills,
and filled with high edifices
of seven precious substances.
There will be cars of the gods
stationed in the sky ;
the gods will behold men,
and men will behold the gods.
Moreover, monks,
at that time that Buddha-field
shall be exempt
from places of punishment
and from womankind,
as all beings shall
be born by apparitional birth.
They shall lead a spiritual life,
have ideal bodies,
be self-lighting, magical,
moving in the firmament,
strenuous,
of good memory, wise,
possessed
of gold-coloured bodies,
and adorned with
the thirty-two characteristics
of a great man.
And at that time, monks,
the beings
in that Buddha-field will
have two things to feed upon,
namely the delight in the law
and the delight in meditation.
There will be an immense,
incalculable number
of hundred thousands
of myriads of kotis
of Bodhisattvas ;
all endowed with
great transcendent wisdom,
accomplished in the four
distinctive qualifications

of an Arhat,
able in instructing creatures.
He will have
a number of disciples,
beyond all calculation,
mighty in magic, powerful,
masters in the meditation
of the eight emancipations.
So immense
are the good qualities
that Buddha-field
will be possessed of.
And that Æon
shall be called Ratnâvabhâsa
(i.e. radiant with gems),
and that world
Suvisuddha (i.e. very pure).
His lifetime shall last
immense, incalculable Æons ;
and after
the complete extinction
of that Lord Dharmaprabhâsa,
the Tathâgata, &c.,
his true law shall last long,
and his world
shall be full of Stûpas
made of precious substances.
Such inconceivable
good qualities, monks,
shall the Buddha-field
of that Lord be possessed of.

So spoke the Lord,
and thereafter he,
the Sugata, the Master,
added the following stanzas :

1.
Listen to me, monks,
and hear how my son has
achieved his course of duty,
and how he,
well-trained and skilful,
has observed
the course of enlightenment.

2.
Viewing these beings
to be lowly-disposed
and to be startled
at the lofty vehicle,
the Bodhisattvas
become disciples
and exercise
Pratyekabuddhaship.

3.
By many hundreds
of able devices they bring
numerous Bodhisattvas
to full ripeness and declare :
We are but disciples, indeed,
and we are far away
from the highest
and supreme enlightenment.

4.
It is by learning from them
this course of duty
that kotis of beings
arrive at full ripeness,
who at first,
lowly-disposed
and somewhat lazy,
in course of time
all become Buddhas.

5.
They follow a course
in ignorance thinking :
We, disciples,
are of little use, indeed !

In despondency
they descend into all places
of existence successively,
and so clear their own field.

6.
They show
in their own persons
that they are not free
from affection, hatred,
and infatuation ; and
on perceiving other beings
clinging to heretical views,
they go so far
as to accommodate
themselves to those views.

7.
By following such a course
my numerous disciples
skilfully save creatures ;
simple people would go mad,
if they were taught
the whole course of life.

8.
Pûrna here, monks,
my disciple,
has formerly fulfilled
his course of duty
under thousands
of kotis of Buddhas,
he has got possession
of this true law by seeking
after Buddha-knowledge.

9.
And at all periods has he been
the foremost of the disciples,
learned, a brilliant orator,
free from hesitation ;
he has, indeed,
always been able
to excite to gladness
and at all times ready
to perform the Buddha-task.

10.
He has always
been accomplished
in the sublime
transcendent faculties
and endowed
with the distinctive
qualifications of an Arhat ;
he knew the faculties
and range of other beings,
and has always preached
the perfectly pure law.

11.
By exposing
the most eminent of true laws
he has brought
thousands of kotis of beings
to full ripeness
for this supreme,
foremost vehicle,
whilst purifying
his own excellent field.

12.
In future also he shall likewise
honour thousands
of kotis of Buddhas,
acquire knowledge
of the most eminent
of good laws,
and clean his own field.

13.
Always free from timidity
he shall preach the law
with thousands of kotis
of able devices,
and bring many beings
to full ripeness
for the knowledge
of the all-knowing
that is free
from imperfections.

14.
After having paid homage
to the Chiefs of men
and always kept
the most eminent of laws,
he shall in the world
be a Buddha self-born,
widely renowned
everywhere by the name
of Dharmaprabhâsa.

15.
And his field
shall always be very pure
and always set off with
seven precious substances ;
his Æon
shall be called Ratnâvabhâsa,
and his world Suvisuddha.

16.
That world shall be pervaded
with many thousand kotis
of Bodhisattvas,
accomplished masters in the
great transcendent sciences,
pure in every respect,
and endowed
with magical power.

17.
At that period
the Chief shall also have
an assemblage of thousands
of kotis of disciples, endowed
with magical power,
adepts at the meditation
of the eight emancipations,
and accomplished
in the four distinctive
qualifications of an Arhat.

18.
And all beings
in that Buddha-field
shall be pure
and lead a spiritual life.
Springing into existence
by apparitional birth,
they shall all be gold coloured
and display the thirty-two
characteristic signs.

19.
They shall know no other food
but pleasure in the law
and delight in knowledge.
No womankind shall be there,
nor fear of the places
of punishments
or of dismal states.

20.
Such shall be
the excellent field of Pûrna,
who is possessed
of all good qualities ;
it shall abound
with all goodly things,
a small part only of which
has here been mentioned.

Then this thought
arose in the mind
of those twelve hundred
self-controlled Arhats :
We are struck
with wonder and amazement.
How if the Tathâgata
would predict to us severally
our future destiny
as the Lord has done
to those other great disciples ?
And the Lord
apprehending in his own mind
what was going on in the
minds of these great disciples
addressed the venerable
Mahâ-Kâsyapa :
Those twelve hundred
self-controlled hearers
whom I am now beholding
from face to face,
to all those twelve hundred
self-controlled hearers,
Kâsyapa, I will presently
foretell their destiny.
Amongst them, Kâsyapa,
the monk Kaundinya,
a great disciple, shall,
after sixty-two hundred
thousand myriads
of kotis of Buddhas,
become a Tathâgata,
an Arhat, &c.,
under the name
of Samantaprabhâsa,
endowed with science
and conduct,
a Sugata, &c. &c. ;
but of those twelve hundred,
Kâsyapa, five hundred
shall become Tathâgatas
of the same name.
Thereafter shall all those
five hundred great disciples
reach supreme
and perfect enlightenment,
all bearing the name
of Samantaprabhâsa ;
namely Gayâ-Kâsyapa,
Nadî-Kâsyapa,
Uruvilvâ-Kâsyapa, Kâla,
Kâlodâyin, Aniruddha,
Kapphina, Vakkula, Kunda,
Svâgata, and the rest
of the five hundred
self-controlled Arhats.

And on that occasion
the Lord uttered
the following stanzas :

21.
The scion
of the Kundina family,
my disciple here,
shall in future be a Tathâgata,
a Lord of the world,
after the lapse
of an endless period ;
he shall educate hundreds
of kotis of living beings.

22.
After seeing
many endless Buddhas,
he shall in future, after
the lapse of an endless period,
become the Gina
Samantaprabhâsa,
whose field
shall be thoroughly pure.

Five Hundred Monks 165

23.
Brilliant, gifted
with the powers of a Buddha,
with a voice
far resounding in all quarters,
waited upon by thousands
of kotis of beings,
he shall preach supreme
and eminent enlightenment.

24.
There shall be
most zealous Bodhisattvas,
mounted on lofty aerial cars,
and moving, meditative,
pure in morals,
and assiduous in doing good.

25.
After hearing the law
from the highest of men,
they shall invariably
go to other fields, to
salute thousands of Buddhas
and show them great honour.

26.
But ere long they shall return
to the field of the Leader
called Prabhâsa, the Tathâgata.
So great shall be the power
of their course of duty.

27.
The measure of the lifetime
of that Sugata shall be
sixty thousand Æons, and,
after the complete extinction
of that mighty one,
his true law shall remain
twice as long in the world.

28.
And the counterfeit of it
shall continue
three times as long.
When the true law
of that holy one
shall he exhausted,
men and gods shall be vexed.

29.
There shall appear
a complete number
of five hundred Chiefs,
supreme amongst men,
who shall bear
the same name
with that Gina,
Samantaprabha,
and follow one another
in regular succession.

30.
All shall have like divisions,
magical powers,
Buddha-fields,
and hosts of followers.
Their true law
also shall be the same
and stand equally long.

31.
All shall have in this world,
including the gods,
the same voice
as Samantaprabhâsa,
the highest of men,
such as I have
mentioned before.

32.
Moved by benevolence
and compassion
they shall in succession
foretell each other's destiny,
with the words :
This is to be
my immediate successor,
and he is to command
the world as I do at present.

33.
Thus, Kâsyapa,
keep now in view here
these self-controlled Arhats,
no less than
five hundred in number,
as well as my other disciples,
and speak of this matter
to the other disciples.

On hearing from the Lord
the announcement
of their own future destiny,
the five hundred Arhats,
contented, satisfied,
in high spirits and ecstasy,
filled with cheerfulness,
joy, and delight,
went up to the place
where the Lord was sitting,
reverentially saluted
with their heads his feet,
and spoke thus :
We confess our fault,
O Lord,
in having continually
and constantly
persuaded ourselves
that we had arrived
at final Nirvâna,
as persons who are dull,
inept, ignorant of the rules,
For, O Lord,
whereas we should have
thoroughly penetrated
the knowledge
of the Tathâgatas,
we were content
with such a trifling
degree of knowledge.

It is, O Lord,
as if some man
having come
to a friend's house
got drunk or fell asleep,
and that friend bound
a priceless gem
within his garment,
with the thought :
Let this gem be his.
After a while, O Lord,
that man rises from his seat
and travels further ;
he goes to some other country,
where he is befallen
by incessant difficulties,
and has great trouble
to find food and clothing.
By dint of great exertion
he is hardly able to obtain
a bit of food,
with which, however,
he is contented and satisfied.
The old friend of that man,
O Lord,
who bound within
the man's garment
that priceless gem,
happens to see him again
and says :

How is it, good friend,
that thou hast such
difficulty in seeking food
and clothing, while I,
in order that thou shouldst
live in ease, good friend,
have bound within
thy garment a priceless gem,
quite sufficient
to fulfil all thy wishes ?
I have given thee that gem,
my good friend,
the very gem I have bound
within thy garment.
Still thou art deliberating :
What has been bound ?
by whom ?
for what reason and purpose ?
It is something foolish,
my good friend,
to be contented,
when thou hast
with so much difficulty
to procure food and clothing.
Go, my good friend,
betake thyself,
with this gem,
to some great city,
exchange the gem for money,
and with that money do all
that can be done with money.

In the same manner,
O Lord,
has the Tathâgata formerly,
when he still followed
the course of duty
of a Bodhisattva,
raised in us also ideas
of omniscience, but we,
O Lord,
did not perceive, nor know it.
We fancied, O Lord,
that on the stage of Arhat
we had reached Nirvâna.
We live in difficulty, O Lord,
because we content ourselves
with such a trifling degree
of knowledge.
But as our strong aspiration
after the knowledge
of the all-knowing
has never ceased,
the Tathâgata
teaches us the right :
'Have no such idea
of Nirvâna, monks ;
there are in your intelligence
roots of goodness
which of yore
I have fully developed.
In this you have to see
an able device of mine
that from the expressions
used by me,
in preaching the law,
you fancy Nirvâna
to take place at this moment.'
And after having taught us
the right in such a way,
the Lord now predicts
our future destiny to supreme
and perfect knowledge.

And on that occasion
the five hundred
self-controlled Arhats,
Âgñâta-Kaundinya
and the rest, uttered
the following stanzas :

34.
We are rejoicing
and delighted to hear
this unsurpassed word
of comfort
that we are destined
to the highest,
supreme enlightenment.
Homage be to thee,
O Lord of unlimited sight !

35.
We confess
our fault before thee ;
we were so childish,
nescient, ignorant
that we were fully contented
with a small part of Nirvâna,
under the mastership
of the Sugata.

36.
This is a case
like that of a certain man
who enters the house
of a friend, which friend,
being rich and wealthy,
gives him much food,
both hard and soft.

37.
After satiating him
with nourishment,
he gives him a jewel
of great value.
He ties it with a knot
within the upper robe
and feels satisfaction
at having given that jewel.

38.
The other man, unaware of it,
goes forth and from that place
travels to another town.
There he is befallen
with misfortune and,
as a miserable beggar,
seeks his food in affliction.

39.
He is contented
with the pittance he gets
by begging without caring
for dainty food ;
as to that jewel,
he has forgotten it ;
he has not
the slightest remembrance
of its having been tied
in his upper robe.

40.
Under these circumstances
he is seen by his old friend
who at home
gave him that jewel.
This friend properly
reprimands him
and shows him the jewel
within his robe.

41.
At this sight the man
feels extremely happy.
The value of the jewel
is such that
he becomes a very rich man,
of great power,
and in possession of all that
the five senses can enjoy.

42.
In the same manner, O Lord,
we were unaware
of our former aspiration,
the aspiration laid in us
by the Tathâgata himself
in previous existences
from time immemorial.

43.
And we were living
in this world, O Lord,
with dull understanding
and in ignorance,
under the mastership
of the Sugata ;
for we were contented
with a little of Nirvâna ;
we required nothing higher,
nor even cared for it.

44.
But the Friend of the world
has taught us better :
'This is no blessed Rest at all ;
the full knowledge
of the highest men,
that is blessed Rest,
that is supreme beatitude.'

45.
After hearing this sublime,
grand, splendid,
and matchless prediction,
O Lord,
we are greatly elated with joy,
when thinking
of the prediction
we shall have to make
to each other
in regular succession.

Chapter IX
Announcement of the Future Destiny of Ânanda, Râhula, and the Two Thousand Monks

On that occasion
the venerable Ânanda
made this reflection:
Should we also receive
a similar prediction?
Thus thinking,
pondering, wishing,
he rose from his seat,
prostrated himself
at the Lord's feet
and uttered
the following words.
And
the venerable Râhula also,
in whom rose
the same thought
and the same wish
as in Ânanda,
prostrated himself
at the Lord's feet,
and uttered these words:
'Let it be our turn also,
O Lord;
let it be our turn also,
O Sugata.
The Lord
is our father and procreator,
our refuge and protection.
For in this world,
including men,
gods, and demons,
O Lord, we are
particularly distinguished,
as people say:
These are the Lord's sons,
the Lord's attendants;
these are the keepers of
the law-treasure of the Lord.
Therefore, Lord,
it would seem meet,
were the Lord
ere long to predict
our destiny to supreme
and perfect enlightenment.'

Two thousand other monks,
and more, both such
as were still under training
and such as were not,
likewise rose from their seats,
put their upper robes
upon one shoulder,
stretched their joined hands
towards the Lord and
remained gazing up to him,
all preoccupied
with the same thought,
namely of
this very Buddha-knowledge:
Should
we also receive a prediction
of our destiny to supreme
and perfect enlightenment.

Then the Lord addressed
the venerable Ânanda
in these words:
Thou, Ânanda,
shalt in future
become a Tathâgata
by the name of
Sâgaravaradhara-
buddhivikrîditâbhigña,

an Arhat, &c.,
endowed with science
and conduct, &c.
After having honoured,
respected, venerated,
and worshipped
sixty-two kotis of Buddhas,
kept in memory the true law
of those Buddhas
and received this command,
thou shalt arrive at supreme
and perfect enlightenment,
and bring to full ripeness
for supreme,
perfect enlightenment
twenty hundred thousand
myriads of kotis
of Bodhisattvas
similar to the sands
of twenty Ganges.
And thy Buddha-field
shall consist of lapis lazuli
and be superabundant.
The sphere shall be named
Anavanâmita-vaigayanta
and the Æon
Manogñasabdâbhigargita.
The lifetime of that Lord
Sâgaravaradhara-
buddhivikrîditâbhigña,
the Tathâgata, &c.,
shall measure an immense
number of Æons,
Æons the term of which is not
to be found by calculation.
So many hundred thousand
myriads of kotis
of incalculable Æons
shall last the lifetime
of that Lord.
Twice as long, Ânanda,
after the complete
extinction of that Lord,
shall his true law stand,
and twice as long again
shall continue its counterfeit.
And further, Ânanda,
many hundred thousand
myriads of kotis of Buddhas,
similar to the sands
of the river Ganges,
shall in all directions
of space speak
the praise of that Tathâgata
Sâgaravaradhara-
buddhivikrîditâbhigña,
the Arhat, &c.

1.
I announce to you,
congregated monks,
that Ânanda-Bhadra,
the keeper of my law,
shall in future become a Gina,
after having worshipped
sixty kotis of Sugatas.

2.
He shall be widely renowned
by the name of
Sâgarabuddhidhârin
Abhigñaprâpta in a beautiful,
thoroughly clear field,
termed
Anavanatâ Vaigayantî
(i.e. triumphal banner
unlowered).

3.
There shall be Bodhisattvas
like the sands of the Ganges
and even more,
whom he shall
bring to full ripeness;
he shall be a Gina endowed
with great magical power,
whose word
shall widely resound
in all quarters of the world.

4.
The duration of his life
shall be immense.
He shall always be benign
and merciful to the world.
After the complete
extinction of that Gina
and mighty saint,
his true law
shall stand twice as long.

5.
The counterfeit
shall continue twice as long
under the rule of that Gina.
Then also shall beings
like grains of sand
of the Ganges
produce in this world
what is the cause
of Buddha-enlightenment.

In that assembly
were eight thousand
Bodhisattvas who had
newly entered the vehicle.
To them this thought
presented itself:
Never before did we have
such a sublime prediction
to Bodhisattvas,
far less to disciples.
What may be the cause of it?
what the motive?
The Lord, who apprehended
in his mind
what was going on
in the minds
of those Bodhisattvas,
addressed them
in these words:
Young men of good family,
I and Ânanda
have in the same moment,
the same instant conceived
the idea of supreme
and perfect enlightenment in
the presence of the Tathâgata
Dharmagahanâ-
bhyudgatarâga,
the Arhat, &c.
At that period,
young men of good family,
Ânanda constantly
and assiduously applied
himself to great learning,
whereas I was applying
myself to strenuous labour.
Hence
I sooner arrived at supreme
and perfect enlightenment,
whilst Ânanda-Bhadra was
the keeper of the law-treasure
of the Lords Buddhas;
that is to say,
young men of good family,
he made a vow
to bring Bodhisattvas
to full development.

When the venerable Ânanda,
heard from the Lord
the announcement
of his own destiny to supreme
and perfect enlightenment,
when he learned
the good qualities of his
Buddha-field and its divisions,
when he heard of the vow
he had made in the past,
he felt pleased, exultant,
ravished, joyous,
filled with cheerfulness
and delight.
And at that juncture
he remembered the true law
of many hundred thousand
myriads of kotis of Buddhas
and his own vow of yore.

And on that occasion
the venerable Ânanda
uttered the following stanzas :

6.
Wonderful,
boundless are the Ginas
who remind us of the law
preached by the extinct Ginas
and mighty saints.
Now I remember it
as if it had happened
to-day or yesterday.

7.
I am freed from all doubts ;
I am ready for enlightenent.
Such is my skilfulness,
as I am the servitor,
and keep the true law
for the sake of enlightenment.

Thereupon the Lord
addressed
the venerable Râhula-Bhadra
in these words :
Thou, Râhula,
shalt be in future
a Tathâgata of the name of
Saptaratnapadma-
vikrântagâmin,
an Arhat, &c., endowed
with science and conduct, &c.
After having honoured,
respected, venerated,
worshipped a number
of Tathâgatas, &c.,
equal to the atoms
of ten worlds,
thou shalt always be
the eldest son
of those Lords Buddhas,
just as thou
art mine at present.
And, Râhula,
the measure
of the lifetime of that Lord
Saptaratnapadma-
vikrântagâmin,
the Tathâgata, &c.,
and the abundance
of all sorts of good qualities
belonging to him shall be
exactly the same
as of the Lord
Sâgaravaradhara-
buddhivikrîditâbhigña,
the Tathâgata, &c. ;
likewise shall the divisions
of the Buddha-field
and its qualities
be the same as those

possessed by that Lord.
And, Râhula,
thou shalt be the eldest son
of that Tathâgata
Sâgaravaradhara-
buddhivikrîditâbhigña,
the Arhat, &c.
Afterwards thou shalt
arrive at supreme
and perfect enlightenment.

8.
Râhula here,
my own eldest son,
who was born to me
when I was a prince royal,
he, my son,
after my reaching
enlightenment,
is a great Seer,
an heir to the law.

9.
The great number
of kotis of Buddhas
which he shall see in future,
is immense.
To all these Ginas
he shall be a son,
striving after enlightenment.

10.
Unknown
is this course of duty
to Râhula,
but I know his former vow.
He glorifies
the Friend of the world
by saying :
I am, forsooth,
the Tathâgata's son.

11.
Innumerable myriads
of kotis of good qualities,
the measure of which
is never to be found,
appertain to this Râhula,
my son ; for it has been said :
He exists by reason
of enlightenment.

The Lord now again regarded
those two thousand disciples,
both such as were
still under training
and such as were not,
who were looking up to him
with serene, mild,
placid minds.
And the Lord then addressed
the venerable Ânanda :
Seest thou, Ânanda,
these two thousand disciples,
both such
as are still under training
and such as are not ?
'I do, Lord ; I do, Sugata.'
The Lord proceeded :
All these
two thousand monks,
Ânanda,
shall simultaneously
accomplish the course
of Bodhisattvas,
and after honouring,
respecting, venerating,
worshipping Buddhas
as numerous as the atoms
of fifty worlds,
and after acquiring
the true law,
they shall,

in their last bodily existence,
attain supreme
and perfect enlightenment
at the same time,
the same moment,
the same instant,
the same juncture
in all directions of space,
in different worlds,
each in his own Buddha-field.
They shall become
Tathâgatas, Arhats, &c.,
by the name
of Ratnaketurâgas.
Their lifetime
shall last a complete Æon.
The division
and good qualities
of their Buddha-fields
shall be equal ;
equal also shall be the number
of the congregation
of their disciples
and Bodhisattvas ;
equal also shall
be their complete extinction,
and their true law
shall continue an equal time.

And on that occasion
the Lord uttered
the following stanzas :

12.
These two thousand disciples,
Ânanda,
who here
are standing before me,
to them, the sages,
I now predict that in future
they shall become Tathâgatas,

13.
After having paid eminent
worship to the Buddhas,
by means of infinite
comparisons and examples,
they shall, when standing
in their last bodily existence,
reach
my extreme enlightenment.

14.
They shall all,
under the same name,
in every direction,
at the same moment
and instant,
and sitting at the foot
of the most exalted tree,
become Buddhas,
after they shall have
reached the knowledge.

15.
All shall bear the same name
of Ketus of the Ratna,
by which they shall be
widely famed in this world.
Their excellent fields
shall be equal,
and equal the congregation
of disciples and Bodhisattvas.

16.
Strong in magic power,
they shall all simultaneously,
in every direction of space,
reveal the law in this world
and all at once become extinct ;
their true law
shall last equally long.

And the disciples,
both such
as were still under training
and such as were not,
on hearing from the Lord,
face to face,
the prediction
concerning each of them,
were pleased, exultant,
ravished, joyous,
filled with
cheerfulness and delight,
and addressed the Lord
with the following stanzas :

17.
We are satisfied,
O Light of the world,
to hear this prediction ;
we are pleased, O Tathâgata,
as if sprinkled with nectar.

18.
We have no doubt,
no uncertainty that we shall
become supreme
amongst men ;
to-day we have
obtained felicity,
because we have heard
that prediction.

Chapter X
The Preacher

The Lord then addressed
the eighty thousand
Bodhisattvas Mahâsattvas
by turning to Bhaishagyarâga
as their representative.
Seest thou, Bhaishagyarâga,
in this assembly
the many gods,
Nâgas, goblins,
Gandharvas, demons,
Garudas, Kinnaras,
great serpents,
men, and beings not human,
monks, nuns, male
and female lay devotees,
votaries of the vehicle
of disciples,
votaries of the vehicle
of Pratyekabuddhas,
and those of the vehicle
of Bodhisattvas,
who have heard
this Dharmaparyâya from
the mouth of the Tathâgata ?
'I do, Lord ;
I do, Sugata.'
The Lord proceeded :
Well, Bhaishagyarâga,
all those
Bodhisattvas Mahâsattvas
who in this assembly
have heard,
were it but a single stanza,
a single verse or word,
or who even
by a single rising thought
have joyfully accepted
this Sûtra,
to all of them,
Bhaishagyarâga,
among the four classes
of my audience
I predict their destiny
to supreme
and perfect enlightenment.
And all whosoever,
Bhaishagyarâga, who,
after the complete extinction
of the Tathâgata,
shall hear
this Dharmaparyâya
and after hearing,
were it but a single stanza,
joyfully accept it,
even with
a single rising thought,
to those also,
Bhaishagyarâga,
be they young men or
young ladies of good family,
I predict their destiny
to supreme
and perfect enlightenment.
Those young men
or ladies of good family,
Bhaishagyarâga,
shall be worshippers
of many hundred
thousand myriads
of kotis of Buddhas.
Those young men
or ladies of good family,
Bhaishagyarâga,
shall have made a vow
under hundred thousands
of myriads of kotis
of Buddhas.
They must be considered
as being reborn

amongst the people
of Gambudvîpa,
out of compassion
to all creatures.
Those who shall take,
read, make known, recite,
copy, and after copying
always keep in memory
and from time to time
regard were it
but a single stanza
of this Dharmaparyâya ;
who by that book
shall feel veneration
for the Tathâgatas,
treat them with the respect
due to Masters,
honour, revere, worship them ;
who shall worship that book
with flowers, incense,
perfumed garlands,
ointment, powder, clothes,
umbrellas, flags, banners,
music, &c.,
and with acts of reverence
such as bowing
and joining hands ;
in short,
Bhaishagyarâga,
any young men
or young ladies of good family
who shall keep
or joyfully accept
were it but a single stanza
of this Dharmaparyâya,
to all of them,
Bhaishagyarâga,
I predict their being destined
to supreme
and perfect enlightenment.

Should some man or woman,
Bhaishagyarâga,
happen to ask :
How now have those creatures
to be who in future
are to become
Tathâgatas, Arhats, &c. ?
then that man or woman
should be referred
to the example
of that young man
or young lady of good family.
'Whoever is able to keep,
recite, or teach,
were it but a single stanza
of four lines,
and whoever shows respect
for this Dharmaparyâya,
that young man or young lady
of good family shall in future
become a Tathâgata, &c. ;
be persuaded of it.'
For, Bhaishagyarâga,
such a young man
or young lady of good family
must be considered
to be a Tathâgata,
and by the whole world,
including the gods,
honour should be done
to such a Tathâgata
who keeps were it
but a single stanza
of this Dharmaparyâya,
and far more, of course,
to one who grasps, keeps,
comprehends, makes known,
copies, and after copying
always retains in his memory
this Dharmaparyâya
entirely and completely,

and who honours that book
with flowers, incense,
perfumed garlands,
ointment, powder, clothes,
umbrellas, flags, banners,
music, joined hands,
reverential bows
and salutations.
Such a young man
or young lady of good family,
Bhaishagyarâga,
must be held
to be accomplished
in supreme
and perfect enlightenment ;
must be held to be
the like of a Tathâgata,
who out of compassion and
for the benefit of the world,
by virtue of a former vow,
makes his appearance
here in Gambudvîpa,
in order to make
this Dharmaparyâya
generally known.
Whosoever,
after leaving his own lofty
conception of the law
and the lofty Buddha-field
occupied by him,
in order to make
generally known
this Dharmaparyâya,
after my complete Nirvâna,
may be deemed
to have appeared
in the predicament
of a Tathâgata,
such a one,
Bhaishagyarâga,
be it a young man or
a young lady of good family,
must be held to perform
the function of the Tathâgata,
to be a deputy
of the Tathâgata.
As such, Bhaishagyarâga,
should be acknowledged
the young man or the
young lady of good family,
who communicates
this Dharmaparyâya,
after the complete Nirvâna
of the Tathâgata,
were it but in secret
or by stealth
or to one single creature that
he communicated or told it.

Again, Bhaishagyarâga,
if some creature vicious,
wicked, and cruel-minded
should in the current Age
speak something injurious
in the face of the Tathâgata,
and if some should utter
a single harsh word,
founded or unfounded,
to those irreproachable
preachers of the law
and keepers of this Sûtrânta,
whether lay devotees
or clergymen,
I declare that the latter sin
is the graver.
For, Bhaishagyarâga,
such a young man or young
lady of good family
must be held to be adorned
with the apparel
of the Tathâgata.
He carries the Tathâgata

on his shoulder,
Bhaishagyarâga,
who after having copied
this Dharmaparyâya
and made a volume of it,
carries it on his shoulder.
Such a one,
wherever he goes,
must be saluted by all beings
with joined hands,
must be honoured,
respected, worshipped,
venerated, revered by
gods and men with flowers,
incense, perfumed garlands,
ointment, powder, clothes,
umbrellas, flags, banners,
musical instruments,
with food, soft and hard,
with nourishment and drink,
with vehicles,
with heaps of choice
and gorgeous jewels.
That preacher of the law
must be honoured
by heaps of gorgeous jewels
being presented
to that preacher of the law.
For it may be that
by his expounding
this Dharmaparyâya,
were it only once,
innumerable,
incalculable beings
who hear it shall soon become
accomplished in supreme
and perfect enlightenment.

And on that occasion
the Lord uttered
the following stanzas :

1.
He who wishes
to be established
in Buddhahood
and aspires to the knowledge
of the Self-born must honour
those who keep this doctrine.

2.
And he who is desirous
of omniscience and thinks :
How shall I soonest reach it ?
must try to know
this Sûtra by heart,
or at least honour one
who knows it.

3.
He has been sent
by the Lord of the world
to convert or catechise men,
he who out of compassion
for mankind recites this Sûtra.

4.
After giving up
a good position,
that great man
has come hither,
he who out of compassion
for mankind
keeps this Sûtra in memory.

5.
It is by force of his position,
that in the last times
he is seen preaching
this unsurpassed Sûtra.

6.
That preacher of the law
must be honoured with divine
and human flowers
and all sorts of perfumes ;
be decked with divine cloth
and strewed with jewels.

7.
One should always
reverentially salute him
with joined hands,
as if he were
the Chief of Ginas
or the Self-born,
he who
in these most dreadful,
last days keeps this Sûtra
of the Extinct Buddha.

8.
One should give food,
hard and soft,
nourishment and drink,
lodging in a convent,
kotis of robes
to honour the son of Gina,
when he has propounded,
be it but once, this Sûtra.

9.
He performs the task
of the Tathâgatas
and has been sent by me
to the world of men,
he who in the last days
shall copy, keep,
or hear this Sûtra.

10.
The man who
in wickedness of heart
or with frowning brow
should at any time
of a whole Æon
utter something
injurious in my presence,
commits a great sin.

11.
But one who reviles
and abuses those guardians
of this Sûtrânta,
when they
are expounding this Sûtra,
I say that he commits
a still greater sin.

12.
The man who,
striving for
superior enlightenment,
shall in a complete Æon
praise me in my face
with joined hands,
with many myriads
of kotis of stanzas,

13.
Shall thence derive
a great merit,
since he has glorified me
in gladness of heart.
But a still greater merit
shall he acquire
who pronounces the praise
of those preachers.

14.
One who shall
during eighteen thousand
kotis of Æons pay worship
to those objects of veneration,
with words, visible things,
flavours, with divine scents
and divine kinds of touch,

15.
If such a one,
by his paying that worship
to the objects of veneration
during eighteen thousand
kotis of Æons,
happens to hear this Sûtra,
were it only once,
he shall obtain
an amazingly great advantage.

I announce to thee,
Bhaishagyarâga,
I declare to thee,
that many
are the Dharmaparyâyas
which I have propounded,
am propounding,
and shall propound.
And among all those
Dharmaparyâyas,
Bhaishagyarâga,
it is this which is apt to meet
with no acceptance
with everybody,
to find no belief
with everybody.
This, indeed,
Bhaishagyarâga,
is the transcendent spiritual
esoteric lore of the law,
preserved by
the power of the Tathâgatas,
but never divulged;
it is an article of creed
not yet made known.
By the majority of people,
Bhaishagyarâga,
this Dharmaparyâya
is rejected during
the lifetime of the Tathâgata;
in far higher degree
such will be the case
after his complete extinction.

Nevertheless,
Bhaishagyarâga,
one has to consider
those young men
or young ladies of good family
to be invested with
the robes of the Tathâgata;
to be regarded and blessed
by the Tathâgatas
living in other worlds,
that they shall have the force
of individual persuasion, the
force that is rooted in virtue,
and the force of a pious vow.
They shall dwell apart
in the convents
of the Tathâgata,
Bhaishagyarâga,
and shall have their
heads stroked by the hand
of the Tathâgata,
those young men and
young ladies of good family,
who after the complete
extinction of the Tathâgata
shall believe, read, write,
honour this Dharmaparyâya
and recite it to others.

Again, Bhaishagyarâga,
on any spot of the earth
where this Dharmaparyâya
is expounded, preached,
written, studied,
or recited in chorus,
on that spot,
Bhaishagyarâga,
one should build
a Tathâgata-shrine,
magnificent, consisting
of precious substances,
high, and spacious ;
but it is not necessary
to depose in it relics
of the Tathâgata.
For the body
of the Tathâgata is, so to say,
collectively deposited there.
Any spot of the earth
where this Dharmaparyâya
is expounded or taught
or recited or rehearsed
in chorus or written
or kept in a volume,
must be honoured, respected,
revered, worshipped
as if it were a Stûpa,
with all sorts of flowers,
incense, perfumes, garlands,
ointment, powder, clothes,
umbrellas, flags, banners,
triumphal streamers,
with all kinds of song,
music, dancing,
musical instruments,
castanets,
and shouts in chorus.
And those, Bhaishagyarâga,
who approach
a Tathâgata-shrine
to salute or see it,
must be held to be
near supreme
and perfect enlightenment.
For, Bhaishagyarâga,
there are many laymen
as well as priests
who observe the course
of a Bodhisattva
without, however,
coming so far as to see,
hear, write or worship
this Dharmaparyâya.
So long as they do not
hear this Dharmaparyâya,
they are not yet
proficient in the course
of a Bodhisattva.
But those who hear
this Dharmaparyâya
and thereupon accept,
penetrate, understand,
comprehend it,
are at the time near supreme,
perfect enlightenment,
so to say,
immediately near it.

It is a case,
Bhaishagyarâga,
similar to that
of a certain man,
who in need
and in quest of water,
in order to get water,
causes a well to be dug
in an arid tract of land.
So long as he sees that
the sand being dug out
is dry and white, he thinks :

the water is still far off.
After some time he sees
that the sand being dug out
is moist, mixed with water,
muddy, with trickling drops,
and that the working men
who are engaged
in digging the well
are bespattered
with mire and mud.
On seeing that foretoken,
Bhaishagyarâga,
the man will be convinced
and certain that water is near.
In the same manner,
Bhaishagyarâga, will these
Bodhisattvas Mahâsattvas
be far away from supreme
and perfect enlightenment
so long as they do not hear,
nor catch, nor penetrate,
nor fathom, nor mind
this Dharmaparyâya.
But when the Bodhisattvas
Mahâsattvas shall hear,
catch, penetrate,
study, and mind
this Dharmaparyâya,
then, Bhaishagyarâga,
they will be, so to say,
immediately near supreme,
perfect enlightenment.
From this Dharmaparyâya,
Bhaishagyarâga,
will accrue to creatures
supreme
and perfect enlightenment.
For this Dharmaparyâya
contains an explanation
of the highest mystery,
the secret article of the law

which the Tathâgatas, &c.,
have revealed
for the perfecting of
the Bodhisattvas Mahâsattvas.
Any Bodhisattva,
Bhaishagyarâga,
who is startled,
feels anxiety,
gets frightened
at this Dharmaparyâya,
may be held,
Bhaishagyarâga,
to have but newly
entered the vehicle.
If, however,
a votary of the vehicle
of the disciples is startled,
feels anxiety,
gets frightened
at this Dharmaparyâya,
such a person,
devoted to the vehicle
of the disciples,
Bhaishagyarâga,
may be deemed
a conceited man.

Any Bodhisattva Mahâsattva,
Bhaishagyarâga,
who after the complete
extinction of the Tathâgata,
in the last times,
the last period shall
set forth this Dharmaparyâya
to the four classes of hearers,
should do so,
Bhaishagyariga,
after having entered
the abode of the Tathâgata,
after having put on
the robe of the Tathâgata,

and occupied
the pulpit of the Tathâgata.
And what
is the abode of the Tathâgata,
Bhaishagyarâga?
It is the abiding in charity
or kindness to all beings;
that is the abode of the
Tathâgata, Bhaishagyarâga,
which the young man
of good family has to enter.
And what is the robe
of the Tathâgata,
Bhaishagyarâga?
It is the apparel
of sublime forbearance;
that is the robe
of the Tathâgata,
Bhaishagyarâga,
which the young man
of good family has to put on.
What is the pulpit
of the Tathâgata,
Bhaishagyarâga?
It is the entering
into the voidness
or complete abstraction
of all laws or things;
that is the pulpit,
Bhaishagyarâga,
on which the young man
of good family has to sit
in order to set forth
this Dharmaparyâya
to the four classes of hearers.
A Bodhisattva
ought to propound
this Dharmaparyâya
with unshrinking mind,
before the face of the
congregated Bodhisattvas,
the four classes of hearers,
who are striving for
the vehicle of Bodhisattvas,
and I,
staying in another world,
Bhaishagyarâga,
will by means
of fictitious creatures
make the minds
of the whole congregation
favorably disposed
to that young man
of good family,
and I will send
fictitious monks, nuns,
male and female lay devotees
in order to hear
the sermon of the preacher,
who are unable to gainsay
or contradict him.
If afterwards he shall
have retired to the forest,
I will send thither many
gods, Nâgas, goblins,
Gandharvas, demons,
Garudas, Kinnaras,
and great serpents
to hear him preach,
while I,
staying in another world,
Bhaishagyarâga,
will show my face
to that young man
of good family,
and the words and syllables
of this Dharmaparyâya
which he happens
to have forgotten
will I again suggest to him
when he repeats his lesson.

And on that occasion
the Lord uttered
the following stanzas :

16.
Let one listen
to this exalted Sûtra,
avoiding all distractedness ;
for rare is the occasion
given for hearing it,
and rare also the belief in it.

17.
It is a case similar
to that of a certain man
who in want of water
goes to dig a well
in an arid tract of land,
and sees how again and again
only dry sand is being dug up.

18.
On seeing which he thinks :
the water is far off ;
a token of its being far off
is the dry white sand
which appears in digging.

19.
But when he afterwards
sees again and again
the sand moist and smooth,
he gets the conviction that
water cannot be very far off.

20.
So, too, are those men far from
Buddha-knowledge
who have not heard
this Sûtra and have failed
to repeatedly meditate on it.

21.
But those who have heard
and oft meditated
on this profound
king amongst Sûtras,
this authoritative
book for disciples,

22.
Are wise and near
Buddha-knowledge,
even as from
the moisture of sand
may be inferred
that water is near.

23.
After entering
the abode of the Gina,
putting on his robe
and sitting down on my seat,
the preacher should,
undaunted,
expound this Sûtra.

24.
The strength of charity
or kindness is my abode ;
the apparel
of forbearance is my robe ;
and voidness or complete
abstraction is my seat ;
let the preacher take
his stand on this and preach.

25.
Where clods, sticks, pikes,
or abusive words and threats
fall to the lot of the preacher,
let him be patient,
thinking of me.

26.
My body has existed entire in
thousands of kotis of regions;
during a number
of kotis of Æons
beyond comprehension
I teach the law to creatures.

27.
To that courageous man
who shall proclaim this Sûtra
after my complete extinction
I will also send
many creations.

28.
Monks, nuns, lay devotees,
male and female,
will honour him as well as
the classes of the audience.

29.
And should there be
some to attack him
with clods, sticks,
injurious words,
threats, taunts,
then the creations
shall defend him.

30.
And when he shall stay alone,
engaged in study,
in a lonely place,
in the forest or the hills,

31.
Then will I show him
my luminous body
and enable him to remember
the lesson he forgot.

32.
While he is living lonely
in the wilderness,
I will send him gods
and goblins in great number
to keep him company.

33.
Such are the advantages
he is to enjoy;
whether he is preaching
to the four classes,
or living, a solitary,
in mountain caverns
and studying his lesson,
he will see me.

34.
His readiness of speech
knows no impediment;
he understands the manifold
requisites of exegesis;
he satisfies thousands
of kotis of beings
because he is,
so to say, inspired
or blessed by the Buddha.

35.
And the creatures
who are entrusted
to his care
shall very soon
all become Bodhisattvas,
and by cultivating
his intimacy
they shall behold Buddhas
as numerous
as the sands of the Ganges.

Chapter XI
Apparition of a Stûpa

Then there arose a Stûpa,
consisting
of seven precious substances,
from the place of the earth
opposite the Lord,
the assembly
being in the middle,
a Stûpa five hundred yoganas
in height and proportionate
in circumference.
After its rising,
the Stûpa,
a meteoric phenomenon,
stood in the sky sparkling,
beautiful, nicely decorated
with five thousand
successive terraces of flowers,
adorned with many
thousands of arches,
embellished
by thousands of banners
and triumphal streamers,
hung with thousands
of jewel-garlands and
with hour-plates and bells,
and emitting the scent
of Xanthochymus and sandal,
which scent
filled this whole world.
Its row of umbrellas
rose so far on high
as to touch the abodes
of the four guardians
of the horizon and the gods.
It consisted
of seven precious substances,
namely gold, silver,
lapis lazuli,
Musâragalva,
emerald, red coral,
and Karketana-stone.
This Stûpa
of precious substances
once formed,
the gods of paradise strewed
and covered it
with Mandârava
and great Mandâra flowers.
And from that Stûpa
of precious substances
there issued this voice :
Excellent, excellent,
Lord Sâkyamuni !
thou hast well expounded
this Dharmaparyâya
of the Lotus of the True Law.
So it is, Lord ;
so it is, Sugata.

At the sight of that great Stûpa
of precious substances,
that meteoric phenomenon
in the sky,
the four classes of hearers
were filled with gladness,
delight, satisfaction and joy.
Instantly they rose
from their seats,
stretched out
their joined hands,
and remained standing
in that position.
Then the Bodhisattva
Mahâsattva Mahâpratibhâna,
perceiving the world,
including gods,
men, and demons,
filled with curiosity,
said to the Lord :

O Lord,
what is the cause,
what is the reason
of so magnificent a Stûpa
of precious substances
appearing in the world ?
Who is it, O Lord,
who causes that sound
to go out from
the magnificent Stûpa
of precious substances ?
Thus asked, the Lord
spake to Mahâpratibhâna,
the Bodhisattva Mahâsattva,
as follows :
In this great Stûpa
of precious substances,
Mahâpratibhâna,
the proper body
of the Tathâgata
is contained condensed ;
his is the Stûpa ;
it is he who causes
this sound to go out.
In the point of space below,
Mahâpratibhâna,
there are innumerable
thousands of worlds.
Further on is the world
called Ratnavisuddha,
there is the Tathâgata
named Prabhûtaratna,
the Arhat, &c.
This Lord of yore
made this vow :
Formerly,
when following the course
of a Bodhisattva,
I have not arrived at supreme,
perfect enlightenment
before I had heard
this Dharmaparyâya
of the Lotus of the True Law,
serving for the instruction
of Bodhisattvas.
But from the moment
that I had heard
this Dharmaparyâya
of the Lotus of the True Law,
I have become
fully ripe for supreme,
perfect enlightenment.
Now, Mahâpratibhâna,
that Lord Prabhûtaratna,
the Tathâgata, &c.,
at the juncture of time
when his complete extinction
was to take place,
announced in presence
of the world,
including the gods :
After my complete extinction,
monks,
one Stûpa must be made
of precious substances
of this frame or form
of the proper body
of the Tathâgata ;
the other Stûpas, again,
should be made in dedication
or in reference to me.
Thereupon, Mahâpratibhâna,
the Lord Prabhûtaratna,
the Tathâgata, &c.,
pronounced this blessing :
Let my Stûpa here,
this Stûpa of my proper
bodily frame or form,
arise wherever
in any Buddha-field
in the ten directions of space,
in all worlds,

the Dharmaparyâya
of the Lotus of the True Law
is propounded, and
let it stand in the sky above
the assembled congregation
when this Dharmaparyâya
of the Lotus of the True Law
is being preached by some
Lord Buddha or another,
and let this Stûpa
of the frame or form
of my proper body
give a shout of applause
to those Buddhas
while preaching
this Dharmaparyâya
of the Lotus of the True Law.
It is that Stûpa,
Mahâpratibhâna,
of the relics
of the Lord Prabhûtaratna,
the Tathâgata, &c., which,
while I was preaching
this Dharmaparyâya
of the Lotus of the True Law
in this Saha-world,
arose above this
assembled congregation and,
standing
as a meteor in the sky,
gave its applause.

Then said Mahâpratibhâna,
the Bodhisattva Mahâsattva,
to the Lord :
Show us, O Lord,
through thy power the frame
of the afore-mentioned
Tathâgata.
Whereon the Lord
spake to the Bodhisattva
Mahâsattva Mahâpratibhâna
as follows :
This Lord Prabhûtaratna,
Mahâpratibhâna, has
made a grave and pious vow.
That vow consisted in this :
When the Lords, the Buddhas,
being in other Buddha-fields,
shall preach
this Dharmaparyâya
of the Lotus of the True Law,
then let this Stûpa of
the frame of my proper body
be near the Tathâgata
to hear from him
this Dharmaparyâya
of the Lotus of the True Law.
And when those Lords,
those Buddhas
wish to uncover the frame of
my proper body and show it
to the four classes of hearers,
let then the Tathâgata-frames,
made by the Tathâgatas
in all quarters,
in different Buddha-fields,
from their own proper body,
and preaching the law
to creatures,
under different names
in several Buddha-fields,
let all those Tathâgata-frames,
made from the proper body,
united together,
along with this Stûpa
containing the frame
of my own body,
be opened and shown
to the four classes of hearers.
Therefore, Mahâpratibhâna,
have I made

many Tathâgata-frames
which in all quarters,
in several Buddha-fields
in thousands of worlds,
preach the law to creatures.
All those ought
to be brought hither.

Thereupon the Bodhisattva
Mahâsattva Mahâpratibhâna
said to the Lord :
Then, O Lord,
shall we reverentially salute
all those bodily emanations
of the Tathâgata
and created by the Tathâgata.

And instantly the Lord
darted from the circle of hair
on his brow a ray,
which was no sooner darted
than the Lords, the
Buddhas stationed in the east
in fifty hundred thousand
myriads of kotis of worlds,
equal to the sands
of the river Ganges,
became all visible,
and the Buddha-fields there,
consisting of crystal,
became visible,
variegated with jewel trees,
decorated
with strings of fine cloth,
replete with many hundred
thousands of Bodhisattvas,
covered with canopies,
decked with a network
of seven precious substances
and gold.
And in those fields
appeared the Lords,
the Buddhas,
teaching with sweet
and gentle voice
the law to creatures ;
and those Buddha-fields
seemed replete
with hundred thousands
of Bodhisattvas.
So, too,
it was in the south-east ;
so in the south ;
so in the south-west ;
so in the west ;
so in the north-west ;
so in the north ;
so in the north-east ;
so in the nadir ;
so in the zenith ;
so
in the ten directions of space ;
in each direction were
to be seen many hundred
thousand myriads
of kotis of Buddha-fields,
similar to the sands
of the river Ganges,
in many worlds
similar to the sands
of the river Ganges,
Lords Buddhas
in many hundred thousand
myriads of kotis
of Buddha-fields.

Those Tathâgatas, &c.,
in the ten directions of space
then addressed
each his own troop
of Bodhisattvas :
We shall have to go,

young men of good family,
to the Saha-world
near the Lord Sâkyamuni,
the Tathâgata, &c.,
to humbly salute
the Stûpa of the relics
of Prabhûtaratna,
the Tathâgata, &c.
Thereupon those Lords,
those Buddhas resorted
with their own satellites,
each with one or two,
to this Saha-world.
At that period
this all-embracing world
was adorned with jewel trees ;
it consisted of lapis lazuli,
was covered with a network
of seven precious substances
and gold, smoking
with the odourous incense
of magnificent jewels,
everywhere strewn
with Mandârava and
great Mandârava flowers,
decorated
with a network of little bells,
showing a checker board
divided by gold threads
into eight compartments,
devoid of villages, towns,
boroughs, provinces,
kingdoms, and royal capitals,
without Kâla-mountain,
without
the mountains Mukilinda
and great Mukilinda,
without a mount Sumeru,
without a Kakravâla
(i.e. horizon)
and great Kakravâla
(i.e. extended horizon),
without
other principal mountains,
without great oceans,
without rivers
and great rivers,
without bodies of gods, men,
and demons, without hells,
without brute creation,
without a kingdom of Yama.
For it must be understood
that at that period all beings
in any of the six states
of existence in this world
had been removed
to other worlds,
with the exception
of those who were assembled
at that congregation.
Then it was that those Lords,
those Buddhas,
attended
by one or two satellites,
arrived at this Saha-world
and went one after the other
to occupy their place close
to the foot of a jewel tree.
Each of the jewel trees
was five hundred
yoganas in height,
had boughs, leaves, foliage,
and circumference
in proportion,
and was provided
with blossoms and fruits.
At the foot of each jewel tree
stood prepared a throne,
five yoganas in height,
and adorned
with magnificent jewels.
Each Tathâgata

went to occupy his throne
and sat on it cross-legged.
And so all the Tathâgatas
of the whole sphere
sat cross-legged
at the foot of the jewel trees.

At that moment
the whole sphere was replete
with Tathâgatas,
but the beings produced
from the proper body
of the Lord Sâkyamuni
had not yet arrived,
not even from
a single point of the horizon.
Then the Lord Sâkyamuni,
the Tathâgata, &c.,
proceeded to make room
for those Tathâgata-frames
that were arriving
one after the other.
On every side
in the eight directions
of space appeared
twenty hundred thousand
myriads of kotis
of Buddha-fields
of lapis lazuli,
decked with a network
of seven precious substances
and gold, decorated
with a fringe of little bells,
strewn with Mandârava and
great Mandârava flowers,
covered with
heavenly awnings,
hung with wreaths
of heavenly flowers,
smoking with
heavenly odourous incense.

All those twenty hundred
thousand myriads of kotis
of Buddha-fields
were without villages, towns,
boroughs, &c. ;
without Kâla-mountain, &c. ;
without great oceans, &c. ;
without bodies of gods, &c.
All those Buddha-fields
were so arranged by him
as to form one Buddha-field,
one soil, even, lovely,
set off with trees
of seven precious substances,
trees five hundred yoganas
in height and circumference,
provided with boughs,
flowers,
and fruits in proportion.
At the foot of each tree
stood prepared a throne,
five yoganas
in height and width,
consisting of celestial gems,
glittering and beautiful.
The Tathâgatas
arriving one after the other
occupied the throne
near the foot of each tree,
and sat cross-legged.
In like manner
the Tathâgata Sâkyamuni
prepared twenty hundred
thousand myriads
of kotis of other worlds,
in every direction of space,
in order to give room
to the Tathâgatas
who were arriving
one after the other.
Those twenty hundred

thousand myriads
of kotis of worlds
in every direction of space
were likewise so made
by him as to be
without villages, towns, &c.
They were without bodies
of gods, &c. ;
all those beings had been
removed to other worlds.
These Buddha-fields
also were of lapis lazuli, &c.
All those jewel trees measured
five hundred yoganas,
and near them were thrones,
artificially made
and measuring five yoganas.
Then those Tathâgatas
sat down cross-legged,
each on a throne
at the foot of a jewel tree.

At that moment
the Tathâgatas produced
by the Lord Sâkyamuni,
who in the east
were preaching the law
to creatures
in hundred thousands
of myriads of kotis
of Buddha-fields,
similar to the sands
of the river Ganges,
all arrived
from the ten points of space
and sat down
in the eight quarters.
Thereupon thirty kotis
of worlds in each direction
were occupied
by those Tathâgatas
from all the eight quarters.
Then, seated on their thrones,
those Tathâgatas
deputed their satellites
into the presence
of the Lord Sâkyamuni,
and after giving them bags
with jewel flowers
enjoined them thus : Go,
young men of good family,
to the Gridhrakûta mountain,
where the Lord Sâkyamuni,
the Tathâgata, &c., is ;
salute him reverentially
and ask, in our name,
after the state of health,
well-being, lustiness,
and comfort both of himself
and the crowd
of Bodhisattvas and disciples.
Strew him with this heap
of jewels and speak thus :
Would the Lord Tathâgata
deign to open
this great Stûpa of jewels ?
It was in this manner
that all those Tathâgatas
deputed their satellites.

And when
the Lord Sâkyamuni,
the Tathâgata,
perceived that his creations,
none wanting, had arrived ;
perceived that they were
severally seated
on their thrones,
and perceived
that the satellites
of those Tathâgatas, &c.,
were present, he,

in consideration
of the wish expressed
by those Tathâgatas, &c.,
rose from his seat
and stood in the sky,
as a meteor.
And all the four classes
of the assembly
rose from their seats,
stretched out
their joined hands,
and stood gazing up
to the face of the Lord.
The Lord then,
with the right fore-finger,
unlocked the middle
of the great Stûpa of jewels,
which showed like a meteor,
and so severed the two parts.
Even as the double doors
of a great city gate separate
when the bolt is removed,
so the Lord
opened the great Stûpa,
which showed like a meteor,
by unlocking it in the middle
with the right fore-finger.
The great Stûpa of jewels
had no sooner been opened
than the Lord Prabhûtaratna,
the Tathâgata, &c.,
was seen sitting cross-legged
on his throne,
with emaciated limbs
and faint body,
as if absorbed
in abstract meditation, and
he pronounced these words :
Excellent, excellent,
Lord Sâkyamuni ;
thou hast well expounded
this Dharmaparyâya
of the Lotus of the True Law.
I repeat,
thou hast well expounded
this Dharmaparyâya
of the Lotus of the True Law,
Lord Sâkyamuni,
to the four classes
of the assembly.
I myself, Lord,
have come hither
to hear the Dharmaparyâya
of the Lotus of the True Law.

Now the four classes
of the assembly,
on perceiving
the Lord Prabhûtaratna,
the Tathâgata, &c.,
who had been extinct
for many hundred thousand
myriads of kotis of Æons,
speaking in this way,
were filled
with wonder and amazement.
Instantly they covered
the Lord Prabhûtaratna,
the Tathâgata, &c.,
and the Lord Sâkyamuni,
the Tathâgata, &c.,
with heaps
of divine and human flowers.
And then the Lord
Prabhûtaratna,
the Tathâgata, &c.,
ceded to the Lord Sâkyamuni,
the Tathâgata, &c.,
the half of the seat
on that very throne within that
same great Stûpa of jewels
and said :

Let the Lord Sâkyamuni,
the Tathâgata, &c.,
sit down here.
Whereon the Lord Sâkyamuni,
the Tathâgata, &c.,
sat down upon
that half-seat together
with the other Tathâgata,
so that both Tathâgatas
were seen as meteors
in the sky,
sitting on the throne
in the middle
of the great Stûpa of jewels.

And in the minds
of those four classes
of the assembly
rose this thought:
We are far off
from the two Tathâgatas;
therefore let us also,
through the power
of the Tathâgata,
rise up to the sky.
As the Lord
apprehended in his mind
what was going on
in the minds of those
four classes of the assembly,
he instantly, by magic power,
established the four classes
as meteors in the sky.
Thereupon the Lord
Sâkyamuni, the Tathâgata,
addressed the four classes:
Who amongst you, monks,
will endeavour to expound
this Dharmaparyâya
of the Lotus of the True Law
in this Saha-world?

The fatal term,
the time of death,
is now at hand;
the Tathâgata longs
for complete extinction, monks,
after entrusting to you
this Dharmaparyâya
of the Lotus of the True Law.

And on that occasion
the Lord uttered
the following stanzas:

1.
Here you see, monks,
the great Seer,
the extinct Chief,
within the Stûpa of jewels,
who now has come
to hear the law.
Who would not call up
his energy for the law's sake?

2.
Albeit completely extinct
for many kotis of Æons,
he yet now comes
to hear the law;
for the law's sake
he moves hither and thither;
very rare and very precious
a law like this.

3.
This Leader
practiced a vow when he was
in a former existence;
even after his complete
extinction he wanders
through this whole world
in all ten points of space.

4.
And all these you here see
are my proper bodies,
by thousands of kotis,
like the sands of the Ganges ;
they have appeared
that the law may be fulfilled
and in order to see
this extinct Master.

5.
After laying out
for each his peculiar field,
as well as
having created all disciples,
men and gods,
in order to preserve
the true law,
as long as the reign
of the law shall last,

6.
I have by magic power
cleared many worlds,
destined as seats
for those Buddhas,
and transported all creatures.

7.
It has always been
my anxious care
how this line of the law
might be manifested.
So you see Buddhas
here in immense number
staying at the foot of trees
like a great multitude
of lotuses.

8.
Many kotis of bases of trees
are brightened by the Leaders
sitting on the thrones
which are perpetually occupied
by them and brightened
as darkness is by fire.

9.
A delicious fragrance
spreads from the Leaders
of the world over all quarters,
a fragrance by which,
when the wind is blowing,
all these creatures
are intoxicated.

10.
Let him who
after my extinction shall
keep this Dharmaparyâya
quickly pronounce
his declaration in the presence
of the Lords of the world.

11.
The Seer Prabhûtaratna who,
though completely extinct,
is awake,
will hear the lion's roar of him
who shall take this resolution.

12.
Myself, in the second place,
as well as the many Chiefs
who have flocked hither
by kotis,
will hear that resolution
from the son of Gina,
who is to exert himself
to expound this law.

13.
And thereby shall I always
be honoured
as well as Prabhûtaratna,
the self-born Gina,
who perpetually wanders
through the quarters
and intermediate quarters
in order to hear
such a law as this.

14.
And these other Lords
of the world here present,
by whom this soil
is so variegated and splendid,
to them also will accrue
ample and manifold honour
from this Sûtra
being preached.

15.
Here on this seat you see me,
together with the Lord
next to me,
in the middle of the Stûpa ;
likewise many other Lords
of the world here present,
in many hundreds of fields.

16.
Ye,
young men of good family,
mind, for mercy's sake
towards all beings,
that it is a very difficult task
to which the Chief urges you.

17.
One might expound
many thousands of Sûtras,
like to the sands
of the Ganges,
without overmuch difficulty.

18.
One who after grasping
the Sumeru in the fist
were to hurl it a distance
of kotis of fields,
would do nothing
very difficult.

19.
Nor would it be
so very difficult
if one could shake
this whole universe
by the thumb to hurl it
a distance of kotis of fields.

20.
Nor would one who,
after taking stand on the limit
of the existing world,
were to expound the law
and thousands
of other Sûtras,
do something so very difficult.

21.
But to keep
and preach this Sûtra
in the dreadful period
succeeding the extinction
of the Chief of the world,
that is difficult.

22.
To throw down
the totality of ether-element
after compressing it in one fist,
and to leave it behind
after having thrown it away,
is not difficult.

23.
But to copy a Sûtra
like this in the period
after my extinction,
that is difficult.

24.
To collect
the whole earth-element
at a nail's end,
cast it away,
and then walk off
to the Brahma-world,

25.
Is not difficult,
nor would it require
a strength surpassing
everybody's strength
to do this work of difficulty.

26.
Something more difficult
than that will he do
who in the last days
after my extinction
shall pronounce this Sûtra,
were it but a single moment.

27.
It will not be difficult for him
to walk in the midst
of the conflagration
at the time of the end
of the world,
even if he carries
with him a load of hay.

28.
More difficult it will be
to keep this Sûtra
after my extinction and
teach it to a single creature.

29.
One may keep
the eighty-four thousand
divisions of the law
and expound them,
with the instructions and such
as they have been set forth,
to kotis of living beings;

30.
This is not so difficult;
nor is it, to train
at the present time monks,
and confirm my disciples
in the five parts
of transcendent knowledge.

31.
But more difficult is it
to keep this Sûtra,
believe in it, adhere to it,
or expound it again and again.

32.
Even he who
confirms many thousands
of kotis of Arhats,
blest with the possession of
the six transcendent faculties,
like sands of the Ganges,

33.
Performs something
not so difficult by far
as the excellent man does
who after my extinction
shall keep my sublime law.

34.
I have often,
in thousands of worlds,
preached the law,
and to-day also I preach it
with the view
that Buddha knowledge
may be obtained.

35.
This Sûtra is declared
the principal of all Sûtras ;
he who keeps in his memory
this Sûtra,
keeps the body of the Gina.

36.
Speak,
O young men of good family,
while the Tathâgata
is still in your presence,
who amongst you
is to exert himself
in later times
to keep the Sûtra.

37.
Not only I myself
shall be pleased,
but the Lords
of the world in general,
if one would keep
for a moment this Sûtra
so difficult to keep.

38.
Such a one
shall ever be praised
by all the Lords of the world,
famed as an eminent hero,
and quick in arriving
at transcendent wisdom.

39.
He shall be entrusted
with the leadership amongst
the sons of the Tathâgatas,
he who, after having reached
the stage of meekness,
shall keep this Sûtra.

40.
He shall be
the eye of the world,
including gods and men,
who shall speak this Sûtra
after the extinction
of the Chief of men.

41.
He is to be
venerated by all beings,
the wise man
who in the last times
shall preach this Sûtra
were it but a single moment.

Thereupon
the Lord addressed
the whole company
of Bodhisattvas
and the world,
including gods and demons,
and said :
Of yore, monks,
in times past I have,

unwearied
and without repose,
sought after the Sûtra
of the Lotus of the True Law,
during immense,
immeasurable Æons ;
many Æons
before I have been a king,
during many
thousands of Æons.
Having once taken
the strong resolution
to arrive at supreme,
perfect enlightenment,
my mind did not swerve
from its aim.
I exerted myself to fulfil
the six Perfections,
bestowing immense alms :
gold, money, gems, pearls,
lapis lazuli, conch-shells,
stones, coral,
gold and silver, emerald,
Musâragalva, red pearls ;
villages, towns, boroughs,
provinces, kingdoms,
royal capitals ;
wives, sons, daughters,
slaves, male and female ;
elephants, horses, cars,
up to the sacrifice
of life and body,
of limbs and members,
hands, feet, head.
And never did the thought
of self-complacency rise in me.
In those days
the life of men lasted long,
so that for a time of many
hundred thousand years
I was exercising the rule
of a King of the Law
for the sake of duty,
not for the sake of enjoyment.
After installing in government
the eldest prince royal,
I went in quest of the best law
in the four quarters,
and had promulgated
with sound of bell
the following proclamation :
He who procures for me
the best laws
or points out what is useful,
to him will I become a servant.
At that time there lived a Seer ;
he told me : Noble king,
there is a Sûtra, called
the Lotus of the True Law,
which is an exposition
of the best law.
If thou consent
to become my servant,
I will teach thee that law.
And I, glad, content,
exulting and ravished
at the words I heard
from the Seer,
became his pupil,
and said :
I will do for thee
the work of a servant.
And so having agreed
upon becoming
the servant of the Seer,
I performed
the duties of a servitor,
such as fetching grass,
fuel, water, bulbs,
roots, fruit, &c.
I held also the office
of a doorkeeper.

When I had done such
kind of work at day-time,
I at night kept his feet while
he was lying on his couch,
and never did I feel fatigue
of body or mind.
In such occupations
I passed a full millennium.

And for the fuller elucidation
of this matter
the Lord on that occasion
uttered the following stanzas :

42.
I have a remembrance
of past ages
when I was Dhârmika,
the King of the Law,
and exercised the royal sway
for duty's sake,
not for love's sake,
in the interest of the best law.

43.
I let go out in all directions
this proclamation :
I will become a servant
to him who shall
explain Dharma.
At that time
there was a far-seeing Sage,
a revealer of the Sûtra
called the True Law.

44.
He said to me :
If thou wish to know Dharma,
become my servant ;
then I will explain it to thee.
As I heard these words
I rejoiced
and carefully performed
such work
as a servant ought to do.

45.
I never felt any bodily
nor mental weariness
since I had become a servant
for the sake of the true law.
I did my best
for real truth's sake,
not with a view
to win honour
or enjoy pleasure.

46.
That king meanwhile,
strenuously
and without engaging
in other pursuits,
roamed in every direction
during thousands
of kotis of complete Æons
without being able to obtain
the Sûtra called Dharma.

Now, monks,
what is your opinion ?
that it was another
who at that time,
at that juncture was the king ?
No, you must
certainly not hold that view.
For it was myself,
who at that time,
at that juncture was the king.
What then, monks,
is your opinion ?
that it was another
who at that time,

at that juncture was the Seer?
No, you must
certainly not hold that view.
For it was this Devadatta
himself, the monk,
who at that time,
at that juncture was the Seer.
Indeed, monks, Devadatta
was my good friend.
By the aid of Devadatta
have I accomplished
the six perfect virtues.
Noble kindness,
noble compassion,
noble sympathy,
noble indifference,
the thirty-two signs
of a great man,
the eighty lesser marks,
the gold-coloured tinge,
the ten powers,
the fourfold absence
of hesitation,
the four articles of sociability,
the eighteen
uncommon properties,
magical power,
ability to save beings
in all directions of space, -
all this have I got after
having come to Devadatta.
I announce to you, monks,
I declare to you:
This Devadatta, the monk,
shall in an age to come,
after immense,
innumerable Æons,
become a Tathâgata
named Devarâga
(i.e. King of the gods),
an Arhat, &c.,
in the world Devasopâna
(i.e. Stairs of the gods).
The lifetime of that Tathâgata
Devarâga, monks,
shall measure
twenty intermediate kalpas.
He shall preach
the law in extension,
and beings equal to the sands
of the river Ganges
shall through him
forsake all evils
and realize Arhatship.
Several beings
shall also elevate their minds
to Pratyekabuddhaship,
whereas beings equal to
the sands of the river Ganges
shall elevate their minds
to supreme,
perfect enlightenment,
and become endowed
with unflinching patience.
Further, monks,
after the complete extinction
of the Tathâgata Devarâgu,
his true law shall stay
twenty intermediate kalpas.
His body shall not
be seen divided
into different parts and relics;
it shall remain
as one mass within a Stûpa
of seven precious substances,
which Stûpa
is to be sixty hundred yoganas
in height and forty yoganas
in extension.
All, gods and men,
shall do worship to it
with flowers, incense,

perfumed garlands,
unguents, powder, clothes,
umbrellas, banners, flags,
and celebrate it
with stanzas and songs.
Those who shall turn round
that Stûpa from left to right
or humbly salute it,
shall some of them
realize Arhatship,
others attain
Pratyekabuddhaship ;
others, gods and men,
in immense number,
shall raise their minds
to supreme,
perfect enlightenment,
never to return.

Thereafter
the Lord again addressed
the assembly of monks :
Whosoever in future, monks,
be he a young man or
a young lady of good family,
shall hear
this chapter of the Sûtra
of the Lotus of the True Law,
and by doing so
be relieved from doubt,
become pure-minded,
and put reliance on it,
to such a one the door
of the three states
of misfortune shall be shut :
he shall not fall so low
as to be born in hell,
among beasts,
or in Yama's kingdom.
When born
in the Buddha-fields
in the ten points of space
he shall at each repeated
birth hear this very Sûtra,
and when born
amongst gods or men
he shall attain
an eminent rank.
And in the Buddha-field
where he is to be born
he shall appear
by metamorphosis on a lotus
of seven precious substances,
face to face
with the Tathâgata.

At that moment
a Bodhisattva
of the name of Pragñâkûta,
having come from beneath
the Buddha-field
of the Tathâgatna,
said to the Tathâgata
Prabhûtaratna : Lord,
let us resort
to our own Buddha-field.
But the Lord Sâkyamuni,
the Tathâgata,
said to the Bodhisattva
Pragñâkûta :
Wait a while,
young man of good family,
first have a discussion with
my Bodhisattva Mañgusrî,
the prince royal,
to settle some point of the law.
And at the same moment, lo,
Mañgusrî, the prince royal,
rose seated
on a centifolious lotus
that was large as a carriage
yoked with four horses,

Apparition of a Stûpa 207

surrounded and attended
by many Bodhisattvas,
from the bosom of the sea,
from the abode
of the Nâga-king Sâgara
(i.e. Ocean).
Rising high into the sky
he went through the air
to the Gridhrakûta mountain
to the presence of the Lord.
There Mañgusrî,
the prince royal,
alighted from his lotus,
reverentially saluted the
feet of the Lord Sâkyamuni
and Prabhûtaratna,
the Tathâgata,
went up to the Bodhisattva
Pragñâkûta and,
after making the usual
complimentary questions
as to his health and welfare,
seated himself
at some distance.
The Bodhisattva Pragñâkûta
then addressed to Mañgusrî,
the prince royal,
the following question :
Mañgusrî,
how many beings
hast thou educated
during thy stay in the sea ?
Mañgusrî answered :
Many, innumerable,
incalculable beings
have I educated,
so innumerable that words
cannot express it,
nor thought conceive it.
Wait a while,
young man of good family,

thou shalt presently
see a token.
No sooner had Mañgusrî,
the prince royal,
spoken these words
than instantaneously
many thousands of lotuses
rose from the bosom
of the sea up to the sky,
and on those lotuses
were seated many thousands
of Bodhisattvas,
who flocked through the air
to the Gridhrakûta mountain,
where they stayed,
appearing as meteors.
All of them had been
educated by Mañgusrî,
the prince royal,
to supreme,
perfect enlightenment.
The Bodhisattvas
amongst them
who had formerly striven
after the great vehicle
extolled the virtues
of the great vehicle
and the six perfect virtues.
Such as had been disciples
extolled the vehicle
of disciples.
But all acknowledged
the voidness or vanity
of all laws or things,
as well as the virtues
of the great vehicle.
Mañgusrî,
the prince royal,
said to
the Bodhisattva Pragñâkûta :
Young man of good family,

while I was staying
in the bosom
of the great ocean
I have by all means
educated creatures,
and here thou seest the result.
Whereupon
the Bodhisattva Pragñâkûta
questioned Mañgusrî,
the prince royal,
in chanting
the following stanzas :

47.
O thou blessed one,
who from thy wisdom
art called the Sage,
by whose power
is it that thou to-day
hast educated
those innumerable beings ?
Tell it me upon my question,
O thou god amongst men.

48.
What law hast thou preached,
or what Sûtra,
in showing
the path of enlightenment,
so that those
who are there with you
have conceived
the idea of enlightenment ?
that,
once having gained
a safe ford,
they have been decisively
established in omniscience ?

Mañgusrî answered :
In the bosom of the sea

I have expounded
the Lotus of the True Law
and no other Sûtra.
Pragñakûta said :
That Sûtra is profound,
subtle, difficult to seize ;
no other Sûtra equals it.
Is there any creature
able to understand
this jewel of a Sûtra
or to arrive at supreme,
perfect enlightenment ?
Mañgusrî replied :
There is,
young man of good family,
the daughter of Sâgara,
the Nâga-king,
eight years old,
very intelligent,
of keen faculties,
endowed with
prudence in acts of body,
speech, and mind,
who has caught
and kept all the teachings,
in substance and form,
of the Tathâgatas,
who has acquired
in one moment a thousand
meditations and proofs
of the essence of all laws.
She does not swerve from
the idea of enlightenment,
has great aspirations,
applies to other beings
the same measure
as to herself ;
she is apt
to display all virtues and
is never deficient in them.
With a bland smile on the face

and in the bloom
of an extremely
handsome appearance
she speaks words
of kindliness and compassion.
She is fit to arrive at supreme,
perfect enlightenment.
The Bodhisattva
Praggakûta said :
I have seen how
the Lord Sâkyamuni,
the Tathâgata,
when he was striving
after enlightenment,
in the state of a Bodhisattva,
performed innumerable
good works,
and during many Æons
never slackened
in his arduous task.
In the whole universe
there is not a single spot
so small as a mustard-seed
where he
has not surrendered his body
for the sake of creatures.
Afterwards he arrived
at enlightenment.
Who then would believe
that she should have been able
to arrive at supreme,
perfect knowledge
in one moment ?

At that very moment
appeared
the daughter of Sâgara,
the Nâga-king,
standing before their face.
After reverentially saluting
the feet of the Lord
she stationed herself
at some distance
and uttered on that occasion
the following stanzas :

49.
Spotless, bright,
and of unfathomable light
is that ethereal body,
adorned with the thirty-two
characteristic signs,
pervading space
in all directions.

50.
He is possessed
of the secondary marks
and praised by every being,
and accessible to all,
like an open market-place.

51.
I have obtained
enlightenment
according to my wish ;
the Tathâgata
can bear witness to it ;
I will extensively
reveal the law that
releases from sufferance.

Then
the venerable Sâriputra said
to that daughter of Sâgara,
the Nâga-king :
Thou hast conceived
the idea of enlightenment,
young lady of good family,
without sliding back,
and art gifted
with immense wisdom,

but supreme,
perfect enlightenment
is not easily won.
It may happen, sister,
that a woman displays
an unflagging energy,
performs good works
for many thousands of Æons,
and fulfills
the six perfect virtues,
but as yet there is no example
of her having reached
Buddhaship,
and that because a woman
cannot occupy the five ranks,
namely
1. the rank of Brahma ;
2. the rank of Indra ;
3. the rank of a chief guardian
of the four quarters ;
4. the rank of Kakravartin ;
5. the rank of a Bodhisattva
incapable of sliding back.

Now the daughter of Sâgara,
the Nâga-king,
had at the time a gem
which in value outweighed
the whole universe.
That gem the daughter
of Sâgara, the Nâga-king,
presented to the Lord,
and the Lord
graciously accepted it.
Then the daughter of Sâgara,
the Nâga-king, said to the
Bodhisattva Pragñâkûta and
the senior priest Sâriputra :
Has the Lord
readily accepted the gem
I presented him or has he not ?

The senior priest answered :
As soon as it was
presented by thee,
so soon it was accepted
by the Lord.
The daughter of Sâgara,
the Nâga-king, replied :
If I were endowed
with magic power,
brother Sâriputra,
I should sooner
have arrived at supreme,
perfect enlightenment,
and there would have been
none to receive this gem.

At the same instant,
before the sight
of the whole world and
of the senior priest Sâriputra,
the female sex
of the daughter of Sâgara,
the Nâga-king, disappeared ;
the male sex appeared
and she manifested herself
as a Bodhisattva,
who immediately
went to the South to sit down
at the foot of a tree made
of seven precious substances,
in the world Vimala
(i.e. spotless),
where he showed himself
enlightened
and preaching the law,
while filling
all directions of space
with the radiance
of the thirty-two
characteristic signs
and all secondary marks.

All beings in the Saha-world
beheld that Lord
while he received
the homage of all,
gods, Nâgas, goblins,
Gandharvas, demons,
Garudas, Kinnaras,
great serpents, men,
and beings not human,
and was engaged
in preaching the law.
And the beings
who heard the preaching
of that Tathâgata
became incapable
of sliding back in supreme,
perfect enlightenment.
And that world Vimala
and this Saha-world
shook in six different ways.
Three thousand living beings
from the congregational circle
of the Lord Sâkyamuni
gained the acquiescence
in the eternal law,
whereas three hundred
thousand beings
obtained the prediction
of their future destiny
to supreme,
perfect enlightenment.

Then
the Bodhisattva Pragñâkûta
and the senior priest Sâriputra
were silent.

Chapter XII
Exertion

Thereafter the
Bodhisattva Bhaishagyarâga
and the
Bodhisattva Mahâpratibhâna,
with a retinue
of twenty hundred thousand
Bodhisattvas,
spoke before
the face of the Lord
the following words :
Let the Lord be at ease
in this respect ;
we will after the extinction
of the Tathâgata
expound this Paryâya
to all creatures,
though we are aware,
O Lord,
that at that period
there shall be malign beings,
having few roots of goodness,
conceited,
fond of gain and honour,
rooted in unholiness,
difficult to tame,
deprived of good will,
and full of unwillingness.
Nevertheless, O Lord,
we will at that period read,
keep, preach,
write, honour,
respect, venerate,
worship this Sûtra ;
with sacrifice of body and life,
O Lord,
we will divulge this Sûtra.
Let the Lord be at ease.

Thereupon five hundred
monks of the assembly,
both such as were
under training
and such as were not,
said to the Lord :
We also, O Lord,
will exert ourselves to divulge
this Dharmaparyâya,
though in other worlds.
Then
all the disciples of the Lord,
both such as were
under training
and such as were not,
who had received
from the Lord
the prediction
as to their future
supreme enlightenment,
all the eight thousand monks
raised their joined hands
towards the Lord and said :
Let the Lord be at case.
We also will divulge
this Dharmaparyâya,
after the complete extinction
of the Lord,
in the last days,
the last period,
though in other worlds.
For in this Saha-world,
O Lord,
the creatures are conceited,
possessed
of few roots of goodness,
always vicious
in their thoughts,
wicked,
and naturally perverse.

Then the noble matron Gautamî, the sister of the Lord's mother, along with six hundred nuns, some of them being under training, some being not, rose from her seat, raised the joined hands towards the Lord and remained gazing up to him. Then the Lord addressed the noble matron Gautamî: Why dost thou stand so dejected, gazing up to the Tathâgata? She replied: I have not been mentioned by the Tathâgata, nor have I received from him a prediction of my destiny to supreme, perfect enlightenment. He said: But, Gautamî, thou hast received a prediction with the prediction regarding the whole assembly. Indeed, Gautamî, thou shalt from henceforward, before the face of thirty-eight hundred thousand myriads of kotis of Buddhas, be a Bodhisattva and preacher of the law. These six thousand nuns also, partly perfected in discipline, partly not, shall along with others become Bodhisattvas and preachers of the law before the face of the Tathâgatas. Afterwards, when thou shalt have completed the course of a Bodhisattva, thou shalt become, under the name of Sarvasattvapriyadarsana (i.e. lovely to see for all beings), a Tathâgata, an Arhat, &c., endowed with science and conduct, &c. &c. And that Tathâgata Sarvasattvapriyadarsana, O Gautamî, shall give a prediction by regular succession to those six thousand Bodhisattvas concerning their destiny to supreme, perfect enlightenment.

Then the nun Yasodharâ, the mother of Râhula, thought thus: The Lord has not mentioned my name. And the Lord comprehending in his own mind what was going on in the mind of the nun Yasodharâ said to her: I announce to thee, Yasodharâ, I declare to thee: Thou also shalt before the face of ten thousand

kotis of Buddhas
become a Bodhisattva
and preacher of the law,
and after regularly
completing the course
of a Bodhisattva
thou shalt become
a Tathâgata, named
Rasmisatasahasra-
paripûrnadhvaga,
an Arhat, &c., endowed with
science and conduct, &c. &c.,
in the world Bhadra ;
and the life time of that Lord
Rasmisatasahasra-
paripûrnadhvaga,
shall be unlimited.

When the noble matron
Gautamî, the nun,
with her suite
of six thousand nuns,
and Yasodharâ, the nun,
with her suite
of four thousand nuns,
heard from the Lord
their future destiny
to supreme,
perfect enlightenment,
they uttered,
in wonder and amazement,
this stanza :

1.
O Lord, thou art the trainer,
thou art the leader ;
thou art the master
of the world,
including the gods ;
thou art the giver of comfort,
thou who art worshipped
by men and gods. Now,
indeed, we feel satisfied.

After uttering this stanza
the nuns said to the Lord :
We also, O Lord,
will exert ourselves to divulge
this Dharmaparyâya
in the last days,
though in other worlds.

Thereafter the Lord
looked towards
the eighty hundred
thousand Bodhisattvas
who were gifted
with magical spells
and capable of moving
forward the wheel
that never rolls back.
No sooner
were those Bodhisattvas
regarded by the Lord
than they rose
from their seats,
raised their joined hands
towards the Lord
and reflected thus :
The Lord invites us
to make known
the Dharmaparyâya.
Agitated by that thought
they asked one another :
What shall we do,
young men of good family,
in order that
this Dharmaparyâya may
in future be made known
as the Lord invites us to do ?
Thereupon those young
men of good family,

in consequence
of their reverence for the Lord
and their own pious vow
in their previous course,
raised a lion's roar
before the Lord :
We, O Lord,
will in future,
after the complete
extinction of the Lord,
go in all directions in order
that creatures shall write,
keep, meditate, divulge
this Dharmaparyâya,
by no other's power
but the Lord's.
And the Lord,
staying in another world,
shall protect, defend,
and guard us.

Then the Bodhisattvas
unanimously in a chorus
addressed the Lord
with the following stanzas :

2.
Be at ease, O Lord.
After thy complete extinction,
in the horrible last period
of the world,
we will proclaim
this sublime Sûtra.

3.
We will suffer,
patiently endure,
O Lord,
the injuries, threats,
blows and threats with sticks
at the hands of foolish men.

4.
At that dreadful last epoch
men will be malign, crooked,
wicked, dull, conceited,
fancying to have
come to the limit
when they have not.

5.
'We do not care
but to live in the wilderness
and wear a patched cloth ;
we lead a frugal life ;'
so will they speak
to the ignorant.

6.
And persons greedily
attached to enjoyments
will preach the law to laymen
and be honoured
as if they possessed
the six transcendent qualities.

7.
Cruel-minded
and wicked men,
only occupied
with household cares,
will enter our retreat
in the forest and become
our calumniators.

8.
The Tîrthikas, themselves
bent on profit and honour,
will say of us that we are so,
and - shame on such monks ! -
they will preach
their own fictions.

9.
Prompted by greed
of profit and honour
they will compose Sûtras
of their own invention
and then,
in the midst of the assembly,
accuse us of plagiarism.

10.
To kings, princes,
king's peers,
as well as to Brahmans
and commoners,
and to monks
of other confessions,

11.
They will speak evil of us
and propagate
the Tîrtha-doctrine.
We will endure
all that out of reverence
for the great Seers.

12.
And those fools
who will not listen to us,
shall sooner or later
become enlightened,
and therefore
will we forbear to the last.

13.
In that dreadful,
most terrible period
of frightful general revolution
will many fiendish monks
stand up as our revilers.

14.
Out of respect
for the Chief of the world
we will bear it,
however difficult it be ;
girded with the girdle
of forbearance
will I proclaim this Sûtra.

15.
I do not care
for my body or life, O Lord,
but as keepers of thine
entrusted deposit
we care for enlightenment.

16.
The Lord himself knows
that in the last period
there are to be wicked monks
who do not understand
mysterious speech.

17.
One will have to
bear frowning looks,
repeated disavowal
or concealment,
expulsion from
the monasteries,
many and manifold abuses.

18.
Yet mindful of the command
of the Lord of the world
we will in the last period
undauntedly proclaim
this Sûtra in the midst
of the congregation.

19.
We will visit towns
and villages everywhere,
and transmit
to those who care for it
thine entrusted deposit,
O Lord.

20.
O Chief of the world,
we will deliver thy message ;
be at ease then,
tranquil and quiet,
great Seer.

21.
Light of the world,
thou knowest
the disposition of all
who have flocked hither
from every direction,
and thou knowest
that we speak a word of truth.

Chapter XIII
Peaceful Life

Mañgusrî, the prince royal,
said to the Lord:
It is difficult, Lord,
most difficult, what these
Bodhisattvas Mahâsattvas
will attempt
out of reverence for the Lord.
How are these Bodhisattvas
Mahâsattvas to promulgate
this Dharmaparyâya
at the end of time,
at the last period?
Whereupon the Lord
answered Mañgusrî,
the prince royal:
A Bodhisattva Mahâsattva,
Mañgusrî,
he who is to promulgate
this Dharmaparyâya
at the end of time,
at the last period,
must be firm in four things.
In which things?
The Bodhisattva Mahâsattva,
Mañgusrî,
must be firm in his conduct
and proper sphere
if he wishes to teach
this Dharmaparyâya.
And how, Mañgusrî,
is a Bodhisattva Mahâsattva
firm in his conduct
and proper sphere?
When the Bodhisattva
Mahâsattva, Mañgusrî,
is patient, meek,
has reached
the stage of meekness;
when he is not rash,
nor envious;
when, moreover, Mañgusrî,
he clings to no law whatever
and sees the real character
of the laws or things;
when he is refraining
from investigating
and discussing these laws,
Mañgusrî;
that is called the conduct
of a Bodhisattva Mahâsattva.
And what is
the proper sphere
of a Bodhisattva Mahâsattva,
Mañgusrî? When the
Bodhisattva Mahâsattva,
Mañgusrî,
does not serve, not court,
not wait upon kings;
does not serve, not court,
not wait upon princes; when
he does not approach them;
when he does not serve,
not court,
not wait upon persons
of another sect,
Karakas, Parivrâgakas,
Âgîvakas, Nirgranthas,
nor persons passionately
fond of fine literature;
when he does not serve,
not court,
not wait upon adepts
at worldly spells,
and votaries
of a worldly philosophy,
nor keep any intercourse
with them;
when he does not go to see
Kândâlas, jugglers,

vendors of pork, poulterers,
deer-hunters, butchers,
actors and dancers, wrestlers,
nor resort to places
whither others flock
for amusement and sport;
when he keeps no intercourse
with them
unless from time to time
to preach the law to them
when they come to him,
and that freely;
when he does not serve,
not court,
not wait upon monks, nuns,
lay devotees,
male and female,
who are adherents
of the vehicle of disciples,
nor keep
intercourse with them;
when he does not
come in contact with them
at the place of promenade
or in the monastery,
unless from time to time
to preach the law to them
when they come to him,
and even that freely.
This, Mañgusrî,
is the proper sphere
of a Bodhisattva Mahâsattva.

Again, Mañgusrî,
the Bodhisattva Mahâsattva
does not take hold of some
favorable opportunity
or another to preach the law to
females every now and anon,
nor is he desirous
of repeatedly seeing females;
nor does he think it proper
to visit families
and then too often
address a girl, virgin,
or young wife,
nor does he greet them
too fondly in return.
He does not preach the law
to a hermaphrodite,
keeps no intercourse
with such a person,
nor greets too friendly
in return.
He does not
enter a house alone
in order to receive alms,
unless having
the Tathâgata in his thoughts.
And when he happens
to preach the law to females,
he does not do so
by passionate attachment
to the law,
far less by passionate
attachment to a woman.
When he is preaching,
he does not display
his row of teeth,
let alone a quick emotion
on his physiognomy.
He addresses no novice,
male or female,
no nun, no monk,
no young boy, no young girl,
nor enters upon
a conversation with them;
he shows no great readiness
in answering their address,
nor cares
to give too frequent answers.
This, Mañgusrî, is called

the first proper sphere
of a Bodhisattva Mahâsattva.

Further, Mañgusrî,
a Bodhisattva Mahâsattva
looks upon all laws
and things as void ;
he sees them duly established,
remaining unaltered,
as they are in reality,
not liable to be disturbed,
not to be moved backward,
unchangeable,
existing in the highest sense
of the word
or in an absolute sense,
having the nature of space,
escaping explanation
and expression
by means of common speech,
not born,
composed and simple,
aggregated and isolated,
not expressible in words,
independently established,
manifesting themselves
owing to a perversion
of perception.
In this way then, Mañgusrî,
the Bodhisattva Mahâsattva
constantly views all laws,
and if he abides in this course,
he remains in his own sphere.
This, Mañgusrî,
is the second proper sphere
of a Bodhisattva Mahâsattva.

And in order to expound
this matter in greater detail,
the Lord uttered
the following stanzas :

1.
The Bodhisattva who,
undaunted and unabashed,
wishes to set forth this Sûtra
in the dreadful period
hereafter,

2.
Must keep
to his course of duty
and proper sphere ;
he must be retired and pure,
constantly avoid intercourse
with kings and princes.

3.
Nor should he
keep up intercourse
with king's servants,
nor with Kândâlas, jugglers,
and Tîrthikas in general.

4.
He ought not
to court conceited men,
but catechise such
as keep to the religion.
He must also
avoid such monks
as follow the precepts
of the Arhat,
and immoral men.

5.
He must be constant
in avoiding a nun who is fond
of banter and chatter ;
he must also avoid
notoriously loose
female lay devotees.

6.
He should shun
any intercourse with
such female lay devotees
as seek
their highest happiness
in this transient world.
This is called the proper
conduct of a Bodhisattva.

7.
But when one comes to him
to question him about the law
for the sake
of superior enlightenment,
he should, at any time,
speak freely,
always firm and undaunted.

8.
He should have
no intercourse with women
and hermaphrodites ;
he should also shun
the young wives
and girls in families.

9.
He must never address them
to ask after their health.
He must also avoid
intercourse with vendors
of pork and mutton.

10.
With any persons who slay
animals of various kind
for the sake of profit,
and with such as sell meat
he should
avoid having any intercourse.

11.
He must shun the society
of whoremongers, players,
musicians, wrestlers,
and other people of that sort.

12.
He should not
frequent whores,
nor other sensual persons ;
he must avoid any exchange
of civility with them.

13.
And when the sage
has to preach for a woman,
he should not enter
into an apartment
with her alone,
nor stay to banter.

14.
When he has often to enter
a village in quest of food,
he must
have another monk with him
or constantly
think of the Buddha.

15.
Herewith have I shown
the first sphere
of proper conduct.
Wise are they who,
keeping this Sûtra
in memory,
live according to it.

16.
And when one
observes no law at all,
low, superior or mean,
composed or uncomposed,
real or not real ;

17.
When the wise man
does not remark,
'This is a woman,'
nor marks,
'This is a man ;'
when in searching
he finds no laws or things,
because they
have never existed ;

18.
This is called the observance
of the Bodhisattvas in general.
Now listen to me
when I set forth
what should be
their proper sphere.

19.
All laws have been declared
to be non-existing,
not appearing,
not produced,
void, immovable,
everlasting ;
this is called
the proper sphere
of the wise.

20.
They have been divided
into existing and non-existing,
real and unreal,
by those
who had wrong notions ;
other laws also,
of permanency,
of being produced,
of birth from something
already produced,
are wrongly assumed.

21.
Let the Bodhisattva
be concentrated in mind,
attentive,
ever firm as the peak
of Mount Sumeru,
and in such a state of mind
look upon all laws
and things as having
the nature of space,

22.
Permanently equal to space,
without essence, immovable,
without substantiality.
These, indeed, are the laws,
all and for ever.
This is called
the proper sphere of the wise.

23.
The monk observing this rule
of conduct given by me may,
after my extinction,
promulgate this Sûtra
in the world,
and shall feel no depression.

24.
Let the sage first,
for some time,
coerce his thoughts,
exercise meditation
with complete absorption,
and correctly perform
all that is required
for attaining spiritual insight,
and then, after rising
from his pious meditation,
preach with unquailing mind.

25.
The kings of this earth
and the princes who listen
to the law protect him.
Others also,
both laymen or burghers
and Brahmans,
will be found together
in his congregation.

Further, Mañgusrî,
the Bodhisattva
Mahâsattva who,
after the complete extinction
of the Tathâgata
at the end of time,
the last period,
the last five hundred years,
when the true law
is in a state of decay,
is going to propound
this Dharmaparyâya,
must be
in a peaceful state of mind
and then preach the law,
whether he knows it
by heart or has it in a book.
In his sermon

he will not be too prone
to carping at others,
not blame
other preaching friars,
not speak scandal
nor propagate scandal.
He does not mention
by name other monks,
adherents
of the vehicle of disciples,
to propagate scandal.
He cherishes even no
hostile feelings against them,
because
he is in a peaceful state.
All who come,
one after the other,
to hear the sermon
he receives with benevolence,
and preaches the law to them
without invidiousness.
He refrains from
entering upon a dispute ;
but if he is asked a question,
he does not answer
in the way of those who follow
the vehicle of disciples ;
on the contrary,
he answers as if he had
attained Buddha-knowledge.

And on that occasion
the Lord uttered
the following stanzas :

26.
The wise man
is always at ease,
and in that state
he preaches the law,
seated on an elevated pulpit

which has been
prepared for him
on a clean and pretty spot.

27.
He puts on a clean,
nice, red robe,
dyed with good colours,
and a black woollen garment
and a long undergarment ;

28.
Having duly washed his feet
and rubbed his head and face
with smooth ointments,
he ascends the pulpit, which
is provided with a footbank
and covered with pieces
of fine cloth of various sorts,
and sits down.

29.
When he is thus seated
on the preacher's pulpit
and all who have gathered
round him are attentive,
he proceeds to deliver
many discourses,
pleasing by variety,
before monks and nuns,

30.
Before male and female
lay devotees,
kings and princes.
The wise man always
takes care to deliver a sermon
diversified in its contents
and sweet,
free from invidiousness.

31.
If occasionally
he is asked some question,
even after he has commenced,
he will explain the matter
anew in regular order,
and he will explain
it in such a way
that his hearers
gain enlightenment.

32.
The wise man
is indefatigable ;
not even the thought
of fatigue will rise in him ;
he knows no listlessness,
and so displays
to the assembly
the strength of charity.

33.
Day and night
the wise man preaches
this sublime law
with myriads of kotis
of illustrations ;
he edifies
and satisfies his audience
without ever
requiring anything.

34.
Solid food, soft food,
nourishment and drink,
cloth, couches, robes,
medicaments for the sick,
all this
does not occupy his thoughts,
nor does he want anything
from the congregation.

35.
On the contrary,
the wise man
is always thinking :
How can I and these beings
become Buddhas ?
I will preach this true law,
upon which the happiness
of all beings depends,
for the benefit of the world.

36.
The monk who,
after my extinction,
shall preach in this way,
without envy,
shall not meet with trouble,
impediment,
grief or despondency.

37.
Nobody shall frighten him,
beat or blame him ;
never shall
he be driven away,
because he is firm
in the strength
of forbearance.

38.
The wise man
who is peaceful,
so disposed as I have just said,
possesses hundreds
of kotis of advantages,
so many that one would not
be able to enumerate them
in hundreds of Æons.

Again, Mañgusrî,
the Bodhisattva Mahâsattva
who lives after the extinction
of the Tathâgata
at the end of time
when the true law is in decay,
the Bodhisattva Mahâsattva
who keeps this Sûtra
is not envious,
not false, not deceitful ;
he does not speak
disparagingly
of other adherents
of the vehicle of Bodhisattvas,
nor defame, nor humble them.
He does not bring forward
the shortcomings
of other monks, nuns,
male and female lay devotees,
neither of the adherents
of the vehicle of disciples
nor of those of the vehicle
of Pratyekabuddhas.
He does not say :
You young men of good family,
you are far off from supreme,
perfect enlightenment ;
you give proof
of not having arrived at it ;
you are too fickle
in your doings
and not capable
of acquiring true knowledge.
He does not in this way
bring forward
the shortcomings
of any adherent of the vehicle
of the Bodhisattvas.
Nor does he show
any delight in disputes
about the law,
or engage in disputes
about the law,

and he never abandons
the strength of charity
towards all beings.
In respect to all Tathâgatas
he feels as if
they were his fathers,
and in respect
to all Bodhisattvas
as if they were his masters.
And as to
the Bodhisattvas Mahâsattvas
in all directions of space,
he is assiduous
in paying homage to them
by good will and respect.
When he preaches the law,
he preaches no less
and no more than the law,
without partial predilection
for any part of the law,
and he does not
show greater favor
to one than to another,
even from love of the law.

Such, Mañgusrî,
is the third quality with which
a Bodhisattva Mahâsattva
is endowed who is to expound
this Dharmaparyâya
after the extinction
of the Tathâgata
at the end of time
when the true law is in decay;
who will live at ease
and not be annoyed
in the exposition
of this Dharmaparyâya.
And in the synod
he will have allies,
and he will find auditors
at his sermons who will listen
to this Dharmaparyâya,
believe, accept, keep,
read, penetrate,
write it and cause it
to be written, and who,
after it has been written
and a volume made of it,
will honour, respect,
esteem, and worship it.

This said the Lord,
and thereafter he,
the Sugata, the Master,
added the following :

39.
The wise man, the preacher,
who wishes to expound
this Sûtra must absolutely
renounce falsehood, pride,
calumny, and envy.

40.
He should never speak
a disparaging word
of anybody ;
never engage in a dispute
on religious belief ;
never say to such
as are guilty of shortcomings,
You will not obtain
superior knowledge.

41.
He is always sincere,
mild, forbearing ;
as a true son of Sugata
he will repeatedly
preach the law without
any feeling of vexation.

42.
'The Bodhisattvas
in all directions of space,
who out of compassion
for creatures
are moving in the world,
are my teachers;'
thus thinking the wise man
respects them as his masters.

43.
Cherishing the memory
of the Buddhas,
the supreme amongst men,
he will always
feel towards them
as if they were his fathers,
and by forsaking
all idea of pride
he will escape hindrance.

44.
The wise man
who has heard this law,
should be constant
in observing it.
If he earnestly strives
after a peaceful life,
kotis of beings
will surely protect him.

Further, Mañgusrî,
the Bodhisattva Mahâsattva,
living at the time
of destruction of the true law
after the extinction
of the Tathâgata,
who is desirous of keeping
this Dharmaparyâya,
should live
as far as possible away
from laymen and friars,
and lead a life of charity.
He must feel affection
for all beings who are
striving for enlightenment
and therefore
make this reflection :
To be sure,
they are greatly
perverted in mind,
those beings who do not hear,
nor perceive, nor understand
the skilfulness and
the mystery of the Tathâgata,
who do not inquire for it,
nor believe in it,
nor even are willing
to believe in it.
Of course,
these beings do not penetrate,
nor understand
this Dharmaparyâya.
Nevertheless will I, who
have attained this supreme,
perfect knowledge,
powerfully bend to it
the mind of every one,
whatever may
be the position he occupies,
and bring about
that he accepts, understands,
and arrives at full ripeness.

By possessing also this
fourth quality, Mañgusrî,
a Bodhisattva Mahâsattva,
who is to expound the law
after the extinction
of the Tathâgata,
will be unmolested, honoured,
respected, esteemed,

venerated by monks, nuns,
and lay devotees,
male and female,
by kings, princes, ministers,
king's officers, by citizens
and country people,
by Brahmans and laymen;
the gods of the sky will,
full of faith,
follow his track
to hear the law,
and the angels
will follow his track
to protect him;
whether he is in a village
or in a monastery,
they will approach him
day and night
to put questions about the law,
and they will be satisfied,
charmed with his explanation.
For this Dharmaparyâya,
Mañgusrî,
has been blessed
by all Buddhas.
With the past, future,
and present Tathâgata,
Mañgusrî,
this Dharmaparyâya
is for ever blessed.
Precious in all worlds,
Mañgusrî,
is the sound, rumour,
or mentioning
of this Dharmaparyâya.

It is a case, Mañgusrî,
similar to that of a king,
a ruler of armies,
who by force has conquered
his own kingdom,
whereupon other kings,
his adversaries,
wage war against him.
That ruler of armies
has soldiers
of various description
to fight with various enemies.
As the king
sees those soldiers fighting,
he is delighted
with their gallantry,
enraptured,
and in his delight and rapture
he makes to his soldiers
several donations,
such as villages
and village grounds,
towns and grounds of a town;
garments and head-gear;
hand-ornaments,
necklaces, gold threads,
earrings, strings of pearls,
bullion, gold, gems, pearls,
lapis lazuli, conch-shells,
stones, corals;
he, moreover, gives elephants,
horses, cars, foot soldiers,
male and female slaves,
vehicles, and litters.
But to none
he makes a present
of his crown jewel,
because that jewel
only fits on the head of a king.
Were the king to give away
that crown jewel,
then that whole royal army,
consisting of four divisions,
would be astonished
and amazed.
In the same manner,

Mañgusrî, the Tathâgata,
the Arhat, &c., exercises
the reign of righteousness
and of the law
in the triple world
which he has conquered
by the power of his arm
and the power of his virtue.
His triple world is assailed
by Mâra, the Evil One.
Then the Âryas,
the soldiers of the Tathâgata,
fight with Mâra.
Then, Mañgusrî,
the king of the law,
the lord of the law,
expounds to the Âryas,
his soldiers,
whom he sees fighting,
hundred thousands of Sûtras
in order to encourage
the four classes.
He gives them
the city of Nirvâna,
the great city of the law ;
he allures them
with that city of Nirvâna,
but he does not preach
to them such
a Dharmaparyâya as this.
Just as in that case,
Mañgusrî, that king,
ruler of armies,
astonished at the great valour
of his soldiers in battle
gives them all his property,
at last even his crown jewel,
and just as that crown jewel
has been kept by the king
on his head to the last, so,
Mañgusrî, the Tathâgata,
the Arhat, &c., who
as the great king of the law
in the triple world
exercises his sway with justice,
when he sees disciples and
Bodhisattvas fighting against
the Mâra of fancies
or the Mâra
of sinful inclinations,
and when he sees
that by fighting they
have destroyed affection,
hatred, and infatuation,
overcome the triple world
and conquered all Mâras,
is satisfied,
and in his satisfaction
he expounds
to those noble ârya soldiers
this Dharmaparyâya
which meets opposition
in all the world,
the unbelief of all the world,
a Dharmaparyâya
never before preached,
never before explained.
And the Tathâgata
bestows on all disciples
the noble crown jewel,
that most exalted
crown jewel which brings
omniscience to all.
For this, Mañgusrî,
is the supreme preaching
of the Tathâgatas ;
this is the last Dharmaparyâya
of the Tathâgatas ;
this is the most profound
discourse on the law,
a Dharmaparyâya meeting
opposition in all the world.

In the same manner,
Mañgusrî,
as that king of righteousness
and ruler of armies
took off the crown jewel
which he had kept
so long a time and gave it
at last to the soldiers, so,
Mañgusrî,
the Tathâgata now reveals this
long-kept mystery of the law
exceeding all others,
the mystery
which must be known
by the Tathâgatas.

And in order to elucidate
this matter more in detail,
the Lord on that occasion
uttered the following stanzas :

45.
Always displaying
the strength of charity,
always filled with compassion
for all creatures,
expounding this law,
the Sugatas have
approved this exalted Sûtra.

46.
The laymen,
as well as
the mendicant friars,
and the Bodhisattvas who
shall live at the end of time,
must all show
the strength of charity,
lest those
who hear the law reject it.

47.
But I, when I shall have
reached enlightenment
and be established
in Tathâgataship,
will initiate others,
and after having
initiated disciples
preach everywhere
this superior enlightenment.

48.
It is a case like that of a king,
ruler of armies,
who gives to his soldiers
various things, gold,
elephants, horses,
cars, foot soldiers ; he
also gives towns and villages,
in token of his contentment.

49.
In his satisfaction he gives
to some hand-ornaments,
silver and gold thread ;
pearls, gems,
conch-shells,
stones, coral ;
he also gives slaves
of various description.

50.
But when he is struck
with the incomparable daring
of one amongst the soldiers,
he says : Thou hast
admirably done this ;
and, taking off his crown,
makes him a present
of the jewel.

51.
Likewise do I, the Buddha,
the king of the law,
I who have
the force of patience and
a large treasure of wisdom,
with justice govern
the whole world, benign,
compassionate, and pitiful.

52.
And seeing how
the creatures are in trouble,
I pronounce thousands
of kotis of Sûtrântas,
when I perceive the heroism
of those living beings
who by pure-mindedness
overcome the sinful
inclinations of the world.

53.
And the king of the law,
the great physician,
who expounds hundreds
of kotis of Paryâyas,
when he recognizes
that creatures are strong,
shows them this Sûtra,
comparable to a crown jewel.

54.
This is the last Sûtra
proclaimed in the world,
the most eminent
of all my Sûtras,
which I have always kept
and never divulged.
Now I am going
to make it known ;
listen all.

55.
There are four qualities
to be acquired by those
who at the period
after my extinction desire
supreme enlightenment
and perform my charge.
The qualities
are such as follows.

56.
The wise man
knows no vexation,
trouble, sickness ;
the colour of his skin
is not blackish ;
nor does he dwell
in a miserable town.

57.
The great Sage
has always a pleasant look,
deserves to be honoured,
as if he were
the Tathâgata himself,
and little angels
shall constantly
be his attendants.

58.
His body
can never be hurt by weapons,
poison, sticks, or clods,
and the mouth of the man
who utters a word of abuse
against him shall be closed.

59.
He is a friend
to all creatures in the world.
He goes
all over the earth as a light,
dissipating the gloom
of many kotis of creatures,
he who keeps this Sûtra
after my extinction.

60.
In his sleep he sees visions
in the shape of Buddha ;
he sees monks and nuns
appearing on thrones
and proclaiming
the many-sided law.

61.
He sees in his dream
gods and goblins,
numerous as the sands
of the Ganges,
as well as demons
and Nâgas of many kinds,
who lift their joined hands
and to whom he expounds
the eminent law.

62.
He sees in his dream
the Tathâgata
preaching the law
to many kotis of beings
with lovely voice,
the Lord with golden colour.

63.
And he stands there
with joined hands
glorifying the Seer,
the highest of men,
whilst the Gina,
the great physician,
is expounding the law
to the four classes.

64.
And he,
glad to have heard the law,
joyfully pays his worship,
and after having soon
reached the knowledge
which never slides back,
he obtains, in dream,
magical spells.

65.
And the Lord of the world,
perceiving is good intention,
announces to him
his destiny of becoming
a leader amongst men :
Young man of good family
says he, thou shalt here reach
in future supreme,
holy knowledge.

66.
Thou shalt
have a large field
and four classes of hearers,
even as myself,
that respectfully
and with joined hands
shall hear from thee
the vast and faultless law.

67.
Again he sees
his own person occupied
with meditating on the law
in mountain caverns;
and by meditating he attains
the very nature of the law and,
on obtaining
complete absorption,
sees the Gina.

68.
And after seeing in his dream
the gold-coloured one,
him who displays
a hundred hallowed signs,
he hears the law,
whereafter he preaches
it in the assembly.
Such is his dream.

69.
And in his dream
he also forsakes
his whole realm, harem,
and numerous kinsfolk;
renouncing all pleasures
he leaves home
to become an ascetic,
and betakes himself
to the place of the terrace
of enlightenment.

70.
There, seated upon a throne
at the foot of a tree
to seek enlightenment,
he will,
after the lapse of seven days,
arrive at the knowledge
of the Tathâgatas.

71.
On having
reached enlightenment
he will rise up from that place
to move forward
the faultless wheel
and preach the law during
an inconceivable number
of thousands of kotis of Æons.

72.
After having revealed
perfect enlightenment
and led many kotis of beings
to perfect rest,
he himself will
be extinguished like a lamp
when the oil is exhausted.
So is that vision.

73.
Endless, Mañgughosha,
are the advantages
which constantly are his
who at the end of time
shall expound this Sûtra
of superior enlightenment
that I have perfectly explained.

Chapter XIV
Issuing of Bodhisattvas From the Gaps of the Earth

Out of the multitude
of Bodhisattvas Mahâsattvas
who had flocked
from other worlds,
Bodhisattvas
eight times equal
to the sands
of the river Ganges then rose
from the assembled circle.
Their joined hands
stretched out towards
the Lord to pay him homage,
they said to him :
If the Lord will allow us,
we also would,
after the extinction
of the Lord,
reveal this Dharmaparyâya
in this Saha-world ;
we would read, write,
worship it,
and wholly devote ourselves
to that law.
Therefore, O Lord,
deign to grant to us also
this Dharmaparyâya.
And the Lord answered : Nay,
young men of good family,
why should you occupy
yourselves with this task ?
I have here in this Saha-world
thousands of Bodhisattvas
equal to the sands
of sixty Ganges rivers,
forming the train
of one Bodhisattva ;
and of such Bodhisattvas
there is a number equal
to the sands
of sixty Ganges rivers,
each of these Bodhisattvas
having an equal number
in their train,
who at the end of time,
at the last period
after my extinction,
shall keep, read, proclaim
this Dharmaparyâya.

No sooner had the Lord
uttered these words
than the Saha-world
burst open on every side,
and from within the clefts
arose many hundred
thousand myriads of kotis
of Bodhisattvas
with gold-coloured bodies
and
the thirty-two characteristic
signs of a great man,
who had been staying
in the element of ether
underneath this great earth,
close to this Saha-world.
These then on hearing
the word of the Lord
came up from below the earth.
Each of these Bodhisattvas
had a train of thousands
of Bodhisattvas
similar to the sands
of sixty Ganges rivers ;
each had a troop,

a great troop,
as teachers of a troop.
Of such Bodhisattvas
Mahâsattvas having a troop,
a great troop,
as teachers of a troop,
there were hundred thousands
of myriads of kotis
equal to the sands
of sixty Ganges rivers,
who emerged
from the gaps of the earth
in this Saha-world.
Much more
there were to be found
of Bodhisattvas Mahâsattvas
having a train of Bodhisattvas
similar to the sands
of fifty Ganges rivers ;
much more there
were to be found
of Bodhisattvas Mahâsattvas
having a train of Bodhisattvas
similar to the sands
of forty Ganges rivers ;
Of 30, 20, 10, 5, 4, 3, 2, 1
Ganges river ;
of 1/2, 1/4, 1/6, 1/10,
1/20, 1/50, 1/100, 1/1000,
1/100,000, 1/10,000,000,
1/100 x 10,000,000, 1/1000
x 10,000,000, 1/100 x 1000
x 10,000,000, 1/100 x 1000
x 10,000 x 10,000,000
part of the river Ganges.
Much more there were
to be found of Bodhisattvas
Mahâsattvas having a train
of many hundred thousand
myriads of kotis
of Bodhisattvas ; of one koli ;
of one hundred thousand ;
of one thousand ;
of 500 ; of 400 ; of 300 ;
of 200 ; of 100 ; of 50 ;
of 40 ; of 30 ; of 20 ;
of 10 ; of 5, 4, 3, 2.
Much more
there were to be found
of Bodhisattvas Mahâsattvas
having one follower.
Much more there
were to be found
of Bodhisattvas Mahâsattvas
standing isolated.
They cannot be numbered,
counted,
calculated, compared,
known by occult science,
the Bodhisattvas
Mahâsattvas who emerged
from the gaps of the earth
to appear in this Saha-world.
And after
they had successively emerged
they went up to the Stûpa
of precious substances
which stood in the sky,
where the Lord Prabhûtaratna,
the extinct Tathâgata,
was seated along with
the Lord Sâkyamuni
on the throne.
Whereafter
they saluted the feet
of both Tathâgatas, &c.,
as well as the images
of Tathâgatas produced
by the Lord Sâkyamuni
from his own body,
who all together were seated
on thrones at the foot

of various jewel trees
on every side in all directions,
in different worlds.
After these Bodhisattvas
had many hundred thousand
times saluted,
and thereon circumambulated
the Tathâgatas, &c.,
from left to right,
and celebrated them with
various Bodhisattva hymns,
they went and kept
themselves at a little distance,
the joined hands
stretched out to honour
the Lord Sâkyamuni,
the Tathâgata, &c.,
and the Lord Prabhûtaratna,
the Tathâgata, &c.

And while those
Bodhisattvas Mahâsattvas
who had emerged
from the gaps of the earth
were saluting and celebrating
the Tathâgatas
by various
Bodhisattva hymns,
fifty intermediate kalpas
in full rolled away,
during which
fifty intermediate kalpas
the Lord Sâkyamuni
remained silent,
and likewise the four classes
of the audience.
Then the Lord produced
such an effect
of magical power
that the four classes
fancied that it had been
no more than one afternoon,
and they saw this Saha-world
assume the appearance
of hundred thousands of worlds
replete with Bodhisattvas.
The four
Bodhisattvas Mahâsattvas
who were the chiefest
of that great host
of Bodhisattvas, namely
the Bodhisattva Mahâsattva
called Visishtakâritra
(i.e. of eminent conduct),
the Bodhisattva Mahâsattva
called Anantakâritra
(i.e. of endless conduct),
the Bodhisattva Mahâsattva
called Visuddhakâritra
(i.e. of correct conduct),
and the Bodhisattva
Mahâsattva called
Supratishthitakâritra
(i.e. of very steady conduct),
these four
Bodhisattvas Mahâsattvas
standing at the head
of the great host,
the great multitude
of Bodhisattvas
stretched out the joined hands
towards the Lord
and addressed him thus :
Is the Lord in good health ?
Does he enjoy well-being
and good ease ?
Are the creatures decorous,
docile, obedient, correctly
performing their task,
so that they give
no trouble to the Lord ?

And those four
Bodhisattvas Mahâsattvas
addressed the Lord with
the two following stanzas :

1.
Does the Lord of the world,
the illuminator, feel at ease ?
Dost thou feel free
from bodily disease,
O Perfect One ?

2.
The creatures, we hope,
will be decorous, docile,
performing the orders
of the Lord of the world,
so as to give no trouble.

And the Lord answered
the four Bodhisattvas
Mahâsattvas who were at
the head of that great host,
that great multitude
of Bodhisattvas : So it is,
young men of good family,
I am in good health,
well-being, and at ease.
And these creatures of mine
are decorous, docile,
obedient, well performing
what is ordered ;
they give no trouble
when I correct them ; and that,
young men of good family,
because these creatures,
owing to their being already
prepared under the ancient,
perfectly enlightened Buddhas,
have but to see and hear me
to put trust in me,
to understand and fathom
the Buddha-knowledge.
And those
who fulfilled their duties
in the stage of disciples
have now
been introduced by me
into Buddha-knowledge
and well instructed
in the highest truth.

And at that time
the Bodhisattvas Mahâsattvas
uttered the following stanzas :

3.
Excellent, excellent,
O great Hero !
we are happy to hear
that those creatures
are decorous, docile,
well performing their duty ;

4.
And that they listen
to thy profound knowledge,
O Leader,
and that after listening to it
they have put trust in it
and understand it.

This said, the Lord declared
his approval to the four
Bodhisattvas Mahâsattvas
who were at the head
of that great host,
that great multitude
of Bodhisattvas Mahâsattvas,
saying : Well done,
young men of good family,
well done,

that you so congratulate
the Tathâgata.

And at that moment
the following thought arose
in the mind of the Bodhisattva
Mahâsattva Maitreya
and the eight hundred
thousand myriads of kotis
of Bodhisattvas
similar to the sands
of the river Ganges :
We never yet saw
so great a host,
so great a multitude
of Bodhisattvas ;
we never yet heard
of such a multitude,
that after issuing
from the gaps of the earth
has stood in the presence
of the Lord to honour,
respect, venerate,
worship him and greet him
with joyful shouts.
Whence have these
Bodhisattvas Mahâsattvas
flocked hither ?

Then the Bodhisattva
Mahâsattva Maitreya,
feeling within himself
doubt and perplexity,
and inferring
from his own thoughts
those of the eight hundred
thousand myriads of kotis
of Bodhisattvas
similar to the sands
of the river Ganges,
stretched out his joined hands
towards the Lord
and questioned him
about the matter by uttering
the following stanzas :

5.
Here are many
thousand myriads of kotis
of Bodhisattvas, numberless,
whom we never saw before ;
tell us, O supreme of men !

6.
Whence and how do these
mighty persons come ?
Whence have they come here
under the form
of great bodies ?

7.
All are great Seers,
wise and strong in memory,
whose outward appearance
is lovely to see ;
whence have they come ?

8.
And each
of those Bodhisattvas,
O Lord of the world,
has an immense train,
like the sands of the Ganges.

9.
The train
of each glorious Bodhisattva
is equal to the sands
of sixty Ganges in full.
All are striving
after enlightenment.

10.
Of such heroes and mighty
possessors of a troop
the followers are equal
to the sands of sixty Ganges.

11.
There are others,
still more numerous,
with an unlimited train,
like the sands of fifty,
forty, and thirty Ganges ;

12., 13.
Who have a train equal to
the sands of twenty Ganges.
Still more numerous are
he mighty sons of Buddha,
who have each a train
equal to the sands of ten,
of five Ganges.
Whence, O Leader,
has such an assembly
flocked hither ?

14.
There are others who have
each a train of pupils
and companions equal
to the sands of four,
three, or two Ganges.

15.
There are others
more numerous yet ;
it would be impossible
to calculate their number
in thousands of kotis of Æons.

16.
Equal to a half Ganges,
one third, one tenth,
one twentieth,
is the train of those heroes,
those mighty Bodhisattvas.

17.
There are yet others
who are incalculable ;
it would be impossible
to count them even
in hundreds of kotis of Æons.

18.
Many more yet there are,
with endless trains ;
they have in their attendance
kotis, and kotis and again
kotis, and also half kotis.

19.
Other great Seers again,
beyond computation,
very wise Bodhisattvas
are seen
in a respectful posture.

20.
They have a thousand,
a hundred,
or fifty attendants ;
in hundreds of kotis of Æons
one would not
be able to count them.

21.
The suite of some of these
heroes consists of twenty,
of ten, five, four, three,
or two ; those are countless.

22.
As to those
who are walking alone
and come to their rest alone,
they have now flocked hither
in such numbers
as to be beyond computation.

23.
Even if one with a magic wand
in his hand would try
for a number of Æons
equal to the sands
of the Ganges to count them,
he would not reach the term.

24.
Where do all those noble,
energetic heroes,
those mighty Bodhisattvas,
come from ?

25.
Who has taught them
the law or duty ?
and by whom
have they been destined
to enlightenment ?
Whose command
do they accept ?
Whose command
do they keep ?

26.
Bursting forth
at all points of the horizon
through the whole extent
of the earth they emerge,
those great Sages
endowed with
magical faculty and wisdom.

27.
This world on every side
is being perforated, O Seer,
by the wise Bodhisattvas,
who at this time are emerging.

28.
Never before have we
seen anything like this.
Tell us the name
of this world, O Leader.

29.
We have repeatedly roamed
in all directions of space,
but never saw
these Bodhisattvas.

30.
We never saw
a single infant of thine,
and now, on a sudden,
these appear to us.
Tell us their history, O Seer.

31.
Hundreds, thousands,
ten thousands
of Bodhisattvas,
all equally filled
with curiosity,
look up to the highest of men.

32.
Explain to us,
O incomparable, great hero,
who knowest no bounds,
where do these heroes,
these wise Bodhisattvas,
come from ?

Meanwhile
the Tathâgatas, &c.,
who had flocked
from hundred thousands
of myriads of kotis of worlds,
they, the creations
of the Lord Sâkyamuni,
who were preaching the law
to the beings in other worlds ;
who all around
the Lord Sâkyamuni,
the Tathâgata, &c.,
were seated with crossed legs
on magnificent jewel thrones
at the foot of jewel trees
in every direction of space ;
as well as the satellites
of those Tathâgatas
were struck with wonder
and amazement
at the sight of that great host,
that great multitude
of Bodhisattvas emerging
from the gaps of the earth
and established
in the element of ether,
and the satellites asked
each their own Tathâgata :
Where, O Lord, do so many
Bodhisattvas Mahâsattvas,
so innumerable,
so countless, come from ?
Whereupon
those Tathâgatas, &c.,
answered severally
to their satellites :
Wait awhile,
young men of good family ;
this Bodhisattva
Mahâsattva here,
called Maitreya,
has just received
from the Lord Sâkyamuni
a revelation about his destiny
to supreme,
perfect enlightenment.
He has questioned
the Lord Sâkyamuni,
the Tathâgata, &c.,
about the matter,
and the Lord Sâkyamuni,
the Tathâgata, &c.,
is going to explain it ;
then you may hear.

Thereupon the Lord
addressed the Bodhisattva
Maitreya : Well done,
Agita, well done ;
it is a sublime subject,
Agita, about which
thou questionest me.
Then the Lord
addressed the entire host
of Bodhisattvas :
Be attentive all,
young men of good family ;
be well prepared
and steady on your post,
you and the entire host
of Bodhisattvas ;
the Tathâgata, the Arhat, &c.,
is now going to exhibit
the sight of the knowledge
of the Tathâgata,
young men of good family,
the leadership
of the Tathâgata,
the work of the Tathâgata,
the sport of the Tathâgata,
the might of the Tathâgata,
the energy of the Tathâgata.

And on that occasion
the Lord pronounced
the following stanzas :

33.
Be attentive all,
young men of good family ;
I am to utter
an infallible word ;
refrain from
disputing about it,
O sages :
the science of the Tathâgata
is beyond reasoning.

34.
Be all steady and thoughtful ;
continue attentive all.
To-day you will hear
a law as yet unknown,
the wonder of the Tathâgatas.

35.
Never have any doubt,
ye sages,
for I shall strengthen you,
I am the Leader
who speaketh infallible truth,
and my knowledge
is unlimited.

36.
Profound are the laws
known to the Sugata,
above reasoning
and beyond argumentation.
These laws
I am going to reveal ; ye,
hear which and how they are.

After uttering these stanzas
the Lord addressed
the Bodhisattva
Mahâsattva Maitreya :
I announce to thee, Agita,
I declare to thee :
These Bodhisattvas
Mahâsattvas, Agita,
so innumerable,
incalculable,
inconceivable,
incomparable,
uncountable,
whom you never saw before,
who just now have issued
from the gaps of the earth,
these
Bodhisattvas Mahâsattvas,
Agita, have I roused,
excited, animated,
fully developed to supreme,
perfect enlightenment
after my having
arrived at supreme, perfect
enlightenment in this world.
I have, moreover,
fully matured,
established, confirmed,
instructed, perfected these
young men of good family
in their Bodhisattvaship.
And these
Bodhisattvas Mahâsattvas,
Agita,
occupy in this Saha-world
the domain
of the ether-element below.
Only thinking of the lesson
they have to study,
and devoted
to thoroughly comprehend it,

these young men
of good family have no liking
for social gatherings,
nor for bustling crowds;
they do not put off their tasks,
and are strenuous.
These young men
of good family, Agita,
delight in seclusion,
are fond of seclusion.
These young men
of good family do not dwell
in the immediate vicinity
of gods and men,
they not being fond
of bustling crowds.
These young men
of good family
find their luxury
in the pleasure of the law,
and apply themselves
to Buddha-knowledge.

And on that occasion
the Lord uttered
the following stanzas:

37.
These Bodhisattvas,
immense, inconceivable
and beyond measure,
endowed with magic power,
wisdom, and learning,
have progressed in knowledge
for many kotis of Æons.

38.
It is I who have brought
them to maturity
for enlightenment,
and it is in my field
that they have their abode;
by me alone have they been
brought to maturity; these
Bodhisattvas are my sons.

39.
All have devoted themselves
to a hermit life
and are assiduous
in shunning places of bustle;
they walk detached,
these sons of mine,
following my precepts
in their lofty course.

40.
They dwell
in the domain of ether,
in the lower portion
of the field,
those heroes who,
unwearied,
are striving day and night
to attain superior knowledge.

41.
All strenuous,
of good memory,
unshaken
in the immense strength
of their intelligence,
those serene sages
preach the law,
all radiant,
as being my sons.

42.
Since the time
when I reached this superior
or foremost enlightenment,
at the town of Gayâ,

at the foot of the tree,
and put in motion
the all-surpassing
wheel of the law,
I have brought to maturity
all of them
for superior enlightenment.

43.
These words I here speak
are faultless, really true ;
believe me,
all of you who hear me :
verily, I have reached
superior enlightenment,
and it is by me alone
that all have been
brought to maturity.

The Bodhisattva
Mahâsattva Maitreya
and those numerous
hundred thousands
of myriads of kotis
of Bodhisattvas were struck
with wonder, amazement,
and surprise, and thought :
How is it possible that
within so short a moment,
within the lapse
of so short a time
so many Bodhisattvas,
so countless,
have been roused
and made fully ripe
to reach supreme,
perfect enlightenment ?
Then the Bodhisattva
Mahâsattva Maitreya
asked the Lord :
How then, O Lord,
has the Tathâgata,
after he left,
when a prince royal,
Kapilavastu,
the town of the Sâkyas,
arrived at supreme,
perfect enlightenment
on the summit of the terrace
of enlightenment,
not far from the town of Gayâ,
somewhat more
than forty years since,
O Lord ?
How then has the Lord,
the Tathâgata,
within so short a lapse of time,
been able to perform
the endless task
of a Tathâgata,
to exercise the leadership
of a Tathâgata,
the energy of a Tathâgata ?
How has the Tathâgata,
within so short a time,
been able to rouse
and bring to maturity
for supreme,
perfect enlightenment
this host of Bodhisattvas,
this multitude
of Bodhisattvas,
a multitude so great
that it would be impossible
to count the whole of it,
even if one
were to continue counting
for hundred thousands
of myriads of kotis of Æons ?
These Bodhisattvas,
so innumerable,
O Lord, so countless,

having long followed
a spiritual course of life
and planted roots
of goodness under
many hundred thousands
of Buddhas,
have in the course
of many hundred
thousands of Æons
become finally ripe.

It is just as if some man,
young and youthful,
a young man with black hair
and in the prime of youth,
twenty-five years of age,
would represent
centenarians as his sons,
and say : 'Here,
young men of good family,
you see my sons ;'
and if those centenarians
would declare :
'This is the father
who begot us !'
Now, Lord,
the speech of that man
would be incredible,
hard to be believed
by the public.
It is the same case
with the Tathâgata,
who but lately
has arrived at supreme,
perfect enlightenment,
and with these
Bodhisattvas Mahâsattvas,
so immense in number,
who for many hundred
thousand myriads
of kotis of Æons,

having observed
a spiritual course of life,
have long since
come to certainty in regard
to Tathâgata-knowledge ;
who are able to plunge in
and again rise
from the hundred thousand
sorts of meditation ;
who are adepts
at the preparatories
to noble transcendent wisdom,
have accomplished
the preparatories to noble
transcendent wisdom ;
who are clever
on the Buddha-ground, able
in the ecclesiastical Council
and in Tathâgata duties ;
who are the wonder
and admiration of the world ;
who are possessed
of great vigour,
strength, and power.
And the Lord says :
From the very beginning
have I roused,
brought to maturity,
fully developed them to be fit
for this Bodhisattva position.
It is I who have displayed
this energy and vigour
after arriving at supreme,
perfect enlightenment.
But, O Lord,
how can we have faith
in the words of the Tathâgata,
when he says :
The Tathâgata
speaks infallible truth ?
The Tathâgata must know

that the Bodhisattvas
who have newly entered
the vehicle are apt to fall
into doubt on this head ;
after the extinction
of the Tathâgata
those who hear
this Dharmaparyâya
will not accept,
not believe,
not trust it.
Hence, O Lord,
they will design acts
tending to the ruin of the law.
Therefore, O Lord,
deign
to explain us this matter,
that we may
be free from perplexity,
and that the Bodhisattvas
who in future shall hear it,
be they young men
of good family
or young ladies,
may not fall into doubt.

On that occasion
the Bodhisattva
Mahâsattva Maitreya
addressed the Lord
with the following stanzas :

44.
When thou wert
born in Kapilavastu,
the home of the Sâkyas,
thou didst leave it
and reach enlightenment
at the town of Gayâ.
That is a short time ago,
O Lord of the world.

45.
And now thou hast
so great a crowd of followers,
these sages
who for many kotis of Æons
have fulfilled their duties,
stood firm in magic power,
unshaken, well disciplined,
accomplished
in the might of wisdom ;

46.
These, who are untainted
as the lotus is by water ;
who to-day
have flocked hither
after rending the earth,
and are standing
all with joined hands,
respectful
and strong in memory,
the sons of the Master
of the world.

47.
How will these Bodhisattvas
believe this great wonder ?
Expel all doubt,
tell the cause,
and show how
the matter really is.

48.
It is as if there
were some man,
a young man with black hair,
twenty years old
or somewhat more,
who presented as his sons
some centenarians,

49.
And the latter,
covered with wrinkles
and gray-haired,
declared the young man
to be their father.
But such a young man
never having sons
of such appearance,
it would be
difficult to believe,
O Lord of the world,
that they were sons
to so young a man.

50.
In the same manner, O Lord,
we are unable to conceive
how these numerous
Bodhisattvas of good memory
and excelling in wisdom,
who have been well instructed
during thousands
of kotis of Æons;

51.
Who are firm,
of keen intelligence,
lovely and agreeable to sight,
free from hesitation
in the decisions on law,
praised by the Leaders
of the world;

52.
Who in freedom
live in the wood;
who unattached
in the element of ether
constantly display
their energy,
who are the sons of Sugata
striving after
this Buddha-ground;

53.
How will this be believed
when the Leader of the world
shall be completely extinct?
After hearing it
from the Lord's own mouth
we shall never more
feel any doubt.

54.
May Bodhisattvas
never come to grief
by having doubt on this head.
Grant us, O Lord,
a truthful account
how these Bodhisattvas
have been brought
to maturity by thee.

Chapter XV
Duration of Life of the Tathâgata

Thereupon the Lord addressed the entire host of Bodhisattvas : Trust me, young men of good family, believe in the Tathâgata speaking a veracious word. A second time the Lord addressed the Bodhisattvas : Trust me, young gentlemen of good family, believe in the Tathâgata speaking a veracious word. A third and last time the Lord addressed the Bodhisattvas : Trust me, young men of good family, believe in the Tathâgata speaking a veracious word. Then the entire host of Bodhisattvas with Maitreya, the Bodhisattva Mahâsattva at their head, stretched out the joined hands and said to the Lord : Expound this matter, O Lord ; expound it, O Sugata ; we will believe in the word of the Tathâgata. A second time the entire host, &c. &c. A third time the entire host, &c. &c.

The Lord, considering that the Bodhisattvas repeated their prayer up to three times, addressed them thus : Listen then, young men of good family. The force of a strong resolve which I assumed is such, young men of good family, that this world, including gods, men, and demons, acknowledges : Now has the Lord Sâkyamuni, after going out from the home of the Sâkyas, arrived at supreme, perfect enlightenment, on the summit of the terrace of enlightenment at the town of Gayâ. But, young men of good family, the truth is that many hundred thousand myriads of kotis of Æons ago I have arrived at supreme, perfect enlightenment. By way of example, young men of good family, let there be the atoms of earth of fifty hundred thousand myriads of kotis of worlds ; let there exist some man who takes one of those atoms of dust and then goes in an eastern direction fifty hundred thousand myriads of kotis of worlds further on, there to deposit that atom of dust ;

Duration of Life 249

let in this manner
the man carry away
from all those worlds
the whole mass of earth,
and in the same manner,
and by the same act
as supposed,
deposit all those atoms
in an eastern direction.
Now, would you think,
young men of good family,
that any one should be able
to imagine, weigh, count,
or determine the number
of those worlds ?
The Lord having thus spoken,
the Bodhisattva Mahâsattva
Maitreya and the entire host
of Bodhisattvas replied :
They are incalculable,
O Lord,
those worlds, countless,
beyond the range of thought.
Not even all the disciples
and Pratyekabuddhas,
O Lord,
with their Ârya-knowledge,
will be able to imagine,
weigh, count,
or determine them.
For us also, O Lord,
who are Bodhisattvas
standing on the place
from whence
there is no turning back,
this point lies
beyond the sphere
of our comprehension ;
so innumerable,
O Lord, are those worlds.

This said, the Lord spoke
to those Bodhisattvas
Mahâsattvas as follows :
I announce to you,
young men of good family,
I declare to you :
However numerous
be those worlds
where that man deposits
those atoms of dust
and where he does not,
there are not,
young men of good family,
in all those hundred
thousands of myriads
of kotis of worlds
so many dust atoms
as there are hundred
thousands of myriads
of kotis of Æons since
I have arrived at supreme,
perfect enlightenment.
From the moment,
young men of good family,
when I began preaching
the law to creatures
in this Saha-world
and in hundred thousands
of myriads of kotis
of other worlds,
and when the other
Tathâgatas, Arhats, &c.,
such as
the Tathâgata Dîpankara
and the rest whom
I have mentioned
in the lapse of time preached,
from that moment have I,
young men of good family,
for the complete Nirvâna
of those Tathâgatas, &c.,

created all that
with the express view
to skilfully preach the law.
Again,
young men of good family,
the Tathâgata, considering
the different degrees
of faculty and strength
of succeeding generations,
reveals at each generation
his own name,
reveals a state
in which Nirvâna
has not yet been reached,
and in different ways
he satisfies the wants
of different creatures through
various Dharmaparyâyas.
This being the case,
young men of good family,
the Tathâgata declares
to the creatures,
whose dispositions
are so various
and who possess
so few roots of goodness,
so many evil propensities :
I am young of age, monks ;
having left my father's home,
monks, I have lately
arrived at supreme,
perfect enlightenment.
When, however,
the Tathâgata,
who so long ago arrived
at perfect enlightenment,
declares himself to have
but lately arrived
at perfect enlightenment,
he does so in order to lead
creatures to full ripeness

and make them go in.
Therefore have
these Dharmaparyâyas
been revealed ;
and it is for the education
of creatures,
young men of good family,
that the Tathâgata
has revealed
all Dharmaparyâyas.
And,
young men of good family,
the word that the Tathâgata
delivers on behalf
of the education of creatures,
either
under his own appearance
or under another's,
either on his own authority
or under the mask of another,
all that the Tathâgata declares,
all those Dharmaparyâyas
spoken by the Tathâgata
are true.
There can be
no question of untruth from
the part of the Tathâgata
in this respect.
For the Tathâgata sees
the triple world as it really is :
it is not born, it dies not ;
it is not conceived,
it springs not into existence ;
it moves not in a whirl,
it becomes not extinct ;
it is not real, nor unreal ;
it is not existing,
nor non-existing ;
it is not such,
nor otherwise,
nor false.

The Tathâgata
sees the triple world,
not as the ignorant,
common people,
he seeing things
always present to him ;
indeed,
to the Tathâgata,
in his position,
no laws are concealed.
In that respect
any word that
the Tathâgata speaks is true,
not false.
But in order to produce
the roots of goodness
in the creatures,
who follow different pursuits
and behave according
to different notions,
he reveals
various Dharmaparyâyas
with various
fundamental principles.
The Tathâgata then,
young men of good family,
does what he has to do.
The Tathâgata
who so long ago
was perfectly enlightened
is unlimited
in the duration of his life,
he is everlasting.
Without being extinct,
the Tathâgata
makes a show of extinction,
on behalf of those
who have to be educated.
And even now,
young gentlemen
of good family,
I have not accomplished my
ancient Bodhisattva-course,
and the measure
of my lifetime is not full.
Nay,
young men of good family,
I shall yet have twice as many
hundred thousand myriads
of kotis of Æons
before the measure
of my lifetime be full.
I announce final extinction,
young men of good family,
though myself I do not
become finally extinct.
For in this way,
young men of good family,
I bring all creatures
to maturity,
lest creatures in whom
goodness is not firmly rooted,
who are unholy, miserable,
eager of sensual pleasures,
blind and obscured
by the film of wrong views,
should,
by too often seeing me,
take to thinking :
'The Tathâgata is staying'
and fancy that all
is a child's play ;
lest they by thinking
'we are near that Tathâgata'
should fail
to exert themselves in order
to escape the triple world
and not conceive how
precious the Tathâgata is.
Hence,
young men of good family,
the Tathâgata

skilfully utters these words :
The apparition
of the Tathâgatas, monks,
is precious and rare.
For in the course
of many hundred thousand
myriads of kotis of Æons
creatures may happen to see
a Tathâgata or not to see him.
Therefore
and upon that ground,
young men of good family,
I say : The apparition
of the Tathâgatas, monks,
is precious and rare.
By being more and more
convinced of the apparition
of the Tathâgatas
being precious or rare
they will feel surprised
and sorry,
and whilst not seeing
the Tathâgata they will
get a longing to see him.
The good roots developing
from their earnest thought
relating to the Tathâgata
will lastingly tend
to their weal, benefit,
and happiness ;
in consideration
of which the Tathâgata
announces final extinction,
though he himself does
not become finally extinct,
on behalf of the creatures
who have to be educated.
Such,
young men of good family,
is the Tathâgata's
manner of teaching ;
when the Tathâgata
speaks in this way,
there is from his part
no falsehood.

Let us suppose
an analogous case,
young men of good family.
There is some physician,
learned, intelligent, prudent,
clever in allaying
all sorts of diseases.
That man has many sons,
ten, twenty, thirty, forty,
fifty, or a hundred.
The physician
once being abroad,
all his children incur a disease
from poison or venom.
Overcome with the grievous
pains caused by that poison
or venom which burns them
they lie rolling on the ground.
Their father, the physician,
comes home
from his journey at the time
when his sons are suffering
from that poison or venom.
Some of them have
perverted notions,
others have right notions,
but all suffer the same pain.
On seeing their father
they cheerfully greet him
and say : Hail, dear father,
that thou art come back
in safety and welfare !
Now deliver us from our evil,
be it poison or venom ;
let us live, dear father.
And the physician,

seeing his sons
befallen with disease,
overcome with pain
and rolling on the ground,
prepares a great remedy,
having the required colour,
smell, and taste,
pounds it on a stone
and gives it
as a potion to his sons,
with these words :
Take this great remedy,
my sons,
which has the required colour,
smell, and taste.
For by taking
this great remedy, my sons,
you shall soon be rid
of this poison or venom ;
you shall recover
and be healthy.
Those amongst the children
of the physician
that have right notions,
after seeing the colour
of the remedy,
after smelling the smell
and tasting the flavour,
quickly take it,
and in consequence of it
are soon totally delivered
from their disease.
But the sons who have
perverted notions cheerfully
greet their father and say :
Hail, dear father,
that thou art come
back in safety and welfare ;
do heal us. So they speak,
but they do not take
the remedy offered,
and that because,
owing to the perverseness
of their notions,
that remedy
does not please them,
in colour, smell, nor taste.
Then the physician
reflects thus :
These sons of mine must
have become perverted
in their notions owing
to this poison or venom,
as they do not take
the remedy nor hail me.
Therefore will I by some
able device induce these
sons to take this remedy.
Prompted by this desire
he speaks to those sons
as follows : I am old,
young men of good family,
decrepit, advanced in years,
and my term of life
is near at hand ;
but be not sorry,
young men of good family,
do not feel dejected ;
here have I prepared
a great remedy for you ;
if you want it,
you may take it. Having
thus admonished them,
he skilfully betakes himself
to another part of the country
and lets his sick sons know
that he has departed life.
They are extremely sorry
and bewail him extremely :
So then he is dead,
our father and protector ;
he who begat us ;

he, so full of bounty !
now are we left
without a protector.
Fully aware
of their being orphans
and of having no refuge,
they are continually
plunged in sorrow, by
which their perverted notions
make room for right notions.
They acknowledge
that remedy possessed
of the required colour,
smell, and taste to have
the required colour,
smell, and taste,
so that they instantly take it,
and by taking it
are delivered from their evil.
Then,
on knowing that these sons
are delivered from evil,
the physician
shows himself again. Now,
young men of good family,
what is your opinion ?
Would any one charge
that physician
with falsehood on account
of his using that device ?
No, certainly not, Lord ;
certainly not, Sugata.
He proceeded :
In the same manner,
young men of good family,
I have arrived at supreme,
perfect enlightenment
since an immense,
incalculable number
of hundred thousands
of myriads of kotis of Æons,

but from time to time
I display such able devices
to the creatures,
with the view
of educating them,
without there being
in that respect
any falsehood on my part.

In order to set forth
this subject more extensively
the Lord on that occasion
uttered the following stanzas :

1.
An inconceivable number
of thousands of kotis of Æons,
never to be measured,
is it since I reached superior
or first enlightenment and
never ceased to teach the law.

2.
I roused many Bodhisattvas
and established them
in Buddha-knowledge.
I brought myriads of kotis
of beings, endless,
to full ripeness
in many kotis of Æons.

3.
I show the place of extinction,
I reveal to all beings
a device to educate them,
albeit I do not
become extinct at the time,
and in this very place
continue preaching the law.

4.
There I rule myself
as well as all beings, I.
But men of perverted minds,
in their delusion,
do not see me standing there.

5.
In the opinion that my body
is completely extinct,
they pay worship,
in many ways,
to the relics,
but me they see not.
They feel, however,
a certain aspiration by which
their mind becomes right.

6.
When such upright or pious,
mild, and gentle creatures
leave off their bodies,
then I assemble the crowd
of disciples and show myself
here on the Gridhrakûta.

7.
And then I speak thus to them,
in this very place :
I was not completely extinct
at that time ;
it was but a device of mine,
monks ;
repeatedly am I born
in the world of the living.

8.
honoured by other beings,
I show them
my superior enlightenment,
but you would not obey
my word,
unless the Lord of the world
enter Nirvâna.

9.
I see how the creatures
are afflicted,
but I do not show them
my proper being.
Let them first
have an aspiration to see me ;
then I will reveal
to them the true law.

10.
Such has always been
my firm resolve
during an inconceivable
number of thousands
of kotis of Æons,
and I have not left
this Gridhrakûta
for other abodes.

11.
And when creatures
behold this world
and imagine that it is burning,
even then my Buddha-field
is teeming with gods and men.

12.
They dispose of manifold
amusements,
kotis of pleasure gardens,
palaces, and aerial cars ;
this field is embellished
by hills of gems
and by trees abounding
with blossoms and fruits.

13.
And aloft gods are striking
musical instruments
and pouring a rain
of Mandâras by which
they are covering me,
the disciples and other sages
who are striving
after enlightenment.

14.
So is my field here,
everlastingly ; but others
fancy that it is burning ;
in their view this world
is most terrific, wretched,
replete with number of woes.

15.
Ay, many kotis of years
they may pass without ever
having mentioned my name,
the law, or my congregation.
That is the fruit
of sinful deeds.

16.
But when mild
and gentle beings are born
in this world of men,
they immediately
see me revealing the law,
owing to their good works.

17.
I never speak to them
of the infinitude of my action.
Therefore, I am, properly,
existing since long,
and yet declare :
The Ginas are rare.

18.
Such is the glorious power
of my wisdom
that knows no limit,
and the duration
of my life is as long
as an endless period ;
I have acquired it
after previously
following a due course.

19.
Feel no doubt concerning it,
O sages,
and leave off all uncertainty :
the word I here pronounce
is really true ;
my word is never false.

20.
For even as that physician
skilled in devices,
for the sake of his sons whose
notions were perverted,
said that he had died
although he was still alive,
and even as no sensible man,
would charge that physician
with falsehood.

21.
So am I
the father of the world,
the Self born,
the Healer,
the Protector of all creatures.
Knowing them
to be perverted,
infatuated, and ignorant
I teach final rest,
myself not being at rest.

22.
What reason should I have to
continually manifest myself ?
When men become
unbelieving, unwise,
ignorant, careless,
fond of sensual pleasures,
and from thoughtlessness
run into misfortune,

23.
Then I, who know
the course of the world,
declare : I am so and so,
and consider :
How can I incline them
to enlightenment ?
how can they
become partakers
of the Buddha-laws ?

Chapter XVI
Of Piety

While this exposition
of the duration
of the Tathâgata's lifetime
was being given,
innumerable,
countless creatures
profited by it.
Then the Lord
addressed the Bodhisattva
Mahâsattva Maitreya :
While this exposition
of the duration
of the Tathâgata's lifetime
was being given, Agita,
sixty-eight hundred
thousand myriads
of kotis of Bodhisattvas,
comparable
to the sands of the Ganges,
have acquired the faculty
to acquiesce in the law
that has no origin.
A thousand times more
Bodhisattvas Mahâsattvas
have obtained Dhâranî ;
and other
Bodhisattvas Mahâsattvas,
equal to the dust atoms
of one third of a macrocosm,
have by hearing
this Dharmaparyâya
obtained the faculty
of unhampered view.
Other Bodhisattvas
Mahâsattvas again,
equal to the dust atoms
of two-third parts
of a macrocosm,
have by hearing
this Dharmaparyâya
obtained the Dhâranî
that makes hundred thousand
kotis of revolutions.
Again, other
Bodhisattvas Mahâsattvas,
equal to the dust atoms
of a whole macrocosm,
have by hearing
this Dharmaparyâya
moved forward the wheel
that never rolls back.
Some
Bodhisattvas Mahâsattvas,
equal to the dust atoms
of a mean universe,
have by hearing
this Dharmaparyâya
moved forward the wheel
of spotless radiance.
Other
Bodhisattvas Mahâsattvas,
equal to the dust atoms
of a small universe, have by
hearing this Dharmaparyâya
come so far that they
will reach supreme,
perfect enlightenment
after eight births.
Other
Bodhisattvas Mahâsattvas,
equal to the dust atoms
of four worlds
of four continents,
have by hearing
this Dharmaparyâya
become such as to require
four births more
before reaching supreme,
perfect enlightenment.

Other Bodhisattvas Mahâsattvas, equal to the dust atoms of three four-continental worlds, have by hearing this Dharmaparyâya become such as to require three births more before reaching supreme, perfect enlightenment. Other Bodhisattvas Mahâsattvas, equal to the dust atoms of two four-continental worlds, have by hearing this Dharmaparyâya become such as to require two births more before reaching supreme, perfect enlightenment. Other Bodhisattvas Mahâsattvas, equal to the dust atoms of one four-continental world, have by hearing this Dharmaparyâya become such as to require but one birth before reaching supreme, perfect enlightenment. Other Bodhisattvas Mahâsattvas, equal to the dust atoms of eight macrocosms consisting of three parts, have by hearing this Dharmaparyâya conceived the idea of supreme, perfect enlightenment.

No sooner had the Lord given this exposition determining the duration and periods of the law, than there fell from the upper sky a great rain of Mandârava and great Mandârava flowers that covered and overwhelmed all the hundred thousand myriads of kotis of Buddhas who were seated on their thrones at the foot of the jewel trees in hundred thousands of myriads of kotis of worlds. It also covered and overwhelmed the Lord Sâkyamuni, the Tathâgata, &c., and the Lord Prabhûtaratna, the Tathâgata, &c., the latter sitting fully extinct on his throne, as well as that entire host of Bodhisattvas and the four classes of the audience. A rain of celestial powder of sandal and agallochum. trickled down from the sky, whilst higher up in the firmament the great drums resounded, without being struck, with a pleasant, sweet, and deep sound. Double pieces of fine heavenly cloth fell down by hundreds and thousands

from the upper sky;
necklaces,
half-necklaces,
pearl necklaces,
gems, jewels,
noble gems,
and noble jewels were seen
high in the firmament,
hanging down
from every side
in all directions of space,
while all around
thousands of jewel censers,
containing priceless,
exquisite incense,
were moving
of their own accord.
Bodhisattvas Mahâsattvas
were seen holding
above each Tathâgata,
high aloft,
a row of jewel umbrellas
stretching as high
as the Brahma-world.
So acted
the Bodhisattvas Mahâsattvas
in respect
to all the innumerable
hundred thousands of
myriads of kotis of Buddhas.
Severally
they celebrated these Buddhas
in appropriate stanzas,
sacred hymns
in praise of the Buddhas.

And on that occasion
the Bodhisattva
Mahâsattva Maitreya
uttered the following stanzas:

1.
Wonderful is the law
which the Sugata
has expounded, the law
we never heard before;
how great the majesty
of the Leaders is,
and how infinite
the duration of their life!

2.
And on hearing such a law
imparted by the Sugata
from face to face,
thousands of kotis
of creatures, the genuine sons
of the Leader of the world,
have been pervaded
with gladness.

3.
Some have reached the point
of supreme enlightenment
from whence
there is no return,
others are standing
on the lower stage;
some have reached
the standpoint of having
an unhampered view,
and others have obtained
thousands of kotis
of Dhâranîs.

4.
There are others, as atoms,
who have reached supreme
Buddha-knowledge. Some,
again, will after eight births
become Ginas
seeing the infinite.

5.
Among those who hear
this law from the Master,
some will
obtain enlightenment
and see the truth
after four births,
others after three,
others after two.

6.
Some among them
will become all-knowing
after one birth, in the next
following existence.
Such will be the perfect result
of learning the duration
of life of the Chief.

7.
Innumerable,
countless as the atoms
of the eight fields,
are the kotis of beings
who by hearing this law
have conceived the idea
of superior enlightenment.

8.
Such is the effect
produced by the great Seer,
when he reveals
this Buddha-state
that is endless
and has no limit,
which is as immense
as the element of ether.

9.
Many thousand kotis
of angels, Indras,
and Brahma-angels,
like the sands of the Ganges,
have flocked hither
from thousands of kotis
of distant fields
and have poured a rain
of Mandâravas.

10.
They move in
the sky like birds,
and strew fragrant powder
of sandal and agallochum,
to cover ceremoniously
the Chief of Ginas withal.

11.
High aloft tymbals
without being struck
emit sweet sounds ;
thousands of kotis of white cloth
whirl down upon the Chiefs.

12.
Thousands of kotis
of jewel censers of costly incense
move of their own accord
on every side to honour
the mighty Lord of the world.

13.
Innumerable wise Bodhisattvas
hold myriads of kotis
of umbrellas,
elevated
and made of noble jewels,
like chaplets,
up to the Brahma-world.

14.
The sons of Sugata,
in their great joy,
have attached beautiful
triumphal streamers
at the top of the banner staffs
in honour of the Leaders
whom they celebrate
in thousands of stanzas.

15.
Such a marvellous,
extraordinary, prodigious,
splendid phenomenon,
O Leader, is being displayed
by all those beings
who are gladdened by
the exposition of the duration
of life of the Tathâgata.

16.
Grand is the matter
now occurring
in the ten points of space,
and great the sound
raised by the Leaders ;
thousands of kotis
of living beings are refreshed
and gifted with virtue
for enlightenment.

Thereupon the Lord
addressed the Bodhisattva
Mahâsattva Maitreya :
Those beings, Agita,
who during the exposition
of this Dharmaparyâya
in which the duration
of the Tathâgata's life
is revealed have entertained,
were it
but a single thought of trust,
or have put belief in it,
how great a merit
are they to produce,
be they young men and
young ladies of good family ?
Listen then, and mind it well,
how great the merit is
they shall produce.
Let us suppose the case,
Agita, that some young man
or young lady of good family,
desirous of supreme,
perfect enlightenment,
for eight hundred thousand
myriads of kotis of Æons
practices the five perfections
of virtue (Pâramitâs),
to wit, perfect charity in alms,
perfect morality,
perfect forbearance,
perfect energy,
perfect meditation
- perfect wisdom
being excepted ;
let us, on the other hand,
suppose the case, Agita,
that a young man
or young lady of good family,
on hearing
this Dharmaparyâya
containing the exposition
of the duration
of the Tathâgata's life,
conceives were it
but a single thought of trust
or puts belief in it ;
then that former
accumulation of merit,
that accumulation of good
connected with

the five perfections of virtue,
that accumulation
which has come
to full accomplishment
in eight hundred thousand
myriads of kotis of Æons,
does not equal
one hundredth part
of the accumulation
of merit in the second case ;
it does not equal
one thousandth part ;
it admits of no calculation,
no counting,
no reckoning,
no comparison,
no approximation,
no secret teaching.
One who is possessed of such
an accumulation of merit,
Agita, be he a young man or
a young lady of good family,
will not miss supreme,
perfect enlightenment ;
no, that is not possible.

And on that occasion
the Lord uttered
the following stanzas :

17.
Let a man who is seeking
after this knowledge,
superior Buddha-knowledge,
undertake to practice
in this world
the five perfect virtues ;

18.
Let him,
during eight thousand
kotis of complete Æons,
continue giving repeated alms
to Buddhas and disciples ;

19.
Regaling Pratyekabuddhas
and kotis of Bodhisattvas
by giving meat,
food and drink,
clothing and lodging ;

20.
Let him build on earth
refuges and monasteries
of sandal-wood,
and pleasant
convent gardens
provided with walks ;

21.
Let him
after so bestowing gifts,
various and diversified,
during thousands
of kotis of Æons,
direct his mind
to enlightenment ;

22.
Let him then,
for the sake
of Buddha-knowledge,
keep unbroken the pure
moral precepts which
have been recommended
by the perfect Buddhas and
acknowledged by the wise ;

23.
Let him further develop
the virtue of forbearance,
be steady
in the stage of meekness,
be constant, of good memory,
and patiently endure
many censures;

24.
Let him, moreover, for the sake
of Buddha-knowledge,
bear the contemptuous words
of unbelievers
who are rooted in pride;

25.
Let him, always zealous,
strenuous, studious,
of good memory,
without any other
pre-occupation in his mind,
practice meditation,
during kotis of Æons;

26.
Let him,
whether living in the forest
or entering upon
a vagrant life, go about,
avoiding sloth and torpor,
for kotis of Æons;

27.
Let him as a philosopher,
a great philosopher
who finds his delight
in meditation,
in concentration of mind,
pass eight thousand
kotis of Æons;

28.
Let him energetically
pursue enlightenment
with the thought
of his reaching
all-knowingness,
and so arrive
at the highest
degree of meditation;

29.
Then the merit accruing
to those who practice
the virtues oft described,
during thousands
of kotis of Æons,

30.
Is less than that,
of a man or a woman who,
on hearing
the duration of my life,
for a single moment
believes in it;
this merit is endless.

31.
He who renouncing doubt,
vacillation,
and misgiving shall believe
even for a short moment,
shall obtain such a reward.

32.
The Bodhisattvas also,
who have practiced
those virtues
during kotis of Æons,
will not be startled at hearing
of this inconceivably
long life of mine.

33.
They will bow their
heads and think:
'May I also in future become
such a one and release kotis
of living beings!

34.
'As the Lord Sâkyamuni,
the Lion of the Sâkya race,
after he had occupied
his seat on the terrace
of enlightenment,
raised his lion's roar;

35.
'So may I in future
be sitting on the terrace
of enlightenment,
honoured by all mortals,
to teach so long a life!'

36.
Those who are possessed
of firmness of intention and
have learnt the principles,
will understand the mystery
and feel no uncertainty.

Again, Agita,
he who after hearing
this Dharmaparyâya,
which contains
an exposition of the duration
of the Tathâgata's life,
apprehends it,
penetrates and understands it,
will produce a yet more
immeasurable accumulation
of merit conducive
to Buddha-knowledge;
unnecessary to add that
he who hears such
a Dharmaparyâya as this
or makes others hear it;
who keeps it in memory,
reads, comprehends or
makes others comprehend it;
who writes or has it written,
collects or has it
collected into a volume,
honours, respects,
worships it with flowers,
incense, perfumed garlands,
ointments, powder, cloth,
umbrellas, flags, streamers,
lighted oil lamps,
ghee lamps or lamps
filled with scented oil,
will produce
a far greater accumulation
of merit conducive
to Buddha-knowledge.

And, Agita, as a test
whether that young man
or young lady of good family
who hears this exposition
of the duration
of the Tathâgata's life
most decidedly believes in it
may be deemed the following.
They will behold me
teaching the law
here on the Gridhrakûta,
surrounded
by a host of Bodhisattvas,
attended by a host
of Bodhisattvas,
in the centre
of the congregation
of disciples.

They will behold
here my Buddha-field
in the Saha-world,
consisting of lapis lazuli
and forming a level plain ;
forming a chequered board
of eight compartments
with gold threads ;
set off with jewel trees.
They will behold the towers
that the Bodhisattvas
use as their abodes.
By this test, Agita,
one may know if a young man
or young lady of good family
has a most decided belief.
Moreover, Agita,
I declare that
a young man of good family
who, after the complete
extinction of the Tathâgata,
shall not reject,
but joyfully accept
this Dharmaparyâya
when hearing it, that such
a young man of good family
also is earnest in his belief ;
far more one who keeps it
in memory or reads it.
He who after collecting
this Dharmaparyâya
into a volume carries it
on his shoulder carries
the Tathâgata on his shoulder.
Such a young man or young
lady of good family, Agita,
need make no Stûpas for me,
nor monasteries ;
need not give
to the congregation of monks
medicaments for the sick
or other requisites.
For, Agita,
such a young man
or young lady of good family
has spiritually built
for the worship
of my relics Stûpas
of seven precious substances
reaching up to
the Brahma-world in height,
and with a circumference
in proportion,
with the umbrellas
thereto belonging,
with triumphal streamers,
with tinkling
bells and baskets ;
has shown manifold
marks of respect
to those Stûpas of relics
with diverse celestial
and earthly flowers,
incense, perfumed garlands,
ointments, powder, cloth,
umbrellas, banners, flags,
triumphal streamers,
by various sweet, pleasant,
clear-sounding tymbals
and drums, by the tune,
noise, sounds of musical
instruments and castanets,
by songs, nautch and dancing
of different kinds, of many,
innumerable kinds ;
has done those acts of worship
during many, innumerable
thousands of kotis of Æons.
One who keeps in memory
this Dharmaparyâya
after my complete extinction,
who reads, writes,

promulgates it,
Agita, shall also
have built monasteries,
large, spacious, extensive,
made of red sandal-wood,
with thirty-two pinnacles,
eight stories,
fit for a thousand monks,
adorned
with gardens and flowers,
having walks
furnished with lodgings,
completely
provided with meat,
food and drink
and medicaments for the sick,
well equipped
with all comforts.
And those numerous,
innumerable beings,
say a hundred or a thousand
or ten thousand or a koti
or hundred kotis
or thousand kotis
or hundred thousand kotis
or ten thousand times
hundred thousand kotis,
they must be considered
to form the congregation
of disciples seeing me
from face to face,
and must be considered
as those whom
I have fully blessed.
He who,
after my complete extinction,
shall keep
this Dharmaparyâya,
read, promulgate, or write it,
he, I repeat, Agita,
need not build
Stûpas of relics,
nor worship
the congregation ;
not necessary to tell, Agita,
that the young man
or young lady of good family
who,
keeping this Dharmaparyâya,
shall crown it by charity
in alms, morality,
forbearance, energy,
meditation, or wisdom,
will produce a much greater
accumulation of merit ;
it is, in fact, immense,
incalculable, infinite.
Just as the element of ether,
Agita, is boundless,
to the east, south, west, north,
beneath, above, and
in the intermediate quarters,
so immense and incalculable
an accumulation of merit,
conducive
to Buddha-knowledge,
will be produced
by a young man
or young lady of good family
who shall keep, read, write,
or cause to be written,
this Dharmaparyâya.
He will be zealous
in worshipping
the Tathâgata shrines ;
he will laud
the disciples of the Tathâgata,
praise the hundred
thousands of myriads
of kotis of virtues of the
Bodhisattvas Mahâsattvas,
and expound them to others ;

he will be accomplished
in forbearance, be moral,
of good character,
agreeable to live with,
and tolerant, modest,
not jealous of others,
not wrathful,
not vicious in mind,
of good memory,
strenuous and always busy,
devoted to meditation
in striving after
the state of a Buddha,
attaching great value
to abstract meditation,
frequently engaging
in abstract meditation,
able in solving questions
and in avoiding hundred
thousands of myriads
of kotis of questions.
Any Bodhisattva
Mahâsattva, Agita, who,
after the Tathâgata's
complete extinction, shall
keep this Dharmaparyâya,
will have the good qualities
I have described.
Such a young man
or young lady of good family,
Agita, must be considered
to make for the terrace
of enlightenment ;
that young man
or young lady of good family
steps towards the foot
of the tree of enlightenment
in order
to reach enlightenment.
And where that
young man or young lady
of good family, Agita, stands,
sits, or walks, there one
should make a shrine,
dedicated to the Tathâgata,
and the world,
including the gods,
should say :
This is a Stûpa of relics
of the Tathâgata.

And on that occasion
the Lord uttered
the following stanzas :

37.
An immense mass of merit,
as I have repeatedly
mentioned, shall be his who,
after the complete extinction
of the Leader of men,
shall keep this Sûtra.

38.
He will have
paid worship to me,
and built Stûpas of relics,
made of precious substances,
variegated, beautiful,
and splendid ;

39.
In height coming up
to the Brahma-world,
with rows of umbrellas,
great in circumference
gorgeous, and decorated
with triumphal streamers ;

40.
Resounding
with the clear ring of bells,
and decorated
with silk bands, while
jingles moved by the wind
form another ornament
at the shrines of Gina relics.

41.
He will have
shown great honour to them
by flowers, perfumes,
and ointments ; by music,
clothes, and the repeated
sound of tymbals.

42.
He will have sweet
musical instruments
struck at those relics,
and lamps with scented oil
kept burning all around.

43.
He who at the period
of depravation shall keep
and teach this Sûtra,
he will have paid me such
an infinitely varied worship.

44.
He has built many kotis
of excellent monasteries
of sandal-wood,
with thirty-two pinnacles,
and eight terraces high ;

45.
Provided with couches,
with food hard and soft ;
furnished
with excellent curtains,
and having cells by thousands.

46.
He has given hermitages
and walks embellished
by flower-gardens ;
many elegant objects
of various forms
and variegated.

47.
He has shown
manifold worship
to the host of disciples
in my presence,
he who,
after my extinction,
shall keep this Sûtra.

48.
Let one be ever so good
in disposition,
much greater merit
will he obtain who shall keep
or write this Sûtra.

49.
Let a man cause this
to be written and have it
well put together in a volume ;
let him always worship
the volume with flowers,
garlands, ointments.

50.
Let him constantly
place near it a lamp
filled with scented oil,
along with full-blown lotuses
and suitable oblations
of Michelia Champaka.

51.
The man who pays
such worship to the books
will produce a mass of merit
which is not to be measured.

52.
Even as there is no measure
of the element of ether,
in none of the ten directions,
so there is no measure
of this mass of merit.

53.
How much more
will this be the case
with one who is patient,
meek, devoted,
moral, studious,
and addicted to meditation ;

54.
Who is not irascible,
not treacherous,
reverential
towards the sanctuary,
always humble
towards monks,
not conceited,
nor neglectful ;

55.
Sensible and wise,
not angry
when he is asked a question ;
who, full of compassion
for living beings,
gives such instruction
as suits them.

56.
If there be such a man
who at the same time
keeps this Sûtra,
he will possess a mass of merit
that cannot be measured.

57.
If one meets such a man
as here described,
a keeper of this Sûtra,
one should do homage to him.

58.
One should present him
with divine flowers,
cover him with divine clothes,
and bow the head
to salute his feet,
in the conviction
of his being a Tathâgata.

59.
And at the sight
of such a man one may
directly make the reflection
that he is going towards
the foot of the tree
to arrive at superior,
blessed enlightenment
for the weal of all the world,
including the gods.

60.
And wherever such a sage
is walking, standing,
sitting, or lying down ;
wherever the hero
pronounces were it
but a single stanza
from this Sûtra ;

61.
There one
should build a Stûpa
for the most high of men,
a splendid, beautiful Stûpa,
dedicated to the Lord Buddha,
the Chief,
and then worship it
in manifold ways.

62.
That spot of the earth
has been enjoyed by myself ;
there have I walked myself,
and there have I been sitting ;
where that son of Buddha
has stayed, there I am.

Chapter XVII
Indication of the Meritoriousness of Joyful Acceptance

Thereupon the Bodhisattva
Mahâsattva Maitreya
said to the Lord : O Lord,
one who, after hearing
this Dharmaparyâya
being preached,
joyfully accepts it,
be that person
a young man of good family
or a young lady,
how much merit,
O Lord, will be produced
by such a young man or
young lady of good family ?

And on that occasion
the Bodhisattva Mahâsattva
Maitreya uttered this stanza :

1.
How great will be
the merit of him who,
after the extinction
of the great Hero,
shall hear this exalted Sûtra
and joyfully accept it ?

And the Lord
said to the Bodhisattva
Mahâsattva Maitreya :
If any one, Agita,
either a young man of good
family or a young lady,
after the complete extinction
of the Tathâgata,
hears the preaching
of this Dharmaparyayâ,
let it be a monk or nun,
a male or female lay devotee,
a man of ripe understanding
or a boy or girl ;
if the hearer joyfully accepts it,
and then after the sermon
rises up to go elsewhere,
to a monastery, house,
forest, street, village,
town, or province,
with the motive
and express aim
to expound the law
such as he has understood,
such as he has heard it,
and according
to the measure of his power,
to another person,
his mother, father, kinsman,
friend, acquaintance,
or any other person ;
if the latter, after hearing,
joyfully accepts,
and, in consequence,
communicates it to another ;
if the latter, after hearing,
joyfully accepts, and
communicates it to another ;
if this other,
again, after hearing,
joyfully accepts it,
and so on in succession until
a number of fifty is reached ;
then, Agita,
the fiftieth person to hear
and joyfully accept
the law so heard,
let it be a young man
of good family

Joyful Acceptance 273

or a young lady,
will have acquired
an accumulation of merit
connected
with the joyful acceptance,
Agita,
which I am going
to indicate to thee.
Listen,
and take it well to heart;
I will tell thee.

It is, Agita,
as if the creatures existing
in the four hundred thousand
Asankhyeyas of worlds,
in any
of the six states of existence,
born from an egg,
from a womb,
from warm humidity,
or from metamorphosis,
whether they have
a shape or have not,
be they conscious
or unconscious,
neither conscious
nor unconscious,
footless,
two-footed, four-footed,
or many-footed,
as many beings
as are contained
in the world of creatures,
as if all those
had flocked together
to one place.
Further,
suppose some man appears,
a lover of virtue,
a lover of good,

who gives
to that whole body
the pleasures, sports,
amusements, and enjoyments
they desire, like, and relish.
He gives to each of them
all Gambudvîpa
for his pleasures,
sports, amusements,
and enjoyments;
gives bullion, gold, silver,
gems, pearls, lapis lazuli,
conches, stones, coral,
carriages yoked with horses,
with bullocks, with elephants;
gives palaces and towers.
In this way, Agita,
that master of munificence,
that great master
of munificence
continues spending his gifts
for fully eighty years.
Then, Agita,
that master of munificence,
that great master
of munificence
reflects thus:
All these beings
have I allowed to sport
and enjoy themselves,
but now they
are covered with wrinkles
and gray-haired, old,
decrepit, eighty years of age,
and near the term of their life.
Let me therefore initiate them
in the discipline of the law
revealed by the Tathâgata,
and instruct them.
Thereupon, Agita,
the man exhorts

all those beings,
thereafter initiates them
in the discipline of the law
revealed by the Tathâgata,
and makes them adopt it.
Those beings
learn the law from him,
and in one moment,
one instant, one bit of time,
all become Srotaâpannas,
obtain the fruit
of the rank of Sakridâgâmin
and of Anâgâmin,
until they become Arhats,
free from all imperfections,
adepts in meditation,
adepts in great meditation
and in the meditation
with eight emancipations.
Now, what is thine opinion,
Agita, will that master
of munificence,
that great master
of munificence,
on account of his doings,
produce great merit,
immense,
incalculable merit ?
Whereupon the Bodhisattva
Mahâsattva Maitreya
said in reply to the Lord :
Certainly, Lord ; certainly,
Sugata ; that person, Lord,
will already produce
much merit on that account,
because he gives to the beings
all that is necessary
for happiness ;
how much more then
if he establishes them
in Arhatship !

This said,
the Lord spoke
to the Bodhisattva
Mahâsattva Maitreya
as follows :
I announce to thee, Agita,
I declare to thee ;
take on one side
the master of munificence,
the great master
of munificence,
who produces merit
by supplying all beings
in the four hundred
thousand Asankhyeyas
of worlds with all
the necessaries for happiness
and by establishing them
in Arhatship ;
take on the other side
the person who, ranking
the fiftieth in the series
of the oral tradition of the law,
hears,
were it but a single stanza,
a single word,
from this Dharmaparyâya
and joyfully accepts it ;
if we compare
the mass of merit connected
with the joyful acceptance
and the mass of merit
connected with the charity
of the master of munificence,
the great master
of munificence,
then the greater merit
will be his who,
ranking the fiftieth
in the series

of the oral tradition of the law,
after hearing were it
but a single stanza,
a single word,
from this Dharmaparyâya,
joyfully accepts it.
Against
this accumulation of merit,
Agita,
this accumulation
of roots of goodness connected
with that joyful acceptance,
the former accumulation
of merit connected
with the charity
of that master
of munificence,
that great master
of munificence,
and connected
with the confirmation
in Arhatship,
does not fetch
the 1/100 part,
not the 1/100,000
not the 1/10,000,000
not the 1/1000,000,000
not the 1/1000 x 10,000,000
not the
1/100,000 x 10,000,000,
not the 1/100,000 x
10,000 x 10,000,000 part ;
it admits of no calculation,
no counting,
no reckoning,
no comparison,
no approximation,
no secret teaching.
So immense,
incalculable,
Agita,

is the merit which a person,
ranking the fiftieth
in the series
of the tradition of the law,
produces
by joyfully accepting,
were it but a single stanza,
a single word,
from this Dharmaparyâya ;
how much more
then will he produce, Agita,
who hears
this Dharmaparyâya
in my presence
and then joyfully accepts it ?
I declare, Agita,
that his accumulation of merit
shall be even more immense,
more incalculable.

And further, Agita,
if a young man of good
family or a young lady,
with the design to hear
this discourse on the law,
goes from home
to a monastery,
and there hears
this Dharmaparyâya
for a single moment,
either standing or sitting,
then that person,
merely by the mass of merit
resulting from that action,
will after the termination
of his present life,
and at the time
of his second existence when
he receives another body,
become a possessor
of carriages yoked

with bullocks, horses,
or elephants, of litters,
vehicles yoked with bulls,
and of celestial aerial cars.
If further that same person
at that preaching sits down,
were it but a single moment,
to hear this Dharmaparyâya,
or persuades another
to sit down
or shares with him his seat,
he will by the store of merit
resulting from that action
gain seats of Indra,
seats of Brahma,
thrones of a Kakravartin.
And, Agita, if some one,
a young man of good
family or a young lady,
says to another person :
Come, friend, and hear
the Dharmaparyâya
of the Lotus of the True Law,
and if that other person
owing to that exhortation
is persuaded to listen,
were it but a single moment,
then the former will by virtue
of that root of goodness,
consisting in that exhortation,
obtain the advantage
of a connection
with Bodhisattvas
who have acquired Dhâranî.
He will become
the reverse of dull,
will get keen faculties,
and have wisdom ;
in the course of a hundred
thousand existences he will
never have a fetid mouth,
nor an offensive one ;
he will have no diseases
of the tongue,
nor of the mouth ;
he will have no black teeth,
no unequal,
no yellow,
no ill-ranged,
no broken teeth,
no teeth fallen out ;
his lips will not be pendulous,
not turned inward,
not gaping,
not mutilated,
not loathsome ;
his nose will not be flat,
nor wry ;
his face will not be long,
nor wry, nor unpleasant.
On the contrary, Agita,
his tongue, teeth,
and lips will be delicate
and well-shaped ;
his nose long ;
his face perfectly round ;
the eyebrows well-shaped ;
the forehead well-formed.
He will receive
a very complete
organ of manhood.
He will have
the advantage that
the Tathâgata renders
sermons intelligible to him
and soon come
in connection with Lords,
Buddhas.
Mark, Agita,
how much good is produced
by one's inciting were it
but a single creature ;

Joyful Acceptance 277

how much more then by him
who reverentially hears,
reverentially reads,
reverentially preaches,
reverentially
promulgates the law !

And on that occasion
the Lord uttered
the following stanzas :

2.
Listen how great the merit
is of one who,
the fiftieth in the series
of tradition,
hears a single stanza
from this Sûtra
and with placid mind
joyfully adopts it.

3.
Suppose there is a man
in the habit of giving alms
to myriads of kotis of beings,
whom I have herebefore
indicated by way
of comparison ;
all of them he satisfies
during eighty years.

4.
Then seeing that old age
has approached for them,
that their brow is wrinkled
and their head gray he thinks :
Alas,
how all beings come to decay !
Let me
therefore admonish them
by speaking of the law.

5.
He teaches them the law
here on earth
and points to the state
of Nirvâna hereafter.
'All existences' he says
'are like a mirage ;
hasten to become disgusted
with all existence.'

6.
All creatures,
by hearing the law
from that charitable person,
become at once Arhats,
free from imperfections,
and living their last life.

7.
Much more merit
than by that person
will be acquired by him
who through
unbroken tradition
shall hear were it
but a single stanza
and joyfully receive it.
The mass of merit
of the former
is not even so much
as a small particle
of the latter's.

8.
So great will be one's merit,
endless, immeasurable,
owing to one's hearing
merely a single stanza,
in regular tradition ;
how much more then
if one hears from face to face !

9.
And if somebody
exhorts were it
but a single creature and says :
Go, hear the law,
for this Sûtra is rare
in many myriads
of kotis of Æons ;

10.
And if the creature
so exhorted should hear
the Sûtra even for a moment,
hark what fruit
is to result from that action.
He shall never
have a mouth disease ;

11.
His tongue is never sore ;
his teeth shall never fall out,
never be black,
yellow, unequal ;
his lips never
become loathsome ;

12.
His face is not wry,
nor lean, nor long ;
his nose not flat ;
it is well-shaped,
as well as his forehead,
teeth, lips, and round face.

13.
His aspect
is ever pleasant to men ;
his mouth is never fetid,
it constantly emits a smell
sweet as the lotus.

14.
If some wise man,
to hear this Sûtra,
goes from his home
to a monastery
and there listen,
were it
but for a single moment,
with a placid mind,
hear what results from it.

15.
His body is very fair ;
he drives
with horse-carriages,
that wise man,
and is mounted
on elevated carriages
drawn by elephants
and variegated with gems.

16.
He possesses litters
covered with ornaments
and carried
by numerous men.
Such is the blessed fruit
of his going
to hear preaching.

17.
Owing to the performance
of that pious work he shall,
when sitting
in the assembly there,
obtain seats of Indra,
seats of Brahma,
seats of kings.

Chapter XVIII
The Advantages of a Religious Preacher

The Lord then addressed
the Bodhisattva Mahâsattva
Satatasamitâbhiyukta
(i.e. ever
and constantly strenuous).
Any one,
young man of good family,
who shall keep, read, teach,
write this Dharmaparyâya
or have it written,
let that person be
a young man of good family
or a young lady,
shall obtain eight hundred
good qualities of the eye,
twelve hundred of the ear,
eight hundred of the nose,
twelve hundred of the tongue,
eight hundred of the body,
twelve hundred of the mind.
By these many hundred
good qualities
the whole of the six organs
shall be perfect,
thoroughly perfect.
By means of the natural,
carnal eye derived
from his parents
being perfect,
he shall see
the whole triple universe,
outwardly and inwardly,
with its mountains
and woody thickets,
down to the great hell Avîki
and up to the extremity
of existence.
All that he shall
see with his natural eye,
as well as the creatures
to be found in it,
and he shall know
the fruit of their works.

And on that occasion
the Lord uttered
the followng stanzas :

1.
Hear from me
what good qualities
shall belong to him
who unhesitatingly
and undismayed
shall preach this Sûtra
to the congregated assembly.

2.
First, then,
his eye shall possess
eight hundred good qualities
by which it shall be correct,
clear, and untroubled.

3.
With the carnal eye
derived from his parents
he shall see the whole world
from within and without.

4.
He shall see
the Meru and Sumeru,
all the horizon
and other mountains,
as well as the seas.

5.
He, the hero, sees all,
downward to the Avîki
and upward
to the extremity of existence.
Such is his carnal eye.

6.
But he has not yet got
the divine eye,
it having not yet
been produced in him;
such as here described
is the range of his carnal eye.

Further,
Satatasamitâbhiyukta,
the young man of good family
or the young lady
who proclaims
this Dharmaparyâya
and preaches it to others,
is possessed
of the twelve hundred
good qualities of the ear.
The various sounds
that are uttered
in the triple universe,
downward to the great hell
Avîki and upward
to the extremity of existence,
within and without,
such as the sounds of horses,
elephants, cows, peasants,
goats, cars; the sounds
of weeping and wailing;
of horror, of conch-trumpets,
bells, tymbals;
of playing and singing;
of camels, of tigers;
of women, men, boys, girls;
of righteousness (piety) and
unrighteousness (impiety);
of pleasure and pain;
of ignorant men and âryas;
pleasant
and unpleasant sounds;
sounds of gods,
Nâgas, goblins, Gandharvas,
demons, Garudas, Kinnaras,
great serpents, men,
and beings not human;
of monks, disciples,
Pratyekabuddhas,
Bodhisattvas, and Tathâgatas;
as many sounds as are uttered
in the triple world,
within and without,
all those he hears
with his natural organ
of hearing when perfect.
Still he does not enjoy
the divine ear,
although he apprehends
the sounds
of those different creatures,
understands,
discerns the sounds
of those different creatures,
and when with
his natural organ of hearing
he hears the sounds
of those creatures,
his ear is not overpowered
by any of those sounds.
Such, Satatasamitâbhiyukta,
is the organ of hearing
that the Bodhisattva
Mahâsattva acquires;
yet he does not
possess the divine ear.

Thus spoke the Lord ;
thereafter he, the Sugata,
the Master, added :

7.
The organ of hearing
of such a person
cleared and perfect,
though as yet it be natural ;
by it he perceives
the various sounds,
without any exception,
in this world.

8.
He perceives the sounds
of elephants, horses, cars,
cows, goats, and sheep ;
of noisy kettle-drums,
tabours, lutes,
flutes, Vallakî-lutes.

9.
He can hear singing,
lovely and sweet,
and, at the same time,
is constant enough
not to allow himself
to be beguiled by it ;
he perceives the sounds
of kotis of men,
whatever and wherever
they are speaking.

10.
He, moreover,
always hears the voice
of gods and Nâgas ;
he hears the tunes,
sweet and affecting, of song,
as well as the voices
of men and women,
boys and girls.

11.
He hears the cries
of the denizens
of mountains and glens ;
the tender notes
of Kalavinkas, cuckoos,
peafowls, pheasants,
and other birds.

12.
He also hears
the heart-rending cries
of those who are suffering
pains in the hells,
and the yells uttered
by the Spirits,
vexed as they are
by the difficulty to get food ;

13.
Likewise the different cries
produced by the demons
and the inhabitants
of the ocean.
All these sounds
the preacher is able to hear
from his place on earth,
without being
overpowered by them.

14.
From where he is stationed
here on the earth
he also hears the different
and multifarious sounds
through which the inhabitants
of the realm of brutes are
conversing with each other.

15.
He apprehends all the sounds,
without any exception,
whereby the numerous angels
living in the Brahma-world,
the Akanishthas
and Âbhâsvaras,
call one another.

16.
He likewise
always hears the sound
which the monks on earth
are raising
when engaged in reading,
and when preaching the law
to congregations,
after having taken orders
under the command
of the Sugatas.

17.
And when
the Bodhisattvas
here on earth
have a reading together
and raise their voices
in the general synods,
he hears them severally.

18.
The Bodhisattva
who preaches this Sûtra shall,
at one time,
also hear the perfect law
of that the Lord Buddha,
the tamer of men,
announces to the assemblies.

19.
The numerous sounds
produced by all beings
in the triple world,
in this field,
within and without,
downward to the Avîki
and upward
to the extremity of existence,
are heard by him.

20.
In short, he perceives
the voices of all beings,
his ear being open.
Being in the possession
of his six senses,
he will discern
the different sources of sound,
and that while
his organ of hearing
is the natural one ;

21.
The divine ear
is not yet operating in him ;
his ear continues
in its natural state.
Such as here told
are the good qualities
belonging to the wise man
who shall be a keeper
of this Sûtra.

Further,
Satatasamitâbhiyukta,
the Bodhisattva Mahâsattva
who keeps, proclaims, studies,
writes this Dharmaparyâya
becomes possessed
of a perfect organ of smell

with eight hundred
good qualities.
By means of that organ
he smells the different smells
that are found
in the triple world,
within and without,
such as fetid smells,
pleasant
and unpleasant smells,
the fragrance
of diverse flowers,
as the great-flowered jasmine,
Arabian jasmine,
Michelia Chainpaka,
trumpet-flower;
likewise the different scents
of aquatic flowers,
as the blue lotus, red lotus,
white esculent water-lily
and white lotus.
He smells the odour
of fruits and blossoms
of various trees bearing
fruits and blossoms,
such as sandal,
Xanthochymus,
Tabernæmontana,
agallochum.
The manifold
hundred-thousand
mixtures of perfumes
he smells and discerns,
without moving
from his standing-place.
He smells the diverse smells
of creatures, as elephants,
horses, cows, goats, beasts,
as well as the smell
issuing from the body
of various living beings
in the condition of brutes.
He perceives the smells
exhaled by the body
of women and men,
of boys and girls.
He smells,
even from a distance,
the odour of grass,
bushes, herbs, trees.
He perceives those smells
such as they really are,
and is not surprised
nor stunned by them.
Staying on this very earth
he smells the odour of gods
and the fragrance
of celestial flowers,
such as Erythrina, Bauhinia,
Mandârava and great
Mandârava, Mañgûsha
and great Mañgûsha.
He smells the perfume
of the divine powders
of sandal and agallochum,
as well as that
of the hundred-thousands
of mixtures
of different divine flowers.
He smells the odour exhaled
by the body of the gods,
such as Indra,
the chief of the gods,
and thereby knows
whether the god
is sporting, playing,
and enjoying himself
in his palace Vaigayanta
or is speaking the law
to the gods of paradise in
the assembly hall of the gods,
Sudharmâ,

or is resorting
to the pleasure-park for sport.
He smells the odour
proceeding from the body
of the sundry other gods,
as well as that
proceeding from the girls
and wives of the gods,
from the youths and maidens
amongst the gods,
without being surprised
or stunned by those smells.
He likewise smells the odour
exhaled by the bodies
of all Devanikâyas,
Brahmakâyikas,
and Mahâbrahmas.
In the same manner
he perceives the smells
coming from disciples,
Pratyekabuddhas,
Bodhisattvas, and Tathâgatas.
He smells the odour
arising from the seats
of the Tathâgatas
and so discovers
where those Tathâgatas,
Arhats, &c. abide.
And by none of all
those different smells
is his organ of smell hindered,
impaired, or vexed ;
and, if required,
he may give an account
of those smells to others
without his memory
being impaired by it.

And on that occasion
the Lord uttered
the following stanzas :

22.
His organ of smell
is quite correct,
and he perceives the manifold
and various smells,
good or bad,
which exist in this world ;

23.
The fragrance of
the great-flowered jasmine,
Arabian jasmine,
Xanthochymus,
sandal, agallochum,
of several blossoms and fruits.

24.
He likewise perceives
the smells exhaled by men,
women, boys, and girls,
at a considerable distance,
and by the smell
he knows where they are.

25.
He recognizes emperors,
rulers of armies,
governors of provinces,
as well as royal princes
and ministers,
and all the ladies
of the harem
by their peculiar scent.

26.
It is by the odour
that the Bodhisattva discovers
sundry jewels of things,
such as are found on the earth
and such as serve
as jewels for women.

27.
That Bodhisattva likewise
knows by the odour
the various kinds
of ornament that women
use for their body, robes,
wreaths, and ointments.

28.
The wise man who keeps
this exalted Sûtra recognizes,
by the power
of a good-smelling organ,
a woman standing,
sitting, or lying ;
he discovers wanton sport
and magic power.

29.
He perceives at once
where he stands,
the fragrance of scented oils,
and the different odours
of flowers and fruits,
and thereby knows
from what source
the odour proceeds.

30.
The discriminating man
recognizes by the odour
the numerous sandal-trees
in full blossom in the glens
of the mountains,
as well as all creatures
dwelling there.

31.
All the beings living within
the compass of the horizon
or dwelling
in the depth of the sea
or in the bosom of the earth
the discriminating man
knows how to distinguish
from the peculiar smell.

32.
He discerns
the gods and demons,
and the daughters of demons ;
he discovers
the sports of demons
and their luxury.
Such, indeed,
is the power
of his organ of smell.

33.
By the smell
he tracks the abodes
of the quadrupeds
in the woods,
lions, tigers, elephants,
snakes, buffaloes,
cows, gayals.

34.
He infers from the odour,
whether the child that women,
languid from pregnancy,
bear in the womb
be a boy or a girl.

35.
He can discern
if a woman is big
with a dead child ;
he discerns
if she is subject to throes,
and, further,
if a woman,

the pains being removed,
shall be delivered
of a healthy boy.

36.
He guesses
the various designs of men,
he smells, so to say,
an air of design ;
he finds out the odour
of passionate,
wicked,
hypocritical,
or quiet persons.

37.
That Bodhisattva
by the scent smells treasures
hidden in the ground,
money, gold, bullion, silver,
chests, and metal pots.

38.
Necklaces of two sorts,
gems, pearls,
nice priceless jewels
he knows by the scent,
as well as things priceless
and brilliant in general.

39.
That great man
from his very place on earth
smells the flowers
here above in the sky
with the gods,
such as Mandâravas,
Mañgûshakas,
and those growing
on the coral tree.

40.
By the power
of his organ of smell he,
without leaving
his stand on earth,
perceives how and whose
are the aerial cars,
of lofty, low,
and middling size,
and other brilliant forms
shooting through
the firmament.

41.
He likewise
finds out the paradise, the
gods in the hall of Sudharmâ
and in the most glorious
palace of Vaigayanta,
and the angels who there
are diverting themselves.

42.
He perceives, here on earth,
an air of them ; by the scent
he knows the angels,
and where each of them
is acting, standing,
listening, or walking.

43.
That Bodhisattva
tracks by the scent
the houris who are decorated
with many flowers,
decked with wreaths
and ornaments
and in full attire ;
he knows wherever
they are dallying
or staying at the time.

44.
By smell
he apprehends the gods,
Brahmas,
and Brahmakâyas moving
on aerial cars aloft,
upwards to the extremity
of existence ;
he knows whether they
are absorbed in meditation
or have risen from it.

45.
He perceives
the Âbhâsvara angels
falling and shooting
and appearing,
even those
that he never saw before.
Such is the organ of smell
of the Bodhisattva
who keeps this Sûtra.

46.
The Bodhisattva
also recognizes all monks
under the rule of the Sugata,
who are strenuously
engaged in their walks
and find their delight
in their lessons and reading.

47.
Intelligent as he is,
he discerns those among the
sons of Gina who are disciples
and those who used to live
at the foot of trees,
and he knows that the monk
so and so is staying
in such and such a place.

48.
The Bodhisattva knows
by the odour whether other
Bodhisattvas
are of good memory,
meditative,
delighting in their lessons
and reading,
and assiduous in preaching
to congregations.

49.
In whatever point of space
the Sugata,
the great Seer,
so benign and bounteous,
reveals the law
in the midst of the crowd
of attending disciples,
the Bodhisattva
by the odour recognizes him
as the Lord of the universe.

50.
Staying on earth,
the Bodhisattva
also perceives those beings
who hear the law
and rejoice at it,
and the whole assembly
of the Gina.

51.
Such is the power
of his organ of smell.
Yet it is not the divine organ
he possesses,
but the natural one
prior to the perfect,
divine faculty of smell.

Further,
Satatasamitâbhiyukta,
the young man of good family
or the young lady who keeps,
teaches, proclaims,
writes this Dharmaparyâya
shall have an organ of taste
possessed of twelve hundred
good faculties of the tongue.
All flavours
he takes on his tongue
will yield a divine,
exquisite relish.
And he tastes in such a way
that he is not to relish
anything unpleasant ; and
even the unpleasant flavours
that are taken on his tongue
will yield a divine relish.
And whatever he shall
preach in the assembly,
the creatures
will be satisfied by it ;
they will be content,
thoroughly content,
filled with delight.
A sweet, tender,
agreeable,
deep voice goes out from him,
an amiable voice
which goes to the heart,
at which those creatures
will be ravished and charmed ;
and those
to whom he preaches,
after having heard
his sweet voice,
so tender and melodious,
will, even if they are gods,
be of opinion
that they ought to go and see,
venerate, and serve him.
And the angels and houris
will be of opinion, &c.
The Indras, Brahmas,
and Brahmakâyikas
will be of opinion, &c.
The Nâgas and Nâga girls
will be of opinion, &c.
The demons and their girls
will be of opinion, &c.
The Garudas and their girls
will be of opinion, &c.
The Kinnaras and their girls,
the great serpents
and their girls,
the goblins and their girls,
the imps and their girls
will be of opinion
that they ought to go and see,
venerate, serve him,
and hear his sermon,
and all will show him honour,
respect, esteem, worship,
reverence, and veneration.
Monks and nuns,
male and female lay devotees
will likewise
be desirous of seeing him.
Kings, royal princes,
and grandees
or ministers will also
be desirous of seeing him.
Kings ruling armies
and emperors possessed
of the seven treasures,
along with the princes royal,
ministers,
ladies of the harem,
and their retinue
will be desirous of seeing him
and paying him their homage.

So sweet will be
the speech delivered
by that preacher,
so truthful and according to
the teaching of the Tathâgata
will be his words.
Others also,
Brahmans and laymen,
citizens and peasants,
will always and ever
follow that preacher
till the end of life.
Even the disciples
of the Tathâgata
will be desirous
of seeing him ;
likewise the Pratyekabuddhas
and the Lords Buddhas.
And wherever that
young man of good family
or young lady shall stay,
there he or she will preach,
the face turned
to the Tathâgata,
and he or she will
be a worthy vessel
of the Buddha-qualities.
Such, so pleasant,
so deep will be
the voice of the law
going out from him.

And on that occasion
the Lord uttered
the following stanzas :

52.
His organ of taste
is most excellent,
and he will never relish
anything of inferior flavour ;
the flavours are no sooner
put on his tongue
than they become divine and
possessed of a divine taste.

53.
He has a tender voice
and delivers sweet words,
pleasant to hear,
agreeable, charming ;
in the midst of the assembly
he is used to speak with
a melodious and deep voice.

54.
And
whosoever hears him when
he is delivering a sermon
with myriads of kotis
of examples,
feels a great joy
and shows him
an immense veneration.

55.
The gods, Nâgas,
demons, and goblins
always long to see him,
and respectfully listen
to his preaching.
All those good qualities
are his.

56.
If he would, he might
make his voice heard
by the whole of this world ;
his voice is so fine, sweet,
deep, tender, and winning.

57.
The emperors on earth,
along
with their children and wives,
go to him with the purpose
of honouring him,
and listen all the time
to his sermon
with joined hands.

58.
He is constantly
followed by goblins,
crowds of Nâgas,
Gandharvas, imps,
male and female,
who honour,
respect,
and worship him.

59.
Brahma himself becomes
his obedient servant;
the gods Îsvara
and Mahesvara,
as well as Indra
and the numerous
heavenly nymphs,
approach him.

60.
And the Buddhas,
benign
and merciful for the world,
along with their disciples,
hearing his voice,
protect him
by showing their face,
and feel satisfaction
in hearing him preaching.

Further,
Satatasamitâbhiyukta,
the Bodhisattva Mahâsattva
who keeps, reads,
promulgates, teaches,
writes this Dharmaparyâya
shall have the eight hundred
good qualities of the body.
It will be pure,
and show a hue clear
as the lapis lazuli;
it will be pleasant to see
for the creatures.
On that perfect body he will
see the whole triple universe;
the beings
who in the triple world
disappear and appear,
who are low or lofty,
of good or of bad colour,
in fortunate
or in unfortunate condition,
as well as the beings dwelling
within the circular plane
of the horizon
and of the great horizon,
on the chief mountains
Meru and Sumeru, and
the beings dwelling below
in the Avîki and upwards
to the extremity of existence;
all of them he will see
on his own body.
The disciples,
Pratyekabuddhas,
Bodhisattvas,
and Tathâgatas dwelling
in the triple universe,
and the law
taught by those Tathâgatas
and the beings serving

the Tathâgatas,
he will see all of them
on his own body,
because he receives
the proper body
of all those beings,
and that on account
of the perfectness of his body.

And on that occasion
the Lord uttered
the following stanzas :

61.
His body becomes
thoroughly pure,
clear as if consisting
of lapis lazuli ;
he who keeps
this sublime Sûtra
is always a pleasant sight
for all creatures.

62.
As on the surface
of a mirror an image is seen,
so on his body this world.
Being self-born,
he sees no other beings.
Such is the perfectness
of his body.

63.
Indeed, all beings who
are in this world, men,
gods, demons, goblins,
the inhabitants of hell,
the spirits,
and the brute creation
are seen reflected
on that body.

64.
The aerial cars of the gods
up to
the extremity of existence,
the rocks,
the ridge of the horizon,
the Himâlaya,
Sumeru, and great Meru,
all are seen on that body.

65.
He also sees
the Buddhas on his body,
along with the disciples
and other sons of Buddha ;
likewise the Bodhisattvas
who lead a solitary life,
and those who preach
the law to congregations.

66.
Such
is the perfectness of his body,
though he has not yet
obtained a divine body ;
the natural property
of his body is such.

Further,
Satatasamitâbhiyukta,
the Bodhisattva Mahâsattva
who after
the complete extinction
of the Tathâgata
keeps, teaches, writes,
reads this Dharmaparyâya
shall have a mental organ
possessed of twelve hundred
good qualities of intellect.
By this perfect mental organ
he will,

even if he hears
a single stanza,
recognize
its various meanings.
By fully comprehending
the stanza he will find in it
the text to preach upon
for a month,
for four months,
nay, for a whole year.
And the sermon
he preaches will not fade
from his memory.
The popular maxims
of common life,
whether sayings or counsels,
he will know how to reconcile
with the rules of the law.
Whatever creatures
of this triple universe
are subject
to the mundane whirl,
in any of
the six conditions of existence,
he will know their thoughts,
doings, and movements.
He will know
and discern their motions,
purposes, and aims.
Though he has not yet
attained the state of an Ârya,
his intellectual organ
will be thoroughly perfect.
And all he shall preach
after having pondered
on the interpretation
of the law will be really true ;
he speaks what
all Tathâgatas have spoken,
all that has been declared
in the Sûtras of former Ginas.

And on that occasion
the Lord uttered
the following stanzas :

67.
His mental organ is perfect,
lucid, right, and untroubled.
By it he finds out
the various laws,
low, high, and mean.

68.
On hearing the contents
of a single stanza,
the wise man catches
the manifold significations
hidden in it,
and he is able for a month,
four months,
or even a year
to go on expounding
both its conventional
and its true sense.

69.
And the beings
living in this world,
within or without,
gods, men, demons,
goblins, Nâgas, brutes,

70.
The beings stationed
in any of
the six conditions of existence,
all their thoughts the sage
knows instantaneously.
These are the advantages
of keeping this Sûtra.

71.
He also hears
the holy sound of the law
which the Buddha,
marked with
a hundred blessed signs,
preaches all over the world,
and he catches
what the Buddha speaks.

72.
He reflects much
on the supreme law,
and is in the wont
of constantly dilating upon it ;
he is never hesitating.
These are the advantages
of keeping this Sûtra.

73.
He knows
the connections and knots ;
he discerns in all laws
contrarieties ;
he knows the meaning
and the interpretations,
and expounds them
according to his knowledge.

74.
The Sûtra
which since so long a time
has been expounded
by the ancient
Masters of the world
is the law which he,
never flinching,
is always preaching
in the assembly.

75.
Such is the mental organ
of him who keeps
or reads this Sûtra ;
he has not yet the knowledge
of emancipation,
but one that precedes it.

76.
He who keeps this Sûtra
of the Sugata stands
on the stage of a master ;
he may preach to all creatures
and is skilful in kotis
of interpretations.

Chapter IXX
Sadâparibhûta

The Lord then addressed
the Bodhisattva Mahisattva
Mahâsthâmaprâpta.
In a similar way,
Mahâsthâmaprâpta,
one may infer
from what has been said
that he who rejects such
a Dharmaparyâya as this,
who abuses monks, nuns,
lay devotees male or female,
keeping this Sûtra,
insults them,
treats them with false
and harsh words,
shall experience dire results,
to such an extent
as is impossible
to express in words.
But those that keep,
read, comprehend, teach,
amply expound it to others,
shall experience happy results,
such as I have
already mentioned :
they shall attain
such a perfection
of the eye, ear, nose,
tongue, body,
and mind as just described.

In the days of yore,
Mahâsthâmaprâpta,
at a past period,
before incalculable Æons,
nay, more than incalculable,
immense,
inconceivable,
and even long before,
there appeared in the world
a Tathâgata, &c., named
Bhîshmagargitasvararâga,
endowed with science and
conduct, a Sugata, &c. &c.,
in the Æon Vinirbhoga,
in the world Mahâsambhava.
Now, Mahâsthâmaprâpta,
that Lord
Bhîshmagargitasvararâga,
the Tathâgata, &c.,
in that world Vinirbhoga,
showed the law
in the presence of the world,
including gods,
men, and demons ;
the law containing
the four noble truths
and starting from
the chain of causes and effects,
tending to overcome birth,
decrepitude, sickness, death,
sorrow, lamentation, woe,
grief, despondency,
and finally leading
to Nirvâna,
he showed to the disciples ;
the law connected
with the six Perfections
of virtue and terminating
in the knowledge
of the Omniscient, after
the attainment of supreme,
perfect enlightenment,
he showed
to the Bodhisattvas.
The lifetime of that Lord
Bhîshmagargitasvararâga,
the Tathâgata, &c.,
lasted forty hundred thousand

myriads of kotis of Æons
equal to the sands
of the river Ganges.
After his complete extinction
his true law remained
hundred thousands
of myriads of kotis of Æons
equal to the atoms
contained in Gambudvîpa,
and the counterfeit
of the true law continued
hundred thousands
of myriads of kotis of Æons
equal to the dust-atoms
in the four continents.
When the counterfeit
of the true law of the Lord
Bhîshmagargitasvararâga,
the Tathâgata, &c.,
after his complete extinction,
had disappeared
in the world Mahâsambhava,
Mahâsthâmaprâpta,
another Tathâgata
Bhîshmagargitasvararâga,
Arhat, &c.,
appeared, endowed
with science and conduct.
So in succession,
Mahâsthâmaprâpta,
there arose in that world
Mahâsambhava
twenty hundred thousand
myriads of kotis of Tathâgatas,
&c., called
Bhîshmagargitasvararâga.
At the time,
Mahâsthâmaprâpta,
after the complete extinction
of the first Tathâgata
amongst all those of the name
of Bhîshmagargitasvararâga,
Tathâgata, &c.,
endowed with science
and conduct, &c. &c.,
when his true law
had disappeared
and the counterfeit
of the true law was fading;
when the reign of the law
was being oppressed
by proud monks,
there was a monk,
a Bodhisattva Mahâsattva,
called Sadâparibhûta.
For what reason,
Mahâsthâmaprâpta, was
that Bodhisattva Mahâsattva
called Sadâparibhûta?
It was, Mahâsthâmaprâpta,
because
that Bodhisattva Mahâsattva
was in the habit of exclaiming
to every monk or nun,
male or female lay devotee,
while approaching them:
I do not contemn you,
worthies.
You deserve no contempt,
for you all observe
the course of duty
of Bodhisattvas
and are to become
Tathâgatas, &c.
In this way,
Mahâsthâmaprâpta,
that Bodhisattva Mahâsattva,
when a monk,
did not teach nor study;
the only thing he did was,
whenever he descried
from afar a monk or nun,

a male or female lay devotee,
to approach them
and exclaim :
I do not contemn you, sisters.
You deserve no contempt,
for you all observe
the course of duty
of Bodhiattvas
and are to become
Tathâgatas, &c.
So, Mahâsthâmaprâpta,
the Bodhisattva Mahâsattva
at that time used to address
every monk or nun,
male or female devotee.
But all were extremely
irritated and angry at it,
showed him their displeasure,
abused and insulted him :
Why does he, unasked,
declare that he feels
no contempt for us ?
just by so doing
he shows a contempt for us.
He renders himself
contemptible by predicting
our future destiny
to supreme,
perfect enlightenment ;
we do not care
for what is not true.
Many years,
Mahâsthâmaprâpta,
went on during which
that Bodhisattva Mahâsattva
was being abused, but he
was not angry at anybody,
nor felt malignity,
and to those who,
when he addressed them
in the said manner,
cast a clod or stick at him, he
loudly exclaimed from afar :
I do not contemn you.
Those monks and nuns,
male and female lay devotees,
being always and ever
addressed by him
in that phrase
gave him the name
of Sadâparibhûta.

Under those circumstances,
Mahâsthâmaprâpta,
the Bodhisattva Mahâsattva
Sadâparibhûta happened
to hear this Dharmaparyâya
of the Lotus of the True Law
when the end of his life
was impending,
and the moment
of dying drawing near.
It was the Lord
Bhîshmagargitasvararâga,
the Tathâgata, &c.,
who expounded
this Dharmaparyâya
in twenty times twenty
hundred thousand myriads
of kotis of stanzas,
which the Bodhisattva
Mahâsattva Sadâparibhûta
heard from a voice in the sky,
when the time of his death
was near at hand.
On hearing
that voice from the sky,
without there appearing
a person speaking,
he grasped
this Dharmaparyâya
and obtained the perfections

already mentioned :
the perfection of sight,
hearing, smell, taste,
body, and mind.
With the attainment
of these perfections
he at the same time
made a vow to prolong his life
for twenty hundred thousand
myriads of kotis of years,
and promulgated
this Dharmaparyâya
of the Lotus of the True Law.
And all those proud beings,
monks, nuns,
male and female lay devotees
to whom he had said :
I do not contemn you,
and who had given him
the name of Sadâparibhûta,
became all his followers
to hear the law,
after they had seen the power
and strength of his sublime
magic faculties, of his vow,
of his readiness of wit,
of his wisdom.
All those and many hundred
thousand myriads of kotis
of other beings were by him
roused to supreme,
perfect enlightenment.

Afterwards,
Mahâsthâmaprâpta, that
Bodhisattva Mahâsattva
disappeared from that place
and propitiated
twenty hundred kotis
of Tathâgatas, &c.,
all bearing the same name

of Kandraprabhâsvararâga,
under all of whom
he promulgated
this Dharmaparyâya.
By virtue of his previous
root of goodness he,
in course of time,
propitiated twenty hundred
thousand myriads
of kotis of Tathâgatas, &c.,
all bearing the name
of Dundubhisvararâga,
and under all he obtained
this very Dharmaparyâya
of the Lotus of the True Law
and promulgated it
to the four classes.
By virtue of his previous
root of goodness he again,
in course of time,
propitiated twenty
hundred thousand myriads
of kotis of Tathâgatas, &c.,
all bearing the name
of Meghasvararâga,
and under all he obtained
this very Dharmaparyâya
of the Lotus of the True Law
and promulgated it
to the four classes.
And under all of them
he was possessed
of the afore-mentioned
perfectness of sight, hearing,
smell, taste, body, and mind.

Now, Mahâsthâmaprâpta,
that Bodhisattva
Mahâsattva Sadâparibhûta,
after having honoured,
respected, esteemed,

worshipped, venerated, revered so many hundred thousand myriads of kotis of Tathâgatas, and after having acted in the same way towards many hundred thousand myriads of kotis of other Buddhas, obtained under all of them this very Dharmaparyâya of the Lotus of the True Law, and owing to his former root of goodness having come to full development, gained supreme, perfect enlightenment. Perhaps, Mahâsthâmaprâpta, thou wilt have some doubt, uncertainty, or misgiving, and think that he who at that time, at that juncture was the Bodhisattva Mahâsattva called Sadâparibhûta was one, and he who under the rule of that Lord Bhîshmagargitasvararâga, the Tathâgata, &c., was generally called Sadâparibhûta by the four classes, by whom so many Tathâgatas were propitiated, was another. But thou shouldst not think so. For it is myself who at that time, at that juncture was the Bodhisattva Mahâsattva Sadâparibhûta. Had I not formerly grasped and kept this Dharmaparyâya, Mahâsthâmaprâpta, I should not so soon have arrived at supreme, perfect enlightenment. It is because I have kept, read, preached this Dharmaparyâya derived from the teaching of the ancient Tathâgatas, &c., Mahâsthâmaprâpta, that I have so soon arrived at supreme, perfect enlightenment. As to the hundreds of monks, nuns, male and female lay devotees, Mahâsthâmaprâpta, to whom under that Lord the Bodhisattva Mahâsattva Sadâparibhûta promulgated this Dharmaparyâya by saying : I do not contemn you ; you all observe the course of duty of Bodhisattvas ; you are to become Tathâgatas, &c., and in whom awoke a feeling of malignity towards that Bodhisattva, they in twenty hundred thousand myriads of kotis of Æons never saw a Tathâgata, nor heard the call of the law, nor the call of the assembly, and for ten thousand Æons they suffered terrible pain in the great hell Avîki.

Thereafter released from the ban, they by the instrumentality of that Bodhisattva Mahâsattva were all brought to full ripeness for supreme, perfect enlightenment. Perhaps, Mahâsthâmaprâpta, thou wilt have some doubt, uncertainty, or misgiving as to who at that time, at that juncture were the persons hooting and laughing at the Bodhisattva Mahâsattva. They are, in this very assembly, the five hundred Bodhisattvas headed by Bhadrapâla, the five hundred nuns following Simhakandrâ, the five hundred lay devotees following Sugataketanâ, who all of them have been rendered inflexible in supreme, perfect enlightenment. So greatly useful it is to keep and preach this Dharmaparyâya, as it tends to result for Bodhisattvas Mahâsattvas in supreme, perfect enlightenment. Hence, Mahâsthâmaprâpta, the Bodhisattvas Mahâsattvas should, after the complete extinction of the Tathâgata, constantly keep, read, and promulgate this Dharmaparyâya.

And on that occasion the Lord uttered the following stanzas :

1.
I remember a past period, when king Bhîshmasvara, the Gina, lived, very mighty, and revered by gods and men, the leader of men, gods, goblins, and giants.

2.
At the time succeeding the complete extinction of that Gina, when the decay of the true law was far advanced, there was a monk, a Bodhisattva, called by the name of Sadâparibhûta.

3.
Other monks and nuns who did not believe but in what they saw, he would approach and say : I never am to contemn you, for you observe the course leading to supreme enlightenment.

4.
It was his wont always to utter those words, which brought him but abuse and taunts from their part. At the time when his death was impending he heard this Sûtra.

5.
The sage, then,
did not expire;
he resolved upon
a very long life,
and promulgated this Sûtra
under the rule of that leader.

6.
And those many persons
who only acknowledged
the evidence
of sensual perception
were by him brought
to full ripeness
for enlightenment.
Then,
disappearing from that place,
he propitiated thousands
of kotis of Buddhas.

7.
Owing to the successive
good actions
performed by him,
and to his constantly
promulgating this Sûtra,
that son of Gina
reached enlightenment.
That Bodhisattva
then is myself, Sâkyamuni.

8.
And those persons
who only believed
in perception by the senses,
those monks, nuns,
male and female lay devotees
who by the sage
were admonished
of enlightenment,

9.
And who have seen
many kotis of Buddhas,
are the monks
here before me,
- no less than five hundred, -
nuns,
and female lay devotees.

10.
All of them
have been by me brought
to complete ripeness,
and after my extinction
they will all, full of wisdom,
keep this Sûtra.

11.
Not once in many,
inconceivably
many kotis of Æons
has such a Sûtra
as this been heard.
There are, indeed,
hundreds of kotis
of Buddhas,
but they do not
elucidate this Sûtra.

12.
Therefore let one who
has heard this law exposed
by the Self-born himself,
and who has repeatedly
propitiated him,
promulgate this Sûtra
after my extinction
in this world.

Chapter XX
Conception of the Transcendent Power of the Tathâgatas

Thereupon those hundred thousands of myriads of kotis of Bodhisattvas equal to the dust-atoms of a macrocosm, who had issued from the gaps of the earth, all stretched their joined hands towards the Lord, and said unto him : We, O Lord, will, after the complete extinction of the Tathâgata, promulgate this Dharmaparyâya everywhere on every occasion in all Buddha-fields of the Lord, wherever or whenever the Lord shall be completely extinct. We are anxious to obtain this sublime Dharmaparyâya, O Lord, in order to keep, read, publish, and write it.

Thereupon the hundred thousands of myriads of kotis of Bodhisattvas, headed by Mañgusrî ; the monks, nuns, male and female lay devotees living in this world ; the gods, Nâgas, goblins, Gandharvas, demons, Garudas, Kinnaras, great serpents, men, and beings not human, and the many Bodhisattvas Mahâsattvas equal to the sands of the river Ganges, said unto the Lord :
We also, O Lord, will promulgate this Dharmaparyâya after the complete extinction of the Tathâgata. While standing with an invisible body in the sky, O Lord, we will send forth a voice, and plant the roots of goodness of such creatures as have not yet planted roots of goodness.

Then the Lord addressed the Bodhisattva Mahâsattva Visishtakâritra, followed by a troop, a great troop, the master of a troop, who was the very first of those afore-mentioned Bodhisattvas Mahâsattvas followed by a troop, a great troop, masters of a troop :
Very well, Visishtakâritra, very well ; so you should do ; it is for the sake of this Dharmaparyâya that the Tathâgata has brought you to ripeness.

Thereupon the Lord Sâkyamuni,

the Tathâgata, &c.,
and the wholly extinct
Lord Prabhûtaratna,
the Tathâgata, &c.,
both seated on the throne
in the centre of the Stûpa,
commenced smiling
to one another,
and from their
opened mouths stretched
out their tongues,
so that with their tongues
they reached
the Brahma-world,
and from those two tongues
issued many hundred
thousand myriads
of kotis of rays.
From each of those rays
issued many hundred
thousand myriads
of kotis of Bodhisattvas,
with gold-coloured bodies
and possessed of the
thirty-two characteristic signs
of a great man, and
seated on thrones consisting
of the interior of lotuses.
Those Bodhisattvas spread
in all directions in hundred
thousands of worlds,
and while on every side
stationed in the sky
preached the law.
Just as the Lord Sâkyamuni,
the Tathâgata, &c.,
produced a miracle of magic
by his tongue, so, too,
Prabhûtaratna,
the Tathâgata, &c.,
and the other Tathâgatas, &c.,
who, having flocked
from hundred thousands
of myriads of kotis
of other worlds,
were seated on thrones
at the foot of jewel trees,
by their tongues produced
a miracle of magic.

The Lord Sâkyamuni,
the Tathâgata, &c.,
and all those Tathâgatas, &c.,
produced that magical effect
during fully a thousand years.
After the lapse
of that millennium
those Tathâgatas, &c.,
pulled back their tongue,
and all simultaneously,
at the same moment,
the same instant,
made a great noise
as of expectoration
and of snapping the fingers,
by which sounds
all the hundred thousands
of myriads of kotis
of Buddha-fields
in every direction of space
were moved, removed,
stirred, wholly stirred,
tossed, tossed forward,
tossed along, and all beings
in all those Buddha-fields,
gods, Nâgas, goblins,
Gandharvas, demons,
Garudas, Kinnaras,
great serpents, men,
and beings not human beheld,
by the power of the Buddha,
from the place

where they stood,
this Saha-world.
They beheld
the hundred thousands
of myriads of kotis
of Tathâgatas
seated severally
on their throne
at the foot of a jewel tree,
and the Lord Sâkyamuni,
the Tathâgata, &c.,
and the Lord Prabhûtaratna,
the Tathâgata, &c.,
wholly extinct,
sitting on the throne
in the centre of the Stûpa
of magnificent
precious substances,
along with
the Lord Sâkyamuni,
the Tathâgata, &c. ;
they beheld, finally,
those four classes
of the audience.
At this sight they felt struck
with wonder,
amazement, and rapture.
And they heard a voice
from the sky calling :
Worthies,
beyond a distance
of an immense,
incalculable number
of hundred thousands
of myriads of kotis of worlds
there is the world named Saha ;
there the Tathâgata
called Sâkyamuni,
the Arhat, &c.,
is just now revealing to
the Bodhisattvas Mahâsattvas
the Dharmaparyâya
of the Lotus of the True Law,
a Sûtrânta of great extent,
serving to instruct
Bodhisattvas,
and belonging in proper
to all Buddhas.
Ye accept it joyfully
with all your heart,
and do homage
to the Lord Sâkyamuni,
the Tathâgata, &c.,
and the Lord Prabhûtaratna,
the Tathâgata, &c.

On hearing such a voice
from the sky all those beings
exclaimed from the place
where they stood,
with joined hands :
Homage
to the Lord Sâkyamuni,
the Tathâgata.
Then they threw
towards the Saha-world
various flowers, incense,
fragrant wreaths,
ointment, gold, cloth,
umbrellas, flags, banners,
and triumphal streamers,
as well as ornaments,
parures, necklaces,
gems and jewels of all sorts,
in order to worship
the Lord Sâkyamuni,
the Tathâgata,
and this Dharmaparyâya
of the Lotus of the True Law.
Those flowers, incense, &c.,
and those necklaces, &c.,
came down upon

this Saha-world,
where they formed
a great canopy of flowers
hanging in the sky
above the Tathâgatas
there sitting,
as well as those
in the hundred thousands
of myriads of kotis
of other worlds.

Thereupon
the Lord addressed
the Bodhisattvas Mahâsattvas
headed by Visishtakâritra :
Inconceivable,
young men of good family,
is the power
of the Tathâgatas, &c.
In order to transmit
this Dharmaparyâya,
young men of good family,
I might go on for hundred
thousands of myriads
of kotis of Æons explaining
the manifold virtues
of this Dharmaparyâya
through the different
principles of the law,
without reaching the end
of those virtues.
In this Dharmaparyâya
I have succinctly taught
all Buddha-laws
or Buddha-qualities,
all the superiority,
all the mystery,
all the profound conditions
of the Buddhas.
Therefore,
young men of good family,
you should,
after the complete extinction
of the Tathâgata,
with reverence keep, read,
promulgate, cherish,
worship it.
And wherever on earth,
young men of good family,
this Dharmaparyâya
shall be made known,
read, written, meditated,
expounded, studied
or collected into a volume,
be it in a monastery or at home,
in the wilderness or in a town,
at the foot of a tree
or in a palace,
in a building or in a cavern,
on that spot one should erect
a shrine in dedication
to the Tathâgata.
For such a spot
must be regarded
as a terrace of enlightenment ;
such a spot
must be regarded as one
where all Tathâgatas &c.
have arrived at supreme,
perfect enlightenment ;
on that spot have
all Tathâgatas moved forward
the wheel of the law ;
on that spot one may hold that
all Tathâgatas have reached
complete extinction.

And on that occasion
the Lord uttered
the following stanzas :

1.
Inconceivable is the power to
promote the weal of the world
possessed by those who,
firmly established
in transcendent knowledge,
by means
of their unlimited sight
display their magic faculty
in order to gladden
all living beings on earth.

2.
They extend their tongue
over the whole world,
darting thousands of beams
to the astonishment of those
to whom this effect of magic
is displayed
and who are making
for supreme enlightenment.

3.
The Buddhas
made a noise of expectoration
and of snapping the fingers,
and by it called the attention
of the whole world,
of all parts of the world
in the ten directions of space.

4.
Those and other miraculous
qualities they display
in their benevolence and
compassion with the view
that the creatures,
gladly excited at the time,
may also keep the Sûtra
after the complete
extinction of the Sugata.

5.
Even if I continued
for thousands
of kotis of Æons
speaking the praise
of those sons of Sugata
who shall keep
this eminent Sûtra
after the extinction
of the Leader of the world,

6.
I should not have terminated
the enumeration
of their qualities ;
inconceivable as the qualities
of infinite space are the merits
of those who constantly
keep this holy Sûtra.

7.
They behold me
as well as these chiefs,
and the Leader of the world
now extinct ;
they behold all
these numerous Bodhisattvas
and the four classes.

8.
Such a one now here
propitiates me
and all these leaders,
as well as the extinct
chief of Ginas and
the others in every quarter.

9.
The future and past Buddhas stationed
in the ten points of space
will all be seen
and worshipped
by him who keeps this Sûtra.

10.
He who keeps this Sûtra,
the veritable law,
will fathom the mystery
of the highest man ;
will soon comprehend
what truth it was
that was arrived at
on the terrace
of enlightenment.

11.
The quickness
of his apprehension
will be unlimited ;
like the wind he will
nowhere meet impediments ;
he knows the purport
and interpretation of the law,
he who keeps
this exalted Sûtra.

12.
He will, after some reflection,
always find out
the connection of the Sûtras
spoken by the leaders ;
even after the complete
extinction of the leader
he will grasp the real meaning
of the Sûtras.

13.
He resembles
the moon and the sun ;
he illuminates all around him,
and while roaming the earth
in different directions
he rouses many Bodhisattvas.

14.
The wise Bodhisattvas who,
after hearing the enumeration
of such advantages,
shall keep this Sûtra
after my complete extinction
will doubtless
reach enlightenment.

Chapter XXI
Spells

Thereupon the Bodhisattva Mahâsattva Bhaishagyarâga rose from his seat, and having put his upper robe upon one shoulder and fixed the right knee upon the ground lifted his joined hands up to the Lord and said : How great, O Lord, is the pious merit which will be produced by a young man of good family or a young lady who keeps this Dharmaparyâya of the Lotus of the True Law, either in memory or in a book ? Whereupon the Lord said to the Bodhisattva Mahâsattva Bhaishagyarâga : Suppose, Bhaishagyarâga, that some man of good family or a young lady honours, respects, reveres, worships hundred thousands of myriads of kotis of Tathâgatas equal to the sands of eighty Ganges rivers ; dost thou think, Bhaishagyarâga, that such a young man or young lady of good family will on that account produce much pious merit ?

The Bodhisattva Bhaishagyarâga replied : Yes, Lord ; yes, Sugata. The Lord said : I announce to thee, Bhaishagyarâga, I declare to thee : any young man or young lady of good family, Bhaishagyarâga, who shall keep, read, comprehend, and in practice follow, were it but a single stanza from this Dharmaparyâya of the Lotus of the True Law, that young man or young lady of good family, Bhaishagyarâga, will on that account produce far more pious merit.

Then the Bodhisattva Mahâsattva Bhaishagyarâga immediately said to the Lord : To those young men or young ladies of good family, O Lord, who keep this Dharmaparyâya of the Lotus of the True Law in their memory or in a book, we will give talismanic words for guard, defence, and protection ; such as, anye manye mane mamane kitte karite same, samitâvi, sânte, mukte, muktatame, same avishame, samasame, gaye, kshaye, akshine, sânte sanî, dhârani âlokabhâshe,

pratyavekshani, nidhini,
abhyantaravisishte,
utkule mutkule,
asade, parade,
sukânkshî, asamasame,
buddhavilokite,
dharmaparikshite,
sanghanirghoshani,
nirghoshanî
bhayâbhayasodhanî,
mantre mantrâkshayate,
rutakausalye, akshaye,
akshavanatâya,
vakule valoda,
amanyatâya.
These words
of charms and spells,
O Lord,
have been pronounced
by reverend Buddhas
in number equal to the sands
of sixty-two Ganges rivers.
All these Buddhas
would be offended
by any one who
would attack such preachers,
such keepers of the Sûtrânta.

The Lord
expressed his approval
to the Bodhisattva Mahâsattva
Bhaishagyarâga by saying :
Very well, Bhaishagyarâga,
by those talismanic words
being pronounced
out of compassion
for creatures,
the common weal
of creatures is promoted ;
their guard, defence,
and protection is secured.

Thereupon the Bodhisattva
Mahâsattva Pradânasûra
said unto the Lord :
I also, O Lord, will,
for the benefit
of such preachers,
give them talismanic words,
that no one seeking
for an occasion to surprise
such preachers
may find the occasion,
be it a demon, giant, goblin,
sorcerer, imp or ghost ;
that none of these
when seeking and spying
for an occasion to surprise
may find the occasion.
And then
the Bodhisattva Mahâsattva
Pradânasûra instantly
pronounced the following
words of a spell :
gvale mahâgvale,
ukke mukke, ade adâvati,
tritye trityâvati,
itini vitini kitini,
tritti trityâvati svâhâ.
These talismanic words,
O Lord,
have been pronounced
and approved
by Tathâgatas, &c.
in number equal
to the sands
of the river Ganges.
All those Tathâgatas
would be offended
by any one
who would attack
such preachers.

Thereupon Vaisravana,
one of the four rulers
of the cardinal points,
said unto the Lord :
I also, O Lord, will
pronounce talismanic words
for the benefit and weal
of those preachers,
out of compassion to them,
for their guard, defence,
and protection :
atte natte vanatte anade,
nâdi kunadi svâhâ.
With these spells, O Lord,
I shall guard those preachers
over an extent
of a hundred yoganas.
Thus will those young men or
young ladies of good family,
who keep this Sûtrânta,
be guarded, be safe.

At that meeting
was present Virûdhaka,
another of the four rulers
of the cardinal points,
sitting surrounded
and attended
by hundred thousands
of myriads of kotis
of Kumbhândas.
He rose from his seat,
put his upper robe
upon one shoulder,
lifted his joined hands
up to the Lord,
and spoke to him as follows :
I also, O Lord,
will pronounce
talismanic words
for the benefit
of people at large,
and to guard, defend,
protect such preachers
as are qualified,
who keep
the Sûtrânta mentioned ;
namely
agane gane gauri gandhâri
kandâli mâtangi pukkasi
sankule vrûsali svâhâ.
These talismanic words,
O Lord,
have been pronounced
by forty-two hundred
thousand myriads
of kotis of Buddhas.
All those Buddhas
would be offended
by any one who would attack
such preachers
as are qualified.

Thereupon the giantesses
called Lambâ, Vilam'â,
Kûtadantî, Pushpadantî,
Makutadantî, Kesinî,
Akalâ, Mâlâdhârî,
Kuntî, Sarvasattvogahârî,
and Hârîtî,
all with their children
and suite went up to the place
where the Lord was,
and with one voice
said unto him :
We also, O Lord,
will afford guard,
defence, and protection
to such preachers
as keep this Sûtrânta ;
we will afford them safety,

that no one
seeking for an occasion
to surprise those preachers
may find the occasion.
And the giantesses
all simultaneously
and in a chorus
gave to the Lord
the following words of spells :
iti me, iti me, iti me,
iti me, iti me ;
nime nime nime nime nime ;
ruhe ruhe ruhe ruhe ruhe ;
stuhe stuhe stuhe stuhe
stuhe, svâhâ.
No one shall overpower
and hurt such preachers ;
no goblin, giant, ghost,
devil, imp, sorcerer,
spectre, gnome ;
no spirit causing epilepsy,
no sorcerer of goblin race,
no sorcerer
of not-human race,
no sorcerer of human race ;
no sorcerer producing
tertian ague,
quartian ague,
quotidian ague.
Even if in his dreams
he has visions of women,
men, boys or girls,
it shall be impossible
that they hurt him.

And the giantesses
simultaneously
and in a chorus
addressed the Lord
with the following stanzas :

1.
His head shall be split
into seven pieces,
like a sprout
of Symplocos Racemosa,
who after hearing this spell
would attack a preacher.

2.
He shall go the way
of parricides and matricides,
who would attack a preacher.

3.
He shall go the way
of oil-millers
and sesamum-pounders,
who would attack a preacher.

4.
He shall go the way
of those who use
false weights and measures,
who would attack a preacher.

Thereafter the giantesses
headed by Kuntî
said unto the Lord :
We also, O Lord,
will afford protection
to such preachers ;
we will procure them safety ;
we will protect them
against assault and poison.
Whereupon the Lord
said to those giantesses :
Very well, sisters, very well ;
you do well
in affording guard,
defence, and protection
to those preachers,

even to such who shall keep
no more than the name
of this Dharmaparyâya ;
how much more then
to those who shall keep
this Dharmaparyâya
wholly and entirely,
or who, possessing
the text of it in a volume,
honour it with flowers,
incense, fragrant garlands,
ointment, powder, cloth,
flags, banners, lamps
with sesamum oil,
lamps with scented oil,
lamps with
Kampaka-scented oil,
with Vârshikâ scented oil,
with lotus-scented oil,
with jasmine-scented oil ;
who by such-like manifold
hundred thousand manners
of worshipping shall honour,
respect, revere,
venerate this Sûtra,
deserve to be guarded
by thee and thy suite, Kuntî !

And
while this chapter on spells
was being expounded,
sixty-eight thousand
living beings
received the faculty
of acquiescence in the law
that has no origin.

Chapter XXII
Ancient Devotion of Bhaishagyarâga

Thereupon
the Bodhisattva Mahâsattva
Nakshatrararâga-
sankusumitâbhigña
spoke to the Lord as follows :
Wherefore, O Lord,
does the Bodhisattva
Bhaishagyarâga
pursue his course
in this Saha-world,
while he is fully aware of
the many hundred thousands
of myriads of kotis
of difficulties he has to meet ?
Let the Lord,
the Tathâgata, &c.,
deign to tell us any part
of the course of duty
of the Bodhisattva Mahâsattva
Bhaishagyarâga,
that by hearing it the gods,
Nâgas, goblins, Gandharvas,
demons, Garudas, Kinnaras,
great serpents, men,
and beings not human,
as well as
the Bodhisattvas Mahâsattvas
from other worlds
here present,
and these great disciples
here may be content,
delighted, overjoyed.

And the Lord,
out of regard to that request
of the Bodhisattva Mahâsattva
Nakshatrararâga-
sankusumitâbhigña
told him the following :
Of yore,
young man of good family,
at a past epoch,
at a time as many Æons ago
as there are grains
of sand in the river Ganges,
there appeared
in the world a Tathâgata, &c.,
by the name of
Kandravimala-
sûryaprabhâsasrî ,
endowed with science
and conduct,
a Sugata, &c. &c.
Now that Tathâgata, &c.,
Kandravimala-
sûryaprabhâsasrî
had a great assembly
of eighty kotis
of Bodhisattvas Mahâsattvas
and an assembly of disciples
equal to the sands
of seventy-two Ganges rivers.
His spiritual rule was exempt
from the female sex,
and his Buddha-field
had no hell,
no brute creation,
no ghosts, no demons ;
it was level, neat, smooth
as the palm of the hand.
Its floor consisted
of heavenly lapis lazuli,
and it was adorned
with trees of jewel
and sandal-wood ;
inlaid with
a multitude of jewels,

and hung
with long bands of silk,
and scented by censors
made of jewels.
Under each jewel tree,
at a distance
not farther than a bowshot,
was made a small jewel-house,
and on the top of those
small jewel-houses stood
a hundred kotis of angels
performing a concert
of musical instruments
and castanets,
in order to honour the Lord
Kandravimala-
sûryaprabhâsasrî,
the Tathâgata, &c.,
while that Lord
was extensively expounding
this Dharmaparyâya
of the Lotus of the True Law
to the great disciples
and Bodhisattvas,
directing himself
to the Bodhisattva Mahâsattva
Sarvasattvapriyadarsana.
Now,
Nakshatrararâga-
sankusumitâbhigña,
the lifetime of that Lord
Kandravimala-
sûryaprabhâsasrî,
the Tathâgata, &c., lasted
forty-two thousand Æons,
and likewise that of
the Bodhisattvas Mahâsattvas
and great disciples.
It was under the spiritual rule
of that Lord that
the Bodhisattva Mahâsattva
Sarvasattvapriyadarsana
applied himself
to his difficult course.
He wandered twelve
thousand years strenuously
engaged in contemplation.
After the expiration of those
twelve thousand years
he acquired
the Samâdhi termed
Sarvarûpasandarsana
(i.e. the sight or display
of all forms).
No sooner had he acquired
that Samâdhi than satisfied,
glad, joyful, rejoicing,
and delighted he made
the following reflection :
It is owing
to this Dharmaparyâya
of the Lotus of the True Law
that I have acquired
the Samâdhi
of Sarvarûpasandarsana.
Then
he made another reflection :
Let me do homage to the Lord
Kandravimala-
sûryaprabhâsasrî
and this Dharmaparyâya
of the Lotus of the True Law.
No sooner had he entered
upon such a meditation
than a great rain of Mandârava
and great Mandârava flowers
fell from the upper sky.
A cloud of Kâlânusârin
sandal was formed,
and a rain of Uragasâra
sandal poured down.
And the nature of those

essences was so noble that
one karsha of it was worth
the whole Saha-world.

After a while,
Nakshatrararâga-
sankusumitâbhigña,
the Bodhisattva Mahâsattva
Sarvasattvapriyadarsana
rose from that meditation
with memory
and full consciousness,
and reflected thus :
This display of magic power
is not likely to honour
the Lord and Tathâgata
so much as the sacrifice
of my own body will do.
Then
the Bodhisattva Mahâsattva
Sarvasattvapriyadarsana
instantly began to eat
Agallochum, Olibanum,
and the resin
of Boswellia Thurifera,
and to drink
oil of Kampaka. So,
Nakshatrararâga-
sankusumitâbhigña,
the Bodhisattva Mahâsattva
Sarvasattvapriyadarsana
passed twelve years in always
and constantly eating
those fragrant substances
and drinking oil of Kampaka.
After the expiration
of those twelve years
the Bodhisattva Mahâsattva
Sarvasattvapriyadarsana
wrapped his body
in divine garments,
bathed it in oil,
made his last vow,
and thereafter
burnt his town body
with the object to pay worship
to the Tathâgata
and this Dharmaparyâya
of the Lotus of the True Law.
Then,
Nakshatrararâga-
sankusumitâbhigña,
worlds equal to
the sands of the river Ganges
were brightened
by the glare of the flames
from the blazing body of
the Bodhisattva Mahâsattva
Sarvasattvapriyadarsana,
and the eighty Lords Buddhas
equal to the sands
of the Ganges in those worlds
all shouted their applause,
and exclaimed :
Well done, well done,
young man of good family,
that is the real heroism
which the Boddhisattvas
Mahâsattvas should develop ;
that is the real worship
of the Tathâgata,
the real worship of the law.
No worshipping with flowers,
incense, fragrant wreaths,
ointment, powder, cloth,
umbrellas, flags, banners ;
no worshipping
with material gifts or with
Uragasâra sandal equals it.
This,
young man of good family,
is the sublimest gift,

higher than
the abandoning of royalty,
the abandoning
of beloved children and wife.
Sacrificing one's own body,
young man of good family,
is the most distinguished,
the chiefest, the best,
the very best,
the most sublime
worship of the law.
After
pronouncing this speech,
Nakshatrararâga-
sankusumitâbhigña,
those Lords Buddhas
were silent.

The body
of Sarvasattvapriyadarsana
continued blazing
for twelve thousand years
without ceasing to burn.
After the expiration of
those twelve thousand years
the fire was extinguished.
Then,
Nakshatrararâga-
sankusumitâbhigña,
the Bodhisattva Mahâsattva
Sarvasattvapriyadarsana,
having paid such worship
to the Tathâgata,
disappeared from that place,
and reappeared
under the spiritual reign
of that very Lord
Kandravimala-
sûryaprabhâsasrî,
the Tathâgata, &c.,
in the house

of king Vimaladattâ,
by apparitional birth,
and sitting cross-legged.
Immediately
after his appearance
the Bodhisattva Mahâsattva
Sarvasattvapriyadarsana
addressed
his father and mother
in the following stanza :

1.
This, O exalted king,
is the walk in which
I have acquired meditation ;
I have achieved
a heroical feat,
fulfilled a great vote
by sacrificing
my own dear body.

After uttering this stanza,
Nakshatrararâga-
sankusumitâbhigña,
the Bodhisattva Mahâsattva
Sarvasattvapriyadarsana
said to his father and mother :
Even now, father and mother,
the Lord Kandravimala-
sûryaprabhâsasrî ,
the Tathâgata, &c.,
is still living, existing,
staying in the world,
the Lord by worshipping
whom I have obtained the
spell of knowing all sounds
and this Dharmaparyâya
of the Lotus of the True Law,
consisting of eighty hundred
thousand myriads
of kotis of stanzas,

of a hundred Niyutas,
of Vivaras,
of a hundred Vivaras, which
I have heard from that Lord.
Therefore, father and mother,
I should like
to go to that Lord
and worship him again.
Instantaneously,
Nakshatrararâga-
sankusumitâbhigña,
the Bodhisattva Mahâsattva
Sarvasattvapriyadarsana
rose seven tâlas high
into the sky
and sat cross-legged
on the top of a tower
of seven precious substances.
So he went up
to the presence of that Lord,
and having approached him
humbly saluted him,
circumambulated him
seven times from left to right,
stretched the joined hands
towards the Lord,
and after thus paying
his homage addressed him
with the following stanza :

2.
O thou whose face
is so spotless and bright ;
thou, king and sage !
How thy lustre sparkles
in all quarters !
After having anciently
paid thee homage,
O Sugata,
I now come again
to behold thee, O Lord.

Having pronounced this stanza,
the Bodhisattva Mahâsattva
Sarvasattvapriyadarsana
said to the Lord
Kandravimala-
sûryaprabhâsasrî ,
the Tathâgata, &c. :
Thou art then still alive,
Lord ?
Whereon the Lord
Kandravimala-
sûryaprabhâsasrî,
the Tathâgata, &c.,
replied : The time
of my final extinction,
young man of good family,
has arrived ; the time
of my death has arrived.
Therefore,
young man of good family,
prepare my couch ;
I am going to enter
complete extinction.
Then,
Nakshatrararâga-
sankusumitâbhigña,
the Lord
Kandravimala-
sûryaprabhâsasrî
said to
the Bodhisattva Mahâsattva
Sarvasattvapriyadarsana :
I entrust to thee,
young man of good family,
my commandment ;
I entrust to thee these
Bodhisattvas Mahâsattvas,
these great disciples,
this Buddha-enlightenment,
this world, these jewel cars,

these jewel trees,
and these angels,
my servitors.
I entrust to thee also,
young man of good family,
my relics
after my complete extinction.
Thou shouldst pay
a great worship to my relics,
young man of good family,
and also distribute them
and build
many thousands of Stûpas.
And,
Nakshatrararâga-
sankusumitâbhigña,
after the Lord
Kandravimala-
sûryaprabhâsasrî,
the Tathâgata, &c.,
had given
these instructions
to the Bodhisattva Mahâsattva
Sarvasattvapriyadarsana
he in the last watch of the night
entered absolute
final extinction.

Thereupon,
Nakshatrararâga-
sankusumitâbhigña,
the Bodhisattva Mahâsattva
Sarvasattvapriyadarsana,
perceiving that the Lord
Kandravimala-
sûryaprabhâsasrî,
the Tathâgata, &c.,
had expired,
made a pyre
of Uragasâra sandal-wood
and burnt the body
of the Tathâgata.
When he saw
that the body
was burnt to ashes
and the fire extinct,
he took the bones and wept,
cried and lamented.
After having wept,
cried and lamented,
Nakshatrararâga-
sankusumitâbhigña,
the Bodhisattva Mahâsattva
Sarvasattvapriyadarsana
caused to be made
eighty-four thousand urns
of seven precious substances,
deposed in them
the bones of the Tathâgata,
founded eighty-four
thousand Stûpas,
reaching in height
to the Brahma-world,
adorned
with a row of umbrellas,
and equipped
with silk bands and bells.
After founding those Stûpas
he made
the following reflection :
I have paid honour
to the Tathâgata-relics
of the Lord
Kandravimala-
sûryaprabhâsasrî,
but I will pay to those relics
a yet loftier and most
distinguished honour.
Then,
Nakshatrararâga-
sankusumitâbhigña,
the Bodhisattva Mahâsattva

Sarvasattvapriyadarsana
addressed that entire
assembly of Bodhisattvas,
those great disciples,
those gods, Nâgas, goblins,
Gandharvas, demons,
Garudas, Kinnaras,
great serpents,
men, and beings not human :
Ye all,
young men of good family,
unanimously vow
to pay worship
to the relics of the Lord.
Immediately after,
Nakshatrararâga-
sankusumitâbhigña,
the Bodhisattva Mahâsattva
Sarvasattvapriyadarsana,
in presence of those
eighty-four thousand Stûpas,
burnt his own arm
which was marked
by the one hundred
auspicious signs,
and so paid worship
to those Stûpas
containing the relics
of the Tathâgata,
during seventy-two
thousand years.
And while paying worship,
he educated countless
hundred thousands
of myriads of kotis of disciples
from that assembly,
in consequence whereof
all those Bodhisattvas
acquired the Samâdhi
termed Sarvarûpasandarsana.

Then,
Nakshatrararâga-
sankusumitâbhigña,
the entire assembly
of Bodhisattvas
and all great disciples,
seeing
the Bodhisattva Mahâsattva
Sarvasattvapriyadarsana
deprived of a limb,
said, with tears in their eyes,
weeping, crying, lamenting :
The Bodhisattva Mahâsattva
Sarvasattvapriyadarsana,
our master and instructor,
is now deprived of a limb,
deprived of one arm.
But
the Bodhisattva Mahâsattva
Sarvasattvapriyadarsana
addressed
those Bodhisattvas,
great disciples, and angels
in the following terms :
Do not,
young men of good family,
weep, cry, lament
at the sight of my being
deprived of one arm.
All the Lords Buddhas
who be, exist,
live in the endless,
limitless worlds
in every direction of space,
have I taken to witness.
Before their face
have I pronounced
a vow of truth,
and by that truth,
by that word of truth shall I,
after the sacrifice

Bhaishagyarâga 323

of my own arm
in honour of the Tathâgata,
have a body of gold colour.
By this truth,
by this word of truth
let this arm of mine
become such as it was before,
and let the great earth
shake in six different ways,
and let the angels in the sky
pour down a rain of flowers.
No sooner,
Nakshatrararâga-
sankusumitâbhigña,
had the Bodhisattva
Mahâsattva
Sarvasattvapriyadarsana
made that vow of truth,
than the whole
triple macrocosm
was shaken
in six different ways,
and from the sky aloft
fell a great rain of flowers.
The arm
of the Bodhisattva Mahâsattva
Sarvasattvapriyadarsana
became again as it was before,
and that
by the power of knowledge
and by the power
of pious merit
belonging to that
Bodhisattva Mahâsattva.
Perhaps,
Nakshatrararâga-
sankusumitâbhigña,
thou wilt have some doubt,
uncertainty or misgiving,
and think that
the Bodhisattva Mahâsattva
Sarvasattvapriyadarsana
at that time, and that epoch,
was another.
But do not think so ;
for the Bodhisattva
Mahâsattva Bhaishagyarâga
here was at that time,
and that epoch,
the Bodhisattva Mahâsattva
Sarvasattvapriyadarsana.
So many hundred thousand
myriads of kotis
of difficult things,
Nakshatrararâga-
sankusumitâbhigña,
and sacrifices of his body
does this
Bodhisattva Mahâsattva
Sarvasattvapriyadarsana
accomplish.
Now,
Nakshatrararâga-
sankusumitâbhigña,
the young man or young lady
of good family striving
in the Bodhisattva-vehicle
towards the goal
and longing for supreme,
perfect enlightenment,
who at the Tathâgata-shrines
shall burn a great toe, a finger,
a toe, or a whole limb,
such a young man
or young lady of good family,
I assure thee,
shall produce
far more pious merit,
far more than results
from giving up a kingdom,
sons, daughters, and wives,
the whole triple world

with its woods, oceans, mountains, springs, streams, tanks, wells, and gardens. And, Nakshatrararâga-sankusumitâbhigña, the young man or young lady of good family, striving in the Bodhisattva-vehicle for the goal, who after filling with the seven precious substances this whole triple world should give it in alms to all Buddhas, Bodhisattvas, disciples, Pratyekabuddhas, that young man or young lady of good family, Nakshatrararâga-sankusumitâbhigña, does not produce so much pious merit as a young man or young lady of good family who shall keep, were it but a single verse from this Dharmaparyâya of the Lotus of the True Law. I positively declare that the accumulation of merit of the latter is greater than if a person, after filling the whole triple world with the seven precious substances, bestows it in alms on all Buddhas, Bodhisattvas, disciples, or Pratyekabuddhas.

Just as the great ocean, Nakshatrararâga-sankusumitâbhigña, surpasses all springs, streams, and tanks, so, Nakshatrararâga-sankusumitâbhigña, this Dharmaparyâya of the Lotus of the True Law surpasses all Sûtras spoken by the Tathâgata. just as the Sumeru, the king of mountains, Nakshatrararâga-sankusumitâbhigña, all elevations at the cardinal points, horizon circles and great horizons, So, Nakshatrararâga-sankusumitâbhigña, this Dharmaparyâya of the Lotus of the True Law surpasses as a king all the Sûtrântas spoken by the Tathâgata. As the moon, Nakshatrararâga-sankusumitâbhigña, as a luminary, takes the first rank amongst the whole of the asterisms, so, Nakshatrararâga-sankusumitâbhigña, this Dharmaparyâya of the Lotus of the True Law ranks first amongst all Sûtrântas spoken by the Tathâgata,

though it surpasses
hundred thousands
of myriads of kotis of moons.
As the orb of the sun,
Nakshatrararâga-
sankusumitâbhigña,
dispels gloomy darkness,
so,
Nakshatrararâga-
sankusumitâbhigña,
this Dharmaparyâya
of the Lotus of the True Law
dispels all the gloomy
darkness of unholy works.
As Indra,
Nakshatrararâga-
sankusumitâbhigña,
is the chief of the gods
of paradise,
so,
Nakshatrararâga-
sankusumitâbhigña,
this Dharmaparyâya
of the Lotus of the True Law
is the chief of Sûtrântas
spoken by the Tathâgata.
As Brahma Sahâmpati,
Nakshatrararâga-
sankusumitâbhigña,
is the king
of all Brahmakâyika gods
and exercises the function of
a father in the Brahma world,
so,
Nakshatrararâga-
sankusumitâbhigña,
this Dharmaparyâya
of the Lotus of the True Law
exercises the function
of a father to all beings,
whether under training

or past it,
to all disciples,
Pratyekabuddhas,
and those who
in the Bodhisattva-vehicle
are striving for the goal.
As the Srotaâpanna,
Nakshatrararâga-
sankusumitâbhigña,
as well as the Sakridâgâmin,
Anâgâmin,
Arhat, and Pratyekabuddha,
excels the ignorant people
and the profanum vulgus,
so,
Nakshatrararâga-
sankusumitâbhigña,
the Dharmaparyâya
of the Lotus of the True Law
must be held to excel
and surpass all Sûtrântas
spoken by the Tathâgata ;
and such as shall keep
this king of Sûtras,
Nakshatrararâga-
sankusumitâbhigña,
must be held to surpass
others who do not.
As a Bodhisattva
is accounted superior
to all disciples
and Pratyekabuddhas,
so,
Nakshatrararâga-
sankusumitâbhigña,
this Dharmaparyâya
of the Lotus of the True Law
is accounted superior
to all Sûtrântas
spoken by the Tathâgata.
Even as the Tathâgata

is the crowned king
of the law of all disciples,
Pratyekabuddhas,
and Bodhisattvas,
so,
Nakshatrararâga-
sankusumitâbhigña,
this Dharmaparyâya
is a Tathâgata
in respect to those who
in the vehicle of Bodhisattvas
are striving to reach the goal.
This Dharmaparyâya
of the Lotus of the True Law,
Nakshatrararâga-
sankusumitâbhigña,
saves all beings from all fear,
delivers them from all pains.
It is like a tank for the thirsty,
like a fire for those
who suffer from cold,
like a garment for the naked,
like the caravan leader
for the merchants,
like a mother for her children,
like a boat
for those who ferry over,
like a leech for the sick,
like a lamp for those
who are wrapt in darkness,
like a jewel
for those who want wealth,
like the ocean for the rivers,
like a torch
for the dispelling of darkness.
So,
Nakshatrararâga-
sankusumitâbhigña,
this Dharmaparyâya
of the Lotus of the True Law
delivers from all evils,
extirpates all diseases,
releases
from the narrow bonds
of the mundane whirl.
And he who shall hear
this Dharmaparyâya
of the Lotus of the True Law,
who shall write it
and cause it to be written,
will produce an accumulation
of pious merit
the term of which
is not to be arrived at
even by Buddha-knowledge;
so great is the accumulation
of pious merit that will
be produced by a young man
of good family or a young
lady who after teaching
or learning it,
writing it or having it
collected into a volume,
shall honour,
respect, venerate,
worship it with flowers,
incense, fragrant garlands,
ointment, powder,
umbrellas, flags, banners,
triumphal streamers,
with music,
with joining of hands,
with lamps burning
with ghee, scented oil,
Kampaka oil, jasmine oil,
trumpet-flower oil,
Vârshikâ oil
or double jasmine oil.

Great will be the pious merit,
Nakshatrararâga-
sankusumitâbhigña,

to be produced by
a young man of good family
or a young lady
striving to reach the goal
in the Bodhisattva-vehicle,
who shall keep this chapter
of the Ancient Devotion
of Bhaishagyarâga,
who shall read and learn it.
And, Nakshatrarâga,
should a female,
after hearing
this Dharmaparyâya,
grasp and keep it,
then this existence
will be her last existence
as a woman.
Any female,
Nakshatrararâga-
sankusumitâbhigña,
who
in the last five hundred years
of the millennium
shall hear and penetrate
this chapter
of the Ancient Devotion
of Bhaishagyarâga,
will after disappearing
from earth be reborn
in the world Sukhâvatî,
where the Lord Amitâyus,
the Tathâgata, &c.,
dwells, exists,
lives surrounded
by a host of Bodhisattvas.
There will he who formerly
was a female appear seated
on a throne consisting
of the interior of a lotus ;
no affection, no hatred,
no infatuation, no pride,
no envy, no wrath,
no malignity will vex him.
With his birth
he will also receive the five
transcendent faculties,
as well as the acquiescence
in the eternal law, and,
once in possession thereof,
Nakshatrararâga-
sankusumitâbhigña, he
as a Bodhisattva Mahâsattva
will see Tathâgatas
equal to the sands
of seventy-two rivers Ganges.
So perfect will be
his organ of sight
that by means thereof
he shall see
those Lords Buddhas,
which Lords Buddhas
will applaud him and say :
Well done, well done,
young man of good family,
that after hearing
this Dharmaparyâya
of the Lotus of the True Law
which has been promulgated
by the spiritual proclamation
of the Lord Sâkyamuni,
the Tathâgata, &c.,
thou hast studied, meditated,
examined, minded it, and
expounded it to other beings,
other persons.
This accumulation
of thy pious merit,
young man of good family,
cannot be burnt by fire,
nor swept away by water.
Even a thousand Buddhas
would not be able

to determine
this accumulation
of thy pious merit,
young man of good family.
Thou hast subdued
the opposition of the Evil One,
young man of good family.
Thou,
young man of good family,
hast victoriously
emerged from the battle
of mundane existence,
hast crushed the enemies
annoying thee.
Thou,
young man of good family,
hast been superintended
by thousands of Buddhas ;
thine equal,
young man of good family,
is not to be found
in the world,
including the gods,
with the only exception
of the Tathâgata ;
there is no other,
be he disciple,
Pratyekabuddha,
or Bodhisattva,
able to surpass thee
in pious merit, knowledge,
wisdom or meditation.
Such a power of knowledge,
Nakshatrararâga-
sankusumitâbhigña,
will be acquired
by that Bodhisattva.

Any one,
Nakshatrararâga-
sankusumitâbhigña,
who on hearing this chapter
of the ancient devotion of
Bhaishagyarâga approves it,
will emit from his mouth
a breath sweet as of the lotus,
and from his limbs
a fragrance as of sandal-wood.
Such temporal advantages
as I have just now indicated
will belong to him
who approves
this Dharmaparyâya.
On that account then,
Nakshatrararâga-
sankusumitâbhigña,
I transmit to thee this chapter
of the Ancient Devotion
of the Bodhisattva Mahâsattva
Sarvasattvapriyadarsana,
that at the end of time,
the last period,
in the latter half
of the millennium
it may have course here
in Gambudvîpa
and not be lost ;
that neither Mâra the Fiend,
nor the celestial beings
called Mârakâyikas,
Nâgas, goblins, imps may find
the opportunity of hurting it.
Therefore,
Nakshatrararâga-
sankusumitâbhigña,
I bequeath this
Dharmaparyâya ; it is to be
like a medicament for sick
and suffering creatures
in Gambudvîpa.
No sickness shall overpower
him who has heard

this Dharmaparyâya,
no decrepitude,
no untimely death.
Whenever a person
striving to reach the goal
in the vehicle of Bodhisattvas
happens to see such a monk
as keeps this Sûtrânta,
then he should strew him
with sandal-powder
and blue lotuses,
and reflect thus :
This young man
of good family
is going to reach
the terrace
of enlightenment ;
he will spread
the bundle of grass
on the terrace
of enlightenment ;
he will put to flight
the party of Mâra,
blow the conch trumpet
of the law,
beat the drum of the law,
cross the ocean of existence.
Thus,
Nakshatrararâga-
sankusumitâbhigña,
should a young man
of good family,
striving to reach the goal
in the vehicle of Bodhisattva,
reflect when seeing a monk
who keeps this Sûtra,
and he will acquire
such advantages
as have been indicated
by the Tathâgata.

While this chapter
of the Ancient Devotion
of Bhaishagyarâga
was being expounded,
eighty-four
thousand Bodhisattvas
attained the spell
connected with
skill in all sounds.
And the Lord Prabhûtaratna,
the Tathâgata, &c.,
intimated his approval
by saying :
Well done, well done,
Nakshatrararâga-
sankusumitâbhigña ;
thou hast done well
in thus questioning
the Tathâgata,
who is endowed
with such inconceivable
qualities and properties.

Chapter XXIII
Gadgadasvara

At that moment
the Lord Sâkyamuni,
the Tathâgata, &c.,
darted a flash of light
from the circle of hair
between his eyebrows,
one of the characteristic
signs of a great man,
by which flash of light
hundred thousands
of myriads of kotis
of Buddha-fields,
equal to the sands
of eighteen rivers Ganges,
became illuminated.
Beyond those Buddha-fields,
equal, &c., is the world called
Vairokanarasmipratimandita
(i.e. embellished
by the rays of the sun).
There dwells, lives,
exists the Tathâgata named
Kamaladalavimalanakshatra-
râgasankusumitâbhigña,
who,
surrounded and attended
by a large and immense
assembly of Bodhisattvas,
preached the law.
Immediately
the ray of light flashing
from the circle of hair
between the eyebrows
of the Lord Sâkyamuni,
the Tathâgata, &c.,
filled the world
Vairokanarasmipratimandita
with a great lustre.

In that world
Vairokanarasmipratimandita
there was a Bodhisattva
Mahâsattva called
Gadgadasvara,
who had planted
roots of goodness,
who had before
seen similar luminous flashes
emitted by many Tathâgatas,
&c., and who had acquired
many Samâdhis,
such as the Samâdhi
Dhvagâgrakeyûra
(i.e. bracelet at the upper
end of the banner staff),
Saddharma-pundarîka
(i.e. the Lotus of the True Law),
Vimaladattâ
(i.e. given by Vimala),
Nakshatraragâvikrîdita
(i.e. sport of the king
of asterisms, the moon god),
Anilambha, Gñânamudrâ
(i.e. the seal of science),
Kandrapradîpa
(i.e. moon-light),
Sarvarutakausalya
(i.e. skill in all sounds),
Sarvapunyasamukkaya
(i.e. compendium
or collection of all piety),
Prasâdavatî (i.e.
the favorably-disposed lady),
Riddhivikrîdita
(i.e. sport of magic),
Gñanolkâ
(i.e. torch of knowledge),
Vyûharâga
(i.e. king of expansions
or speculations),

Vimalaprabhâ
(i.e. spotless lustre),
Vimalagarbha,
(i.e. of spotless interior part),
Apkritsna,
Sûryâvarta (i.e. sun-turn);
in short,
he had acquired
many hundred thousand
myriads of kotis of Samâdhis
equal to the sands
of the river Ganges.
Now,
the flash of light came down
upon that Bodhisattva
Mahâsattva Gadgadasvara.
Then the Bodhisattva
Mahâsattva Gadgadasvara
rose from his seat,
put his upper robe
upon one shoulder,
fixed his right knee
on the ground,
stretched his joined hands
towards the Lord Buddha,
and said to the Tathâgata
Kamaladalavimalanakshatra-
râgasankusumitâbhigña :
O Lord, I would resort
to the Saha-world to see,
salute, wait upon the Lord
Sâkyamuni,
the Tathâgata, &c. ;
to see and salute Mañgusrî,
the prince royal ;
to see the Bodhisattvas
Bhaishagyarâga,
Pradânasûra,
Nakshatrarâgasan-
kusumitâbhigña,
Visishtakâritra,
Vyûharâga,
Bhaishagyarâgasamudgata.

Then the Lord
Kamaladalavimalanakshatra-
râgasankusumitâbhigña,
the Tathâgata, &c.,
said to the Bodhisattva
Mahâsattva Gadgadasvara :
On coming to the Saha-world,
young man of good family,
thou must not conceive
a low opinion of it.
That world,
young man of good family,
has ups and downs,
consists of earth,
is replete
with mountains of Kâla,
filled with gutters.
The Lord Sâkyamuni,
the Tathâgata, &c.,
is short of stature,
and so are the
Bodhisattvas Mahâsattvas,
whereas thou,
young man of good family,
hast got a body
forty-two hundred
thousand yoganas high,
and myself have got a body
sixty-eight hundred
thousand yoganas high.
And,
young man of good family,
thou art lovely, handsome,
of pleasant appearance,
endowed with a full bloom
of extremely fine colour,
and abundantly blest
with hundred thousands

of holy signs.
Therefore then,
young man of good family,
when you have come
to the Saha-world,
do not conceive
a low opinion
of the Tathâgata,
nor of the Bodhisattvas,
nor of that Buddha-field.

Thus addressed,
the Bodhisattva
Mahâsattva Gadgadasvara
said to the Lord
Kamaladalavimalanaksha-
tarâgasankusumitâbhigña,
the Tathâgata, &c. :
I shall do, Lord,
as the Lord commands ;
I shall go to that Saha-world
by virtue
of the Lord's resolution,
of the Lord's power,
of the Lord's might,
of the Lord's disposal,
of the Lord's foresight.
Whereon the Bodhisattva
Mahâsattva Gadgadasvara,
without leaving
that Buddha-field
and without leaving his seat,
plunged into
so deep a meditation
that immediately after,
on a sudden,
there appeared
before the Tathâgata on
the Gridhrakûta-mountains
in the Saha-world
eighty-four hundred
thousand myriads of kotis
of lotuses on gold stalks
with silver leaves
and with cups
of the hue of rosy lotuses
and Butea Frondosa.

On seeing the appearance
of this mass of lotuses
the Bodhisattva Mahâsattva
Mañgusrî, the prince royal,
asked the Lord Sâkyamuni,
the Tathâgata, &c. :
By what cause and by whom,
O Lord, have been produced
these eighty-four hundred
thousand myriads
of kotis of lotuses
on gold stalks
with silver leaves
and with cups
of the hue of rosy lotuses
and Butea Frondosa ?
Whereon the Lord replied
to Mañgusrî, the prince royal :
It is, Mañgusrî,
the Bodhisattva
Mahâsattva Gadgadasvara,
who accompanied
and attended
by eighty-four hundred
thousand myriads of kotis
of Bodhisattvas
arrives from the east,
from the world
Vairokanarasmipratimandita,
the Buddha-field of the Lord
Kamaladalavimalanaksha-
tarâgasankusumitâbhigña,
the Tathâgata, &c.,
at this Saha-world to see,

salute, wait upon me,
and to hear
this Dharmaparyâya
of the Lotus of the True Law.
Then Mañgusrî,
the prince royal,
said to the Lord :
What mass of roots
of goodness, O Lord,
has that young man
of good family collected,
that he has deserved
to obtain such a distinction ?
And what meditation is it,
O Lord, that
the Bodhisattva practices ?
Let us also learn
that meditation,
O Lord,
and practice that meditation.
And
let us see that Bodhisattva,
Lord ;
see how the colour,
outward shape, character,
figure, and behaviour
of that Bodhisattva is.
May the Lord
deign to produce
such a token that
the Bodhisattva Mahâsattva
be admonished by it
to come to this Saha-world.

Then the Lord Sâkyamuni,
the Tathâgata, &c., said
to the Lord Prabhûtaratna,
the Tathâgata, &c.,
who was completely extinct :
Produce such a token, Lord,
that the Bodhisattva
Mahâsattva Gadgadasvara
be admonished by it
to come to this Saha-world.
And the Lord Prabhûtaratna,
the Tathâgata, &c., who
was completely extinct,
instantly produced a token
in order to admonish
the Bodhisattva Mahâsattva
Gadgadasvara and said :
Come,
young man of good family,
to this Saha-world ;
Mañgusrî, the prince royal,
will hail thy coming.
And the Bodhisattva
Mahâsattva Gadgadasvara,
after humbly saluting the feet
of the Lord
Kamaladalavimalanaksha-
trarâgasankusumitâbhigña,
the Tathâgata, &c.,
and after three times
circumambulating
him from left to right,
vanished from the world
Vairokanarasmipratimandita,
along with eighty-four
hundred thousand
myriads of kotis
of Bodhisattvas
who surrounded
and followed him,
and arrived
at this Saha-world,
among a stir of Buddha-fields,
a rain of lotuses,
a noise of hundred thousands
of myriads of kotis
of musical instruments.
His face showed eyes

resembling blue lotuses,
his body was gold-coloured,
his person marked
by a hundred thousand
of holy signs;
he sparkled with lustre,
glowed with radiance,
had limbs marked
by the characteristic signs,
and a body compact
as Nârâyana's.
Mounted on a tower made
of seven precious substances,
he moved through the sky
to a height of seven Tâlas,
surrounded
by a host of Bodhisattvas,
in the direction
of this Saha-world,
and approached
the Gridhrakûta,
the king of mountains.
At his arrival,
he alighted from the tower,
and went,
with a necklace of pearls
worth a hundred thousands,
to the place
where the Lord was sitting.
After humbly saluting
the feet of the Lord,
and circumambulating him
seven times from left to right,
he offered him the necklace
of pearls in token of homage,
whereafter
he said to the Lord:
The Lord
Kamaladalavimalanaksha-
trarâgasankusumitâbhigña,
the Tathâgata, &c.,
inquires after the Lord's
health, welfare,
and sprightliness;
whether he feels free
from affliction and at ease.
That Lord has also
charged me to ask:
Is there something
thou hast to suffer or allow?
the humours of the body
are not
in an unfavorable state;
thy creatures are
decent in manners, tractable,
and easy to be healed;
their bodies are clean;
They are not too passionate,
I hope, not too irascible, not
too unwise in their doings?
They are not jealous, Lord,
not envious, not ungrateful
to their father and mother,
not impious, not heterodox,
not unsubdued in mind,
not unrestrained
in sexual desires;
Are the creatures
able to resist the Evil One;
Has the Lord Prabhûtaratna,
the Tathâgata, &c.,
who is completely extinct,
come to the Saha-world
in order to hear the law,
sitting in the centre
of a Stûpa made of
seven precious substances;
And as to that,
Lord Prabhûtaratna,
the Tathâgata, &c., the Lord
Kamaladalavimalanaksha-
trarâgasankusumitâbhigña,

inquires:
Is there something that
the Lord Prabhûtaratna, &c.,
has to suffer or allow; Is
the Lord Prabhûtaratna, &c.,
to stay long;
We also, O Lord,
are desirous of seeing
the rudimentary frame
of that Lord Prabhûtaratna,
the Tathâgata, &c.
May the Lord
therefore please to show us
the rudimentary frame
of the Lord Prabhûtaratna,
the Tathâgata, &c.

Then the Lord Sâkyamuni,
the Tathâgata, &c., said
to the Lord Prabhûtaratna,
the Tathâgata, &c.,
who was completely extinct:
Lord, the Bodhisattva
Mahâsattva Gadgadasvara
here wishes to see
the Lord Prabûtaratna,
the Tathâgata, &c.,
who is completely extinct.
Whereon
the Lord Prabhûtaratna,
the Tathâgata, &c.,
spoke to the Bodhisattva
Mahâsattva Gadgadasvara
in this strain:
Well done, well done,
young gentleman,
that thou hast come hither
in the desire to see
the Lord Sâkyamuni,
the Tathâgata, &c.;
to hear this Dharmaparyâya
of the Lotus of the True Law,
and see Mañgusrî,
the prince royal.

Subsequently
the Bodhisattva Mahâsattva
Padmasrî said to the Lord:
What root of goodness
has the Bodhisattva
Mahâsattva Gadgadasvara
formerly planted?
And in presence
of which Tathâgata?
And the Lord Sâkyamuni,
the Tathâgata, &c.,
said to the Bodhisattva
Mahâsattva Padmasrî:
In the days of yore,
young man of good family,
at a past period there
appeared in the world
a Tathâgata called
Meghadundubhisvararâga
(i.e. the king of the
drum-sound of the clouds),
perfectly enlightened,
endowed with science
and conduct, a Sugata, &c.,
in the world
Sarvabuddhasandarsana
(i.e. sight or display
of all Buddhas),
in the Æon Priyadarsana.
To that Lord
Meghadundubhisvararâga
the Bodhisattva
Mahâsattva Gadgadasvara
paid homage
by making resound
hundred thousands
of musical instruments

during twelve thousand years. He presented to him also eighty-four thousand vessels of seven precious substances. Under the preaching of the Tathâgata Meghadundubhisvararâga, young man of good family, has the Bodhisattva Mahâsattva Gadgadasvara obtained such a beauty as he now displays. Perhaps, young man of good family, thou hast some doubt, uncertainty or misgiving, and thinkest that at that time, that epoch, there was another Bodhisattva Mahâsattva called Gadgadasvara, who paid that homage to the Lord Meghadundubhisvararâga, the Tathâgata, and presented him the eighty-four thousand vessels. But, young man of good family, do not think so. For it was the very same Bodhisattva Mahâsattva Gadgadasvara, young man of good family, who paid that homage to the Lord Meghadundubhisvararâga, the Tathâgata, and presented to him the eighty-four thousand vessels. So, young man of good family, the Bodhisattva Mahâsattva Gadgadasvara has waited upon many Buddhas, has planted good roots under many Buddhas, and prepared the soil under each of them. And this Bodhisattva Mahâsattva Gadgadasvara had previously seen Lords Buddhas similar to the sands of the river Ganges. Dost thou see, Padmasrî, how the Bodhisattva Mahâsattva Gadgadasvara now looks ? Padmasrî replied : I do, Lord ; I do, Sugata. The Lord said : Now, Padmasrî, this Bodhisattva Mahâsattva Gadgadasvara preaches this Dharmaparyâya of the Lotus of the True Law under many shapes he assumes ; sometimes or somewhere under the shape of Brahma, sometimes under that of Indra, sometimes under that of Siva, sometimes under that of Kubera,

sometimes
under that of a sovereign,
sometimes
under that of a duke,
sometimes
under that of a chief merchant,
sometimes
under that of a citizen,
sometimes
under that of a villager,
sometimes
under that of a Brahman.
Sometimes again
the Bodhisattva
Mahâsattva Gadgadasvara
preaches this Dharmaparyâya
of the Lotus of the True Law
under a monk's shape,
sometimes under a nun's,
sometimes
under a male lay devotee's,
sometimes
under a female lay devotee's,
sometimes under that
of a chief merchant's wife,
sometimes
under that of a citizen's wife,
sometimes under a boy's,
sometimes
under a girl's shape.
With so many variations
in the manner
to show himself,
the Bodhisattva
Mahâsattva Gadgadasvara
preaches this Dharmaparyâya
of the Lotus of the True Law
to creatures.
He has even assumed
the shape of a goblin
to preach this Dharmaparyâya
to such as were
to be converted by a goblin.
To some he has preached
this Dharmaparyâya
of the Lotus of the True Law
under the shape of a demon,
to some under a Garuda's,
to some under a Kinnara's,
to some under
a great serpent's shape.
Even to the beings
in any of the wretched states,
in the hells, the brute creation,
Yama's realm,
the Bodhisattva
Mahâsattva Gadgadasvara
is a supporter.
Even to the creatures
in the gynæceums
of this Saha-world
has the Bodhisattva
Mahâsattva Gadgadasvara,
after metamorphosing
himself into a woman,
preached this Dharmaparyâya
of the Lotus of the True Law.
Verily, Padmasrî,
the Bodhisattva
Mahâsattva Gadgadasvara is
the supporter of the creatures
living in this Saha-world.
Under so many shapes,
assumed at will,
has the Bodhisattva
Mahâsattva Gadgadasvara
preached this Dharmaparyâya
of the Lotus of the True Law
to creatures.
Yet,
there is no diminution
of wisdom,

nor diminution
of magic power
in that good man.
So many,
young man of good family,
are the manifestations
of knowledge
by which this Bodhisattva
Mahâsattva Gadgadasvara
has made himself known
in this Saha-world.
In other worlds also,
similar to the sands
of the river Ganges,
he preaches the law,
under the shape
of a Bodhisattva
to such as must be converted
by a Bodhisattva ;
under the shape
of a disciple to such as must
be converted by a disciple ;
under the shape
of a Pratyekabuddha
to such as must be converted
by a Pratyekabuddha ;
under the shape
of a Tathâgata to such
as must be converted
by a Tathâgata.
Nay, he will show to those
who must be converted
by a relic of the Tathâgata
himself such a relic,
and to those
who must be converted
by complete extinction
he will show himself
completely extinct.
Such is the powerful
knowledge, Padmasrî,
the Bodhisattva Mahâsattva
is possessed of.

Thereafter the Bodhisattva
Mahâsattva Padmasrî
said to the Lord :
The Bodhisattva
Mahâsattva Gadgadasvara
then has planted good roots,
Lord.
What meditation is it, Lord,
whereby the Bodhisattva
Mahâsattva Gadgadasvara,
with unshaken firmness,
has converted or educated
so many creatures ;
Whereupon
the Lord Sâkyamuni,
the Tathâgata. &c..
replied to the Bodhisattva
Mahâsattva Padmasrî : It is,
young man of good family,
the meditation termed
Sarvarûpasandarsana.
By steadiness in it has
the Bodhisattva
Mahâsattva Gadgadasvara
so immensely promoted
the weal of creatures.

While this chapter
of Gadgadasvara
was being expounded,
all the eighty-four
hundred thousand
myriads of kotis
of Bodhisattvas
Mahâsattvas who,
along with the Bodhisattva
Mahâsattva Gadgadasvara,
had come to the Saha-world,

obtained the meditation
Sarvarûpasandarsana,
and as to the number
of Bodhisattvas Mahâsattvas
of this Saha-world
obtaining the meditation
Sarvarûpasandarsana,
it was beyond calculation.

Then the Bodhisattva
Mahâsattva Gadgadasvara,
after having paid great
and ample worship
to the Lord Sâkyamuni,
the Tathâgata, &c.,
and at the Stûpa of relics
of the Lord Prabhûtaratna,
the Tathâgata, &c.,
again mounted
the tower made
of seven precious substances,
among the stir of the fields,
the rain of lotuses,
the noise
of hundred thousands
of myriads of kotis
of musical instruments,
and with the eighty-four
hundred thousand
myriads of kotis
of Bodhisattvas
surrounding
and following him,
returned
to his own Buddha-field.
At his arrival there
he said to the Lord
Kamaladalavimalanaksha-
trarâgasankusumitâbhigña,
the Tathâgata, &c. :
O Lord,
I have in the Saha-world
promoted
the weal of creatures ;
I have seen and saluted
the Stûpa of relics
of the Lord Prabhûtaratna,
the Tathâgata, &c. ;
I have seen and saluted
the Lord Sâkyamuni,
the Tathâgata, &c. ;
I have seen Mañgusrî,
the prince royal,
as well as the
Bodhisattva Bhaishagyarâga,
who is possessed
of mighty knowledge
and impetuosity,
and the Bodhisattva
Mahâsattva Pradânasûra ;
and these eighty-four
hundred thousand
myriads of kotis
of Bodhisattvas Mahâsattvas
have all obtained
the meditation termed
Sarvarûpasandarsana.

And while this relation
of the going and coming
of the Bodhisattva
Mahâsattva Gadgadasvara
was being delivered,
forty-two thousand
Bodhisattvas acquired
the faculty of acquiescence
in future things,
and the Bodhisattva
Mahâsattva Padmasrî
acquired
the meditation called
the Lotus of the True Law.

Chapter XXIV
The All-sided One

Thereafter the Bodhisattva
Mahâsattva Akshayamati
rose from his seat,
put his upper robe
upon one shoulder,
stretched his joined hands
towards the Lord, and said :
For what reason,
O Lord,
is the Bodhisattva
Mahâsattva Avalokitesvara
called Avalokitesvara ?
So he asked,
and the Lord
answered to the Bodhisattva
Mahâsattva Akshayamati :
All the hundred thousands of
myriads of kotis of creatures,
young man of good family,
who in this world
are suffering troubles will,
if they hear the name
of the Bodhisattva
Mahâsattva Avalokitesvara,
be released from
that mass of troubles.
Those who shall keep
the name of this Bodhisattva
Mahâsattva Avalokitesvara,
young man of good family,
will, if they fall
into a great mass of fire,
be delivered there from
by virtue of the lustre of
the Bodhisattva Mahâsattva.
In case,
young man of good family,
creatures,
carried off
by the current of rivers,
should implore
the Bodhisattva
Mahâsattva Avalokitesvara,
all rivers
will afford them a ford.
In case,
young man of good family,
many hundred thousand
myriads of kotis of creatures,
sailing in a ship on the ocean,
should see their bullion,
gold, gems, pearls, lapis
lazuli, conch shells,
stones, corals, emeralds,
Musâragalvas, red pearls,
and other goods lost,
and the ship by a vehement,
untimely gale cast
on the island of Giantesses,
and if in that ship
a single being implores
Avalokitesvara,
all will be saved from
that island of Giantesses.
For that reason,
young man of good family,
the Bodhisattva Mahâsattva
Avalokitesvara is named
Avalokitesvara.

If a man given up
to capital punishment
implores Avalokitesvara,
young man of good family,
the swords of the executioners
shall snap asunder.
Further,
young man of good family,
if the whole triple chiliocosm

were teeming
with goblins and giants,
they would
by virtue of the name
of the Bodhisattva
Mahâsattva Avalokitesvara
being pronounced
lose the faculty of sight
in their wicked designs.
If some creature,
young man of good family,
shall be bound
in wooden or iron manacles,
chains or fetters,
be he guilty or innocent,
then those manacles,
chains or fetters shall give way
as soon as the name
of the Bodhisattva Mahâsattva
Avalokitesvara is pronounced.
Such,
young man of good family,
is the power
of the Bodhisattva
Mahâsattva Avalokitesvara.
If this whole triple chiliocosm,
young man of good family,
were teeming with knaves,
enemies, and robbers
armed with swords,
and if a merchant leader
of a caravan
marched with a caravan
rich in jewels ;
if then they perceived
those robbers, knaves,
and enemies
armed with swords,
and in their anxiety and fright
thought themselves helpless ;
if, further,
that leading merchant
spoke to the caravan
in this strain :
Be not afraid,
young gentlemen,
be not frightened ;
invoke, all of you,
with one voice
the Bodhisattva
Mahâsattva Avalokitesvara,
the giver of safety ;
then you shall be delivered
from this danger
by which you are threatened
at the hands
of robbers and enemies ;
if then the whole caravan
with one voice invoked
Avalokitesvara
with the words :
Adoration, adoration
be to the giver of safety,
to Avalokitesvara
Bodhisattva Mahâsattva !
then,
by the mere act
of pronouncing that name,
the caravan would be
released from all danger.
Such,
young man of good family,
is the power
of the Bodhisattva
Mahâsattva Avalokitesvara.
In case creatures
act under the impulse
of impure passion,
young man of good family,
they will, after adoring
the Bodhisattva Mahâsattva
Avalokitesvara,

be freed from passion.
Those who act under
the impulse of hatred will,
after adoring
the Bodhisattva Mahâsattva
Avalokitesvara,
be freed from hatred.
Those who act
under the impulse
of infatuation will,
after adoring
the Bodhisattva Mahâsattva
Avalokitesvara,
be freed from infatuation.
So mighty,
young man of good family,
is the Bodhisattva
Mahâsattva Avalokitesvara.
If a woman,
desirous of male offspring,
young man of good family,
adores the Bodhisattva
Avalokitesvara,
she shall get a son, nice,
handsome, and beautiful ;
one possessed
of the characteristics
of a male child,
generally beloved
and winning,
who has planted good roots.
If a woman is desirous
of getting a daughter,
a nice, handsome,
beautiful girl
shall be born to her ;
one possessed
of the good characteristics
of a girl,
generally beloved
and winning,
who has planted good roots.
Such,
young man of good family,
is the power
of the Bodhisattva
Mahâsattva Avalokitesvara.

Those who adore
the Bodhisattva Mahâsattva
Avalokitesvara
will derive from it
an unfailing profit.
Suppose,
young man of good family,
on one hand
some one adoring
the Bodhisattva Mahâsattva
Avalokitesvara
and cherishing his name ;
on the other hand another
adoring a number
of Lords Buddhas
equal to sixty-two times
the sands of the river Ganges,
cherishing their names
and worshipping so many
Lords Buddhas
during their stay, existence,
and life, by giving robes,
alms-bowls, couches,
medicaments for the sick ;
how great is then
in thine opinion,
young man of good family,
the accumulation
of pious merit
which that young gentleman
or young lady will produce
in consequence of it ?
So asked, the Bodhisattva
Mahâsattva Akshayamati

said to the Lord : Great,
O Lord, great, O Sugata,
is the pious merit
which that young gentleman
or young lady will produce
in consequence of it.
The Lord proceeded : Now,
young man of good family,
the accumulation
of pious merit
produced by that
young gentleman
paying homage to so many
Lords Buddhas,
and the accumulation
of pious merit
produced by him
who performs were it
but a single act of adoration
to the Bodhisattva
Mahâsattva Avalokitesvara
and cherishes his name,
are equal.
He who adores a number
of Lords Buddhas
equal to sixty-two times
the sands of the river Ganges
and cherishes their names,
and he who adores
the Bodhisattva Mahâsattva
Avalokitesvara
and cherishes his name,
have an equal accumulation
of pious merit ;
both masses of pious merit
are not easy to be destroyed
even in hundred thousands
of myriads of kotis of Æons.
So immense,
young man of good family,
is the pious merit
resulting from cherishing
the name of the Bodhisattva
Mahâsattva Avalokitesvara.

Again the Bodhisattva
Mahâsattva Akshayamati
said to the Lord :
How, O Lord,
is it that the Bodhisattva
Mahâsattva Avalokitesvara
frequents this Saha-world ?
And how does he
preach the law ?
And which is the range
of the skilfulness
of the Bodhisattva
Mahâsattva Avalokitesvara ?
So asked, the Lord replied
to the Bodhisattva
Mahâsattva Akshayamati :
In some worlds,
young man of good family,
the Bodhisattva
Mahâsattva Avalokitesvara
preaches the law to creatures
in the shape of a Buddha ;
in others he does so in
the shape of a Bodhisattva.
To some beings
he shows the law in the shape
of a Pratyekabuddha ;
to others he does so
in the shape of a disciple ;
to others again under
that of Brahma, Indra,
or a Gandharva.
To those who are
to be converted by a goblin,
he preaches the law
assuming the shape
of a goblin ;

to those who are
to be converted by Îsvara,
he preaches the law
in the shape of Îsvara ;
to those who are to be
converted by Mahesvara,
he preaches assuming
the shape of Mahesvara.
To those who are to be
converted by a Kakravartin,
he shows the law
after assuming
the shape of a Kakravartin ;
to those who are
to be converted by an imp,
he shows the law
under the shape of an imp ;
to those who are to be
converted by Kubera,
he shows the law
by appearing
in the shape of Kubera ;
to those who are
to be converted by Senâpati,
he preaches
in the shape of Senâpati ;
to those who
are to be converted
by assuming a Brahman,
he preaches
in the shape of a Brahman ;
to those who are to be
converted by Vagrapâni,
he preaches
in the shape of Vagrapâni.
With such
inconceivable qualities,
young man of good family,
is the Bodhisattva Mahâsattva
Avalokitesvara endowed.
Therefore then,
young man of good family,
honour the Bodhisattva
Mahâsattva Avalokitesvara.
The Bodhisattva
Mahâsattva Avalokitesvara,
young man of good family,
affords safety
to those who are in anxiety.
On that account one calls him
in this Saha-world
Abhayandada
(i.e. Giver of Safety).

Further, the Bodhisattva
Mahâsattva Akshayamati
said to the Lord :
Shall we give a gift of piety,
a decoration of piety,
O Lord, to the Bodhisattva
Mahâsattva Avalokitesvara ?
The Lord replied : Do so,
if thou thinkest it opportune.
Then the Bodhisattva
Mahâsattva Akshayamati
took from his neck
a pearl necklace,
worth a hundred thousand
gold pieces,
and presented it
to the Bodhisattva
Mahâsattva Avalokitesvara
as a decoration of piety,
with the words :
Receive from me
this decoration of piety,
good man.
But he would not accept it.
Then the Bodhisattva
Mahâsattva Akshayamati
said to the Bodhisattva
Mahâsattva Avalokitesvara :

Out of compassion to us,
young man of good family,
accept this pearl necklace.
Then the Bodhisattva
Mahâsattva Avalokitesvara
accepted the pearl necklace
from the Bodhisattva
Mahâsattva Akshayamati,
out of compassion
to the Bodhisattva Mahâsattva
Akshayamati
and the four classes,
and out of compassion
to the gods, Nâgas, goblins,
Gandharvas demons,
Garudas, Kinnaras,
great serpents, men,
and beings not human.
Thereafter he divided
the necklace into two parts,
and offered one part
to the Lord Sâkyamuni,
and the other
to the jewel Stûpa
of the Lord Prabhûtaratna,
the Tathâgata, &c., who had
become completely extinct.

With such a faculty
of transformation,
young man of good family,
the Bodhisattva
Mahâsattva Avalokitesvara
is moving in this Saha-world.

And on that occasion
the Lord uttered
the following stanzas :

1.
Kitradhvaga
asked Akshayamati
the following question :
For what reason, son of Gina,
is Avalokitesvara so called ?

2.
And Akshayamati,
that ocean of profound insight,
after considering
how the matter stood,
spoke to Kitradhvaga :
Listen to the conduct
of Avalokitesvara.

3.
Hear from my indication
how for numerous,
inconceivable Æons
he has accomplished his vote
under many thousand
kotis of Buddhas.

4.
Hearing, seeing, regularly
and constantly thinking
will infallibly destroy all
suffering, mundane existence,
and grief of living beings
here on earth.

5.
If one be thrown
into a pit of fire,
by a wicked enemy
with the object of killing him,
he has but to think
of Avalokitesvara, and
the fire shall be quenched
as if sprinkled with water.

6.
If one happens to fall
into the dreadful ocean,
the abode of Nâgas,
marine monsters,
and demons,
he has but to think
of Avalokitesvara,
and he shall never sink down
in the king of waters.

7.
If a man happens
to be hurled down
from the brink of the Meru,
by some wicked person
with the object of killing him,
he has but to think
of Avalokitesvara,
and he shall, sunlike,
stand firm in the sky.

8.
If rocks of thunderstone
and thunderbolts are thrown
at a man's head to kill him,
he has but to think
of Avalokitesvara,
and they shall not be able
to hurt one hair of the body.

9.
If a man be surrounded
by a host of enemies
armed with swords,
who have the intention
of killing him,
he has but to think
of Avalokitesvara,
and they shall instantaneously
become kind-hearted.

10.
If a man,
delivered to the power
of the executioners,
is already standing
at the place of execution,
he has but to think
of Avalokitesvara,
and their swords
shall go to pieces.

11.
If a person
happens to be fettered
in shackles of wood or iron,
he has but to think
of Avalokitesvara,
and the bonds shall be
speedily loosened.

12.
Mighty spells, witchcraft,
herbs, ghosts, and spectres,
pernicious to life,
revert thither whence
they come, when one
thinks of Avalokitesvara.

13.
If a man is surrounded
by goblins, Nâgas, demons,
ghosts, or giants,
who are in the habit
of taking away bodily vigour,
he has but to think
of Avalokitesvara,
and they shall not
be able to hurt
one hair of his body.

14.
If a man is surrounded
by fearful beasts
with sharp teeth and claws,
he has but to think
of Avalokitesvara,
and they shall quickly fly
in all directions.

15.
If a man is surrounded by
snakes malicious and frightful
on account of the flames
and fires they emit,
be has but to think
of Avalokitesvara,
and they shall quickly
lose their poison.

16.
If a heavy thunderbolt
shoots from a cloud
pregnant with lightning
and thunder,
one has but to think
of Avalokitesvara,
and the fire of heaven
shall quickly,
instantaneously be quenched.

17.
Avalokitesvara
with his powerful knowledge
beholds all creatures
who are beset
with many hundreds
of troubles and afflicted
by many sorrows,
and thereby is a saviour
in the world,
including the gods.

18.
As he is thoroughly practiced
in the power of magic,
and possessed
of vast knowledge
and skilfulness,
he shows himself
in all directions
and in all regions of the world.

19.
Birth, decrepitude,
and disease
will come to an end
for those who are
in the wretched
states of existence,
in hell, in brute creation,
in the kingdom of Yama,
for all beings in general.

Then Akshayamati
in the joy of his heart
uttered the following stanzas :

20.
O thou whose eyes are clear,
whose eyes are kind,
distinguished
by wisdom and knowledge,
whose eyes are full of pity
and benevolence ;
thou so lovely
by thy beautiful face
and beautiful eyes !

21.
Pure one,
whose shine is spotless bright,
whose knowledge
is free from darkness,

thou shining as the sun,
not to be beaten away,
radiant as the blaze of fire,
thou spreadest
in thy flying course
thy lustre in the world.

22.
O thou
who rejoicest in kindness
having its source
in compassion,
thou great cloud
of good qualities
and of benevolent mind,
thou quenchest the fire
that vexes living beings,
thou pourest out nectar,
the rain of the law.

23.
In quarrel, dispute, war,
battle, in any great danger
one has to think
of Avalokitesvara,
who shall quell
the wicked troop of foes.

24.
One should think
of Avalokitesvara,
whose sound is
as the cloud's
and the drum's,
who thunders
like a rain-cloud,
possesses a good voice
like Brahma,
a voice going through
the whole gamut of tones.

25.
Think,
O think with tranquil mood
of Avalokitesvara,
that pure being;
he is a protector, a refuge,
a recourse in death,
disaster, and calamity.

26.
He who possesses
the perfection of all virtues,
and beholds all beings
with compassion
and benevolence,
he, an ocean of virtues,
Virtue itself,
he, Avalokitesvara,
is worthy of adoration.

27.
He,
so compassionate
for the world,
shall once become a Buddha,
destroying all dangers
and sorrows;
I humbly
bow to Avalokitesvara.

28.
This universal Lord,
chief of kings,
who is a rich mine
of monastic virtues,
he, universally worshipped,
has reached pure,
supreme enlightenment,
after plying his course of duty
during
many hundreds of Æons.

29.
At one time
standing to the right,
at another to the left
of the Chief Amitâbha,
whom he is fanning,
he, by dint of meditation,
like a phantom,
in all regions
honours the Gina.

30.
In the west,
where the pure world
Sukhâkara is situated,
there the Chief Amitâbha,
the tamer of men,
has his fixed abode.

31.
There no women
are to be found ;
there sexual intercourse
is absolutely unknown ;
there the sons of Gina,
on springing into existence
by apparitional birth,
are sitting in
the undefiled cups of lotuses.

32.
And
the Chief Amitâbha himself
is seated on a throne
in the pure
and nice cup of a lotus,
and shines as the Sâla-king.

33.
The Leader of the world,
whose store of merit
has been praised,
has no equal in the triple world.
O supreme of men,
let us soon become like thee !

Thereupon the Bodhisattva
Mahâsattva Dharanindhara
rose from his seat,
put his upper robe
upon one shoulder,
fixed his right knee
against the earth,
stretched his joined hands
towards the Lord and said :
They must be possessed
of not a few good roots, O Lord,
who are to hear this chapter
from the Dharmaparyâya
about
the Bodhisattva Mahâsattva
Avalokitesvara
and this miraculous power
of transformation
of the Bodhisattva Mahâsattva
Avalokitesvara.

And while this chapter
of the All-sided One
was being expounded
by the Lord,
eighty-four thousand
living beings
from that assembly
felt their minds
drawn to that supreme
and perfect enlightenment,
with which nothing else
can be compared.

Chapter XXV
Ancient Devotion

Thereupon
the Lord addressed
the entire assemblage
of Bodhisattvas:
Of yore,
young men of good family,
at a past epoch,
incalculable,
more than
incalculable Æons ago,
at that time
there appeared in the world
a Tathâgata named
Galadharagargitaghos-
hasusvaranakshatrarâ-
gasankusumitâbhigña,
an Arhat, &c.,
endowed with science
and conduct, &c. &c.,
in the Æon Priyadarsana,
in the world
Vairokanarasmipratimandita.
Now, there was,
young men of good family,
under the spiritual rule
of the Tathâgata
Galadharagargitaghos-
hasusvaranakshatrarâ-
gasankusumitâbhigña,
a king called Subhavyûha.
That king Subhavyûha,
young men of good family,
had a wife called
Vimaladattâ, and two sons,
one called Vimalagarbha,
the other Vimalanetra.
These two boys,
who possessed
magical power and wisdom,
applied themselves
to the course of duty
of Bodhisattvas,
namely to the perfect virtues
of alms-giving,
morality, forbearance,
energy, meditation, wisdom,
and skilfulness;
they were accomplished
in benevolence,
compassion,
joyful sympathy
and indifference,
and in all
the thirty-seven constituents
of true knowledge.
They had perfectly mastered
the meditation Vimala
(i.e. spotless),
the meditation
Nakshatrarâgâditya,
the meditation
Vimalanirbhâsa,
the meditation Vimalâbhâsa,
the meditation Alankârasûra,
the meditation
Mahâtegogarbha.
Now at that time,
that period
the said Lord preached
the Dharmaparyâya
of the Lotus of the True Law
out of compassion
for the beings then living
and for the king Subhavyûha.
Then,
young men of good family,
the two young princes
Vimalagarbha
and Vimalanetra

went to their mother,
to whom they said,
after stretching
their joined hands :
We should like to go, mother,
to the Lord
Galadharagargitaghos-
hasusvaranakshatrarâ-
gasankusumitâbhigña,
the Tathâgata, &c.,
and that, mother,
because the Lord
Galadharagargitaghos-
hasusvaranakshatrarâ-
gasankusumitâbhigña,
the Tathâgata, &c.,
expounds, in great extension,
before the world,
including the gods,
the Dharmaparyâya
of the Lotus of the True Law.
We should like to hear it.
Whereupon
the queen Vinialadattâ
said to the two young princes
Vimalagarbha
and Vimalanetra :
Your father,
young gentlemen,
the king Subhavyûha,
favors the Brahmans.
Therefore you will not
obtain the permission
to go and see the Tathâgata.
Then the two young princes
Vimalagarbha
and Vimalanetra,
stretching their joined hands,
said to their mother :
Though born
in a family that adheres,
to a false doctrine,
we feel as sons
to the king of the law.
Then,
young men of good family,
the queen Vimaladattâ
said to the young princes :
Well, young gentlemen,
out of compassion
for your father,
the king Subhavyûha,
display some miracle,
that he may become
favorably inclined to you,
and on that account
grant you the permission
of going to the Lord
Galadharagargitaghos-
hasusvaranakshatrarâ-
gasankusumitâbhigña,
the Tathâgata, &c.

Immediately the young
princes Vimalagarbha
and Vimalanetra
rose into the atmosphere
to a height of seven Tâl trees
and performed miracles
such as are allowed
by the Buddha,
out of compassion
for their father,
the king, Subhavyûha.
They prepared in the sky
a couch and raised dust ;
there they also emitted
from the lower part
of their body
a shower of rain,
and from the upper part
a mass of fire ;

then again they emitted
from the upper part
of their body a shower of rain,
and from the lower part
a mass of fire.
While in the firmament
they became now big,
then small ;
and now small, then big.
Then they vanished
from the sky to come up again
from the earth
and reappear in the air.
Such,
young men of good family,
were the miracles produced
by the magical power
of the two young princes,
whereby their father,
the king Subhavyûha,
was converted.
At the sight
of the miracle produced
by the magical power
of the two young princes,
the king Subhavyûha
was content, in high spirits,
ravished, rejoiced, joyful,
and happy, and,
the joined hands raised,
he said to the boys :
Who is your master,
young gentlemen ?
whose pupils are you ?
And the two young princes
answered
the king Subhavyûha :
There is, noble king,
there exists and lives a Lord
Galadharagargitaghos-
hasusvaranakshatrarâ-
gasankusumitâbhigña,
a Tathâgata, &c. ;
seated on the stool of law
at the foot of
the tree of enlightenment ;
he extensively reveals
the Dharmaparyâya
of the Lotus of the True Law
to the world,
including the gods.
That Lord is our Master,
O noble king ;
we are his pupils.
Then,
young gentlemen
of good family,
the king Subhavyûha
said to the young princes :
I will see your Master,
young gentlemen ;
I am to go myself
to the presence of that Lord.

After the two young princes
had descended from the sky,
young gentlemen,
they went to their mother
and with joined hands
stretched forward said to her :
Mother, we have converted
our father to supreme
and perfect knowledge ;
we have performed
the office of masters
towards him ;
therefore let us go now ;
we wish to enter upon
the ecclesiastical life
in the face of the Lord.
And on that occasion,
young men of good family,

the young princes
Vimalagarbha
and Vimalanetra
addressed their mother
in the following two stanzas :

1.
Allow us, O mother,
to go forth from home
and to embrace
the houseless life ;
ay, we will become ascetics,
for rare to be met with
is a Tathâgata.

2.
As the blossom
of the glomerated fig-tree,
nay, more rare is the Gina.
Let us depart ;
we will renounce the world ;
the favorable moment
is precious or not often
to be met with.

Vimaladattâ said :

3.
Now I grant you leave ;
go, my children,
I give my consent.
I myself will likewise
renounce the world,
for rare to be met with
or precious is a Tathâgata.

Having uttered these stanzas,
young men of good family,
the two young princes
said to their parents :
Pray, father and mother,

you also go together
with us to the Lord
Galadharagargitaghos-
hasusvaranakshatrarâ-
gasankusumitâbhigña,
the Tathâgata, &c.,
in order to see,
humbly salute
and wait upon him,
and to hear the law.
For, father and mother,
the appearance of a Buddha
is rare to be met with
as the blossom
of the glomerated fig-tree,
as the entering
of the tortoise's neck
into the hole of the yoke
formed by the great ocean.
The appearance
of Lords Buddhas,
father and mother, is rare.
Hence,
father and mother,
it is a happy lot
we have been blessed with,
to have been born
at the time of such a prophet.
Therefore,
father and mother,
give us leave ;
we would go
and become ascetics
in presence of the Lord
Galadharagargitaghos-
hasusvaranakshatrarâ-
gasankusumitâbhigña,
the Tathâgata, &c.,
for the seeing of a Tathâgata
is something rare.
Such a king of the law

is rarely met with;
such a favorable
occasion is rarely met with.

Now at that juncture,
young men of good family,
the eighty-four thousand
women of the harem
of the king Subhavyûha
became worthy
of being receptacles
of this Dharmaparyâya
of the Lotus of the True Law.
The young prince
Vimalanetra
exercised himself
in this Dharmaparyâya,
whereas the young prince
Vimalagarbha
for many hundred thousand
myriads of kotis of Æons
practiced the meditation
Sarvasattvapâpagahana,
with the object that all beings
should abandon all evils.
And the mother
of the two young princes,
the queen Vimaladattâ,
acknowledged the harmony
between all Buddhas and all
topics treated by them. Then,
young men of good family,
the king Subhavyûha,
having been converted
to the law of the Tathâgata
by the instrumentality
of the two young princes,
having been initiated
and brought to
full maturity in it,
along with all his relations
and retinue;
the queen Vimaladattâ
with the whole crowd
of women in her suite,
and the two young princes,
the sons
of the king Subhavyûha,
accompanied by forty-two
thousand living beings,
along with the women
of the harem
and the ministers,
went all together
and unanimously to the Lord
Galadharagargitaghos-
hasusvaranakshatrarâ-
gasankusumitâbhigña,
the Tathâgata, &c.
On arriving at the place
where the Lord was,
they humbly saluted his feet,
circumambulated him
three times from left to right
and took their stand
at some distance.

Then,
young men of good family,
the Lord
Galadharagargitaghos-
hasusvaranakshatrarâ-
gasankusumitâbhigña,
the Tathâgata, &c.,
perceiving
the king Subhavyûha,
who had arrived
with his retinue,
instructed, roused, excited,
and comforted him
with a sermon.
And the king Subhavyûha,

Ancient Devotion 355

young men of good family,
after he had been well
and duly instructed, roused,
excited, and comforted
by the sermon of the Lord,
was so content, glad,
ravished, joyful,
rejoiced, and delighted,
that he put his diadem
on the head
of his younger brother
and established him
in the government,
whereafter he himself
with his sons, kinsmen,
and retinue, as well as
the queen Vimaladattâ
and her numerous
train of women,
the two young princes
accompanied by forty-two
thousand living beings
went all together
and unanimously
forth from home
to embrace the houseless life,
prompted as they were
by their faith
in the preaching of the Lord
Galadharagargitaghos-
hasusvaranakshatrarâ-
gasankusumitâbhigña,
the Tathâgata, &c.
Having become an ascetic,
the king Subhavyûha,
with his retinue,
remained for eighty-four
thousand years
applying himself to studying,
meditating,
and thoroughly penetrating
this Dharmaparyâya
of the Lotus of the True Law.
At the end of those eighty
four thousand years,
young men of good family,
the king Subhavyûha
acquired
the meditation termed
Sarvagunâlankâravyûha.
No sooner had
he acquired that meditation,
than he rose seven Tâls
up to the sky,
and while staying in the air,
young men of good family,
the king Subhavyûha
said to the Lord
Galadharagargitaghos-
hasusvaranakshatrarâ-
gasankusumitâbhigña,
the Tathâgata, &c. :
My two sons, O Lord,
are my masters,
since it is owing
to the miracle produced
by their magical power
that I have been diverted
from that great heap
of false doctrines,
been established
in the command of the Lord,
brought to full ripeness in it,
introduced to it,
and exhorted to see the Lord.
They have acted
as true friends to me, O Lord,
those two young princes
who as sons
were born in my house,
certainly to remind me of
my former roots of goodness.

At these words the Lord
Galadharagargitaghos-
hasusvaranakshatrarâ-
gasankusumitâbhigña,
the Tathâgata, &c., spoke
to the king Subhavyûha :
It is as thou sayest, noble
king. Indeed, noble king,
such young men or young
ladies of good family
as possess roots of goodness,
will in any existence, state,
descent, rebirth or place
easily find true friends,
who with them shall
perform the task of a master,
who shall admonish,
introduce,
fully prepare them
to obtain supreme
and perfect enlightenment.
It is an exalted position,
noble king,
the office of a true friend
who rouses another
to see the Tathâgata.
Dost thou see these two
young princes, noble king ?
I do, Lord ; I do, Sugata,
said the king.
The Lord proceeded : Now,
these two young gentlemen,
noble king,
will pay worship
to sixty-five times the number
of Tathâgatas, &c.,
equal to the sands
of the Ganges ;
they will keep
this Dharmaparyâya
of the Lotus of the True Law,
out of compassion for beings
who hold false doctrines,
and with the aim to produce
in those beings
an earnest striving
after the right doctrine.

Thereupon,
young men of good family,
the king Subhavyûha
came down from the sky,
and, having raised
his joined hands,
said to the Lord
Galadharagargitaghos-
hasusvaranakshatrarâ-
gasankusumitâbhigña,
the Tathâgata, &c. :
Please, Lord, deign to tell me,
what knowledge
the Tathâgata is possessed of,
so that the protuberance
on his head is shining ;
that the Lord's eyes
are so clear ;
that between his brows
the Ûrnâ
circle of hair is shining,
resembling in whiteness
the moon ;
that in his mouth
a row of equal
and close-standing teeth
is glittering ;
that the Lord has lips
red as the Bimba
and such beautiful eyes.

As the king Subhavyûha,
young men of good family,

had celebrated the Lord
Galadharagargitaghos-
hasusvaranakshatrarâ-
gasankusumitâbhigña,
the Tathâgata, &c.,
by enumerating
so many good qualities
and hundred thousands
of myriads of kotis of
other good qualities besides,
he said to the Lord
Galadharagargitaghos-
hasusvaranakshatrarâ-
gasankusumitâbhigña,
the Tathâgata, &c. :
It is wonderful, O Lord,
how valuable
the Tathâgata's teaching is,
and with how many
inconceivable virtues
the religious discipline
proclaimed
by the Tathâgata is attended ;
how beneficial
the moral precepts
proclaimed
by the Tathâgata are.
From henceforward, O Lord,
we will no more be slaves
to our own mind ;
no more be slaves
to false doctrine ;
no more slaves to rashness ;
no more slaves
to the sinful thoughts
arising in us.
Being possessed
of so many good qualities,
O Lord,
I do not wish to go away from
the presence of the Lord.

After humbly saluting
the feet of the Lord
Galadharagargitaghos-
hasusvaranakshatrarâ-
gasankusumitâbhigña,
the Tathâgata, &c.,
the king rose up to the sky
and there stood.
Thereupon
the king Subhavyûha
and the queen Vimaladattâ
from the sky,
threw a pearl necklace
worth a hundred thousand
gold pieces upon the Lord ;
and that pearl necklace
no sooner came down upon
the head of the Lord
than it assumed the shape
of a tower with four columns,
regular, well-constructed,
and beautiful.
On the summit of the tower
appeared a couch covered
with many hundred thousand
pieces of fine cloth,
and on the couch
was seen the image
of a Tathâgata
sitting cross-legged.
Then the following thought
presented itself
to the king Subhavyûha :
The Buddha-knowledge
must be very powerful,
and the Tathâgata
endowed with
inconceivable good qualities
that this Tathâgata-image
shows itself

on the summit of the tower,
an image so nice, beautiful,
possessed of an extreme
abundance of good colours.
Then the Lord
Galadharagargitaghos-
hasusvaranakshatrarâ-
gasankusumitâbhigña,
the Tathâgata, &c.,
addressed the four classes
and asked :
Do you see, monks,
the king Subhavyûha who,
standing in the sky,
is emitting a lion's roar ?
They answered : We do, Lord.
The Lord proceeded :
This king Subhavyûha,
monks,
after having become a monk
under my rule
shall become a Tathâgata
in the world,
by the name of Sâlendrarâga,
endowed with science
and conduct, &c. &c.,
in the world Vistîrnavatî ;
his epoch shall be called
Abhyudgatarâga.
That Tathâgata Sâlendrarâga,
monks, the Arhat, &c.,
shall have
an immense congregation
of Bodhisattvas,
an immense
congregation of disciples.
The said world Vistîrnavatî
shall be level as the palm
of the hand,
and consist of lapis lazuli.
So he shall be
an inconceivably
great Tathâgata, &c.
Perhaps,
young men of good family,
you will have some doubt,
uncertainty or misgiving
and think that
the king Subhavyûha
at that time,
that juncture was another.
But you must not think so ;
for it is the very same
Bodhisattva Mahâsattva
Padmasrî here present,
who at that time,
that juncture
was the king Subhavyûha.
Perhaps,
young men of good family,
you will have some doubt,
uncertainty or misgiving
and think that the queen
Vimaladattâ at that time,
that juncture was another.
But you must not think so ;
for it is the very same
Bodhisattva Mahâsattva
called
Vairokanarasmi-
pratimanditarâga,
who at that time,
that juncture
was the queen Vimaladattâ,
and who out of compassion
for the king Subhavyûha
and the creatures
had assumed
the state of being the wife
of king Subhavyûha.
Perhaps,
young men of good family,

you will have some doubt,
uncertainty or misgiving
and think that the two
young princes were others.
But you must not think so ;
for it was Bhaishagyarâga and
Bhaishagyarâgasamudgata,
who at that time,
that juncture were sons
to the king Subhavyûha.
With such inconceivable
qualities,
young men of good family,
were
the Bodhisattvas Mahâsattvas
Bhaishagyarâga and
Bhaishagyarâgasamudgata
endowed, they,
the two good men,
having planted good roots
under many hundred
thousand myriads
of kotis of Buddhas.
Those that shall
cherish the name
of these two good men
shall all become worthy
of receiving homage
from the world,
including the gods.

While this chapter
on Ancient Devotion
was being expounded,
the spiritual insight
of eighty-four thousand
living beings
in respect to the law
was purified
so as to become
unclouded and spotless.

Chapter XXVI
Encouragement
of the Samantabhadra

Thereupon the Bodhisattva
Mahâsattva Samantabhadra,
in the east,
surrounded and followed
by Bodhisattvas Mahâsattvas
surpassing all calculation,
amid the stirring of fields,
a rain of lotuses,
the playing
of hundred thousands
of myriads of kotis
of musical instruments,
proceeded with the great
pomp of a Bodhisattva,
the great display
of transformations proper
to a Bodhisattva,
the great magnificence
of a Bodhisattva,
the great power
of a Bodhisattva,
the great lustre
of a glorious Bodhisattva,
the great stately march
of a Bodhisattva,
the great miraculous display
of a Bodhisattva,
a great phantasmagorical
sight of gods,
Nâgas, goblins,
Gandharvas, demons,
Garudas, Kinnaras,
great serpents, men,
and beings not human,
who,
produced by his magic,
surrounded
and followed him ;
Samantabhadra,
then,
the Bodhisattva,
amid such inconceivable
miracles worked by magic,
arrived at this Saha-world.
He went up to the place
of the Lord
on the Gridhrakûta,
the king of mountains,
and on approaching
he humbly saluted
the Lord's feet,
made seven
circumambulations
from left to right,
and said to the Lord :
I have come hither,
O Lord,
from the field of the
Lord Ratnategobhyudgata,
the Tathâgata, &c.,
as I am aware,
Lord, that here
in the Saha-world
is taught the Dharmaparyâya
of the Lotus of the True Law,
to hear which from the mouth
of the Lord Sâkyamuni
I have come accompanied
by these hundred thousands
of Bodhisattvas Mahâsattvas.
May the Lord
deign to expound,
in extension,
this Dharmaparyâya
of the Lotus of the True Law
to these
Bodhisattvas Mahâsattvas.

So addressed,
the Lord said
to the Bodhisattva
Mahâsattva Samantabhadra :
These Bodhisattvas,
young man of good family,
are, indeed,
quick of understanding,
but this is the Dharmaparyâya
of the Lotus of the True Law,
that is to say,
an unmixed truth.
The Bodhisattvas exclaimed :
Indeed Lord ; indeed, Sugata.
Then in order to confirm,
in the Dharmaparyâya
of the Lotus of the True Law,
the females among the monks,
nuns, and lay devotees
assembled at the gathering,
the Lord again spoke
to the Bodhisattva
Mahâsattva Samantabhadra :
This Dharmaparyâya
of the Lotus of the True Law,
young man of good family,
shall be entrusted
to a female if she be possessed
of four requisites, to wit :
she shall stand
under the superintendence
of the Lords Buddhas ;
she shall have
planted good roots ;
she shall keep steadily
to the mass
of disciplinary regulations ;
she shall,
in order to save creatures,
have the thoughts
fixed on supreme
and perfect enlightenment.
These are the four requisites,
young man of good family,
a female must be possessed of,
to whom this Dharmaparyâya
of the Lotus of the True Law
is to be entrusted.

Then the Bodhisattva
Mahâsattva Samantabhadra
said to the Lord :
At the end of time,
at the end of the period,
in the second half
of the millennium,
I will protect the monks
who keep this Sûtrânta ;
I will take care of their safety,
avert blows,
and destroy poison,
so that no one laying snares
for those preachers
may surprise them,
neither Mâra the Evil One,
nor the sons of Mâra,
the angels called Mârakâyikas,
the daughters of Mâra,
the followers of Mâra, and
all other servitors to Mâra ;
that no gods, goblins,
ghosts, imps, wizards,
spectres laying snares
for those preachers
may surprise them.
Incessantly and constantly,
O Lord,
will I protect such a preacher.
And when a preacher
who applies himself
to this Dharmaparyâya
shall take a walk, then,

O Lord,
will I mount
a white elephant
with six tusks,
and with a train
of Bodhisattvas
betake myself to the place
where that preacher
is walking,
in order to protect
this Dharmaparyâya.
And when that preacher,
applying himself
to this Dharmaparyâya,
forgets,
be it but a single word
or syllable,
then will I mount
the white elephant
with six tusks,
show my face
to that preacher,
and repeat
this entire Dharmaparyâya.
And when the preacher
has seen my proper body
and heard from me
this entire Dharmaparyâya,
he, content, in high spirits,
ravished, rejoiced, joyful,
and delighted,
will the more
do his utmost to study
this Dharmaparyâya,
and immediately
after beholding me
he will acquire meditation
and obtain spells,
termed the talisman
of preservation,
the talisman
of hundred thousand kotis,
and the talisman
of skill in all sounds.

Again, Lord,
the monks, nuns,
male or female lay devotees,
who at the end of time,
at the end of the period,
in the second half
of the millennium,
shall study
this Dharmaparyâya,
when walking
for three weeks,
or twenty-one days,
to them will I show my body,
at the sight of which
all beings rejoice.
Mounted on that same
white elephant with six tusks,
and surrounded
by a troop of Bodhisattvas,
I shall on the twenty-first day
betake myself
to the place where
the preachers are walking ;
there I shall rouse,
excite, and stimulate them,
and give them spells
whereby those preachers
shall become inviolable,
so that no being,
either human or not human,
shall be able to surprise them,
and no women
able to beguile them.
I will protect them,
take care of their safety,
avert blows,
and destroy poison.

I will, besides, O Lord, give those preachers words of talismanic spells, such as, Adande dandapati, dandâvartani dandakusale dandasudhâri dhâri sudhârapati, buddhapasyani dhârani, âvartani samvartani sanghaparîkshite sanghanirghâtani dharmaparîkshite sarvasattvaruta-kausalyânugate simhavikrîdite. The Bodhisattva Mahâsattva, whose organ of hearing is struck by these talismanic words, Lord, shall be aware that the Bodhisattva Mahâsattva Samantabhadra is their ruling power.

Further, Lord, the Bodhisattvas Mahâsattvas to whom this Dharmaparyâya of the Lotus of the True Law shall be entrusted, as long as it continues having course in Gambudvîpa, those preachers, Lord, should take this view: It is owing to the power and grandeur of the Bodhisattva Mahâsattva Samantabhadra that this Dharmaparyâya has been entrusted to us. Those creatures who shall write and keep this Sûtra, O Lord, are to partake of the course of duty of the Bodhisattva Mahâsattva Samantabhadra; they will belong to those who have planted good roots under many Buddhas, O Lord, and whose heads are caressed by the hands of the Tathâgata. Those who shall write and keep this Sûtra; O Lord, will afford me pleasure. Those who shall write this Sûtra, O Lord, and comprehend it, shall, when they disappear from this world, after having written it, be reborn in the company of the gods of paradise, and at that birth shall eighty-four thousand heavenly nymphs immediately come near them. Adorned with a high crown, they shall as angels dwell amongst those nymphs. Such is the mass of merit resulting from writing this Dharmaparyâya; how much greater will

be the mass of merit reaped
by those who recite, study,
meditate, remember it!
Therefore,
young men of good family,
one ought to honour
this Dharmaparyâya
of the Lotus of the True Law,
and write it
with the utmost attention.
He who writes it
with undistracted attention
shall be supported
by the hands
of a thousand Buddhas,
and at the moment
of his death he shall see
another thousand of Buddhas
from face to face.
He shall not sink down
into a state of wretchedness,
and after disappearing
from this world
he shall enter the company
of the Tushita-gods,
where the Bodhisattva
Mahâsattva Maitreya
is residing, and where,
marked by the thirty-two
sublime characteristics,
surrounded by
a host of Bodhisattvas,
and waited upon
by hundred thousands
of myriads of kotis
of heavenly nymphs
he is preaching the law.
Therefore, then,
young men of good family,
a wise young man
or young lady of good family
should respectfully write
this Dharmaparyâya
of the Lotus of the True Law,
respectfully recite it,
respectfully study it,
respectfully treasure it
up in his or her mind.
By writing, reciting, studying
this Dharmaparyâya,
and by treasuring it up
in one's mind,
young men of good family,
one is to acquire
innumerable good qualities.
Hence a wise young man
or young lady of good family
ought to keep
this Dharmaparyâya
of the Lotus of the True Law.
I myself, O Lord,
will superintend
this Dharmaparyâya,
that through
my superintendence
it may here spread
in Gambudvîpa.

Then the Lord Sâkyamuni,
the Tathâgata, &c.,
expressed his approval to
the Bodhisattva Mahâsattva
Samantabhadra:
Very well, very well,
Samantabhadra.
It is happy that thou art
so well disposed to promote
the weal and happiness
of the people at large,
out of compassion
for the people,
for the benefit, weal,

and happiness
of the great body of men;
that thou art endowed with
such inconceivable qualities,
with a mind
so full of compassion,
with intentions
so inconceivably kind,
so that of thine own accord
thou wilt take those preachers
under thy protection.
The young men of good
family who shall cherish
the name of the Bodhisattva
Mahâsattva Samantabhadra
may be convinced that
they have seen Sâkyamuni,
the Tathâgata, &c.;
that they have heard
this Dharmaparyâya
of the Lotus of the True Law
from the Lord Sâkyamuni;
that they have paid homage
to the Tathâgata Sâkyamuni;
that they have
applauded the preaching
of the Tathâgata Sâkyamuni.
They will have
joyfully accepted
this Dharmaparyâya;
the Tathâgata Sâkyamuni
will have laid his hand
upon their head,
and they will have decked
the Lord Sâkyamuni
with their robes.
Those young men
or young ladies
of good family,
Samantabhadra,
must be held to have
accepted the command
of the Tathâgata.
They will have no pleasure
in worldly philosophy;
no persons fondly addicted
to poetry will please them;
no dancers, athletes,
vendors of meat, mutton
butchers, poulterers, pork
butchers, or profligates
will please them.
After having heard,
written, kept,
or read such Sûtrântas as this,
they will find no delight
in those persons.
They must be held
to be possessed
of natural righteousness;
they will be right-minded
from themselves,
possess a power to do good
of their own accord,
and make an agreeable
impression on others.
Such will be the monks
who keep this Sûtrânta.
No passionate attachment
will hinder them, no hatred,
no infatuation, no jealousy,
no envy, no hypocrisy,
no pride, no conceitedness,
no mendaciousness.
Those preachers,
Samantabhadra,
will be content
with what they receive.
He, Samantabhadra,
who at the end of time,
at the end of the period,
in the second half

of the millennium,
sees a monk
keeping this Dharmaparyâya
of the Lotus of the True Law,
must think thus : This
young man of good family
will reach the terrace
of enlightenment ;
this young man will conquer
the troop of the wicked Mâra,
move forward
the wheel of the law,
strike the drum of the law,
blow the conch trumpet
of the law,
spread the rain of the law,
and ascend
the royal throne of the law.
The monks
who at the end of time,
at the end of the period,
in the second half
of the millennium,
keep this Dharmaparyâya,
will not be covetous,
nor greedy of robes
or vehicles.
Those preachers
will be honest,
and possessed
of three emancipations ;
they will refrain
from worldly business.
Such persons
as lead into error monks
who know this Sûtrânta,
shall be born blind ;
and such as openly
defame them,
shall have a spotted body
in this very world.

Those who scoff and hoot
at the monks
who copy this Sûtrânta,
shall have the teeth broken
and separated
far from each other ;
disgusting lips, a flat nose,
contorted hands and feet,
squinting eyes ;
a putrid body,
a body covered
with stinking boils,
eruptions, scabs, and itch.
If one speaks an unkind word,
true or not true,
to such writers, readers,
and keepers of this Sûtrânta,
it must be considered
a very heinous sin.
Therefore then,
Samantabhadra,
people should,
even from afar,
rise from their seats
before the monks who
keep this Dharmaparyâya
and show them
the same reverence
as to the Tathâgata.

While this chapter
of the Encouragement
of Samantabhadra
was being expounded,
hundred thousands of kotis
of Bodhisattvas Mahâsattvas,
equal to the sands
of the river Ganges,
acquired the talismanic spell
Âvarta.

Chapter XXVII
The Period

Thereupon
the Lord Sâkyamuni,
the Tathâgata, &c.,
rose from his pulpit,
collected the Bodhisattvas,
took their right hands
with his own right hand,
which had become strong
by the exercise of magic,
and spoke on that occasion
as follows :
Into your hands,
young men of good family,
I transfer and transmit,
entrust and deposit
this supreme and perfect
enlightenment arrived
at by me after hundred
thousands of myriads of kotis
of incalculable Æons.
Ye, young men of good family,
do your best
that it may grow and spread.

A second time,
a third time the Lord spoke
to the host of Bodhisattvas
after taking them
by the right hands :
Into your hands,
young men of good family,
I transfer and transmit,
entrust and deposit
this supreme
and perfect enlightenment
arrived at by me
after hundred thousands
of myriads of kotis
of incalculable Æons.
Receive it,
young men of good family,
keep, read,
fathom, teach,
promulgate,
and preach it to all beings.
I am not avaricious,
young men of good family,
nor narrow-minded ;
I am confident
and willing to impart
Buddha-knowledge,
to impart the knowledge
of the Tathâgata,
the knowledge
of the Self-born.
I am a bountiful giver,
young men of good family,
and ye,
young men of good family,
follow my example ;
imitate me in liberally
showing this
knowledge of the Tathâgata,
and in skilfulness,
and preach
this Dharmaparyâya
to the young men and
young ladies of good family
who successively
shall gather round you.
And
as to unbelieving persons,
rouse them to accept this law.
By so doing,
young men of good family,
you will acquit your debt
to the Tathâgatas.
So addressed
by the Lord Sâkyamuni,

the Tathâgata, &c.,
the Bodhisattvas
filled with delight and joy,
and with a feeling
of great respect they lowered,
bent, and bowed their body
towards the Lord, and,
the head inclined and the
joined hands stretched out,
they spoke in one voice
to the Lord Sâkyamuni,
the Tathâgata, &c.,
the following words :
We shall do,
O Lord,
what the Tathâgata commands ;
we shall fulfil the command
of all Tathâgatas.
Let the Lord
be at ease as to this,
and perfectly quiet.
A second time,
a third time
the entire host
of Bodhisattvas
spoke in one voice
the same words :
Let the Lord
be at ease as to this,
and perfectly quiet.
We shall do,
O Lord,
what the Tathâgata
commands us ;
we shall fulfil the command
of all Tathâgatas.

Thereupon
the Lord Sâkyamuni,
the Tathâgata, &c.,
dismissed all those
Tathâgatas, &c.,
who had come
to the gathering
from other worlds,
and wished them
a happy existence,
with the words :
May the Tathâgatas, &c.,
live happy.
Then he restored the Stûpa
of precious substances
of the Lord Prabhûtaratna,
the Tathâgata, &c.,
to its place,
and wished him also
a happy existence.

Thus spoke the Lord.
The incalculable,
innumerable Tathâgatas, &c.,
who had come
from other worlds
and were sitting
on their thrones
at the foot of jewel trees,
as well as Prabhûtaratna,
the Tathâgata, &c.,
and the whole host
of Bodhisattvas
headed by Visishtakâritra,
the innumerable,
incalculable
Bodhisattvas Mahâsattvas
who had issued
from the gaps of the earth,
the great disciples,
the four classes, the world,
including gods, men,
demons, and Gandharvas,
in ecstasy applauded
the words of the Lord.

Index

A
Âbhâsvaras 284
Abhayandada 345
Abhigñâgñânâbhibhû 130, 152
Abhigñaprâpta 172
Abhirati 148
Abhyudgatarâga 359
Adhimâtrakârunika 137
Aerial cars 134, 135, 136, 137, 138, 139, 140, 141, 143, 153, 166, 256, 277, 288, 289, 293
Agâtasatru 4
Agita 15, 16, 17, 18, 242, 243, 244, 259, 263, 264, 266, 267, 268, 269, 273, 274, 275, 276, 277
Âgîvakas 219
Âgñâta-Kaundinya 1, 28, 168
Akalâ 313
Akanishthas 284
Âkâsapratishthita 148
Akshayamati 2, 341, 343, 344, 345, 346, 348
Akshobhya 148
Alankârasûra 351
Amitâbha 350
Amitâyus 148
Amoghadarsin 2
Anâbhibhû 152
Anâgâmin 326
Ânanda 1, 171, 172, 173, 174, 175, 176
Anantamati 15
Anantavikrâmin 2
Anavanâmita 172
Anavanatâ 172
Anavatapta 3
Angelic cars 153
Anikshiptadhura 2
Anilambha 331
Aniruddha 1, 165
Anupamamati 2
Apkritsna 332
Arhat 14, 15, 36, 47, 57, 66, 68, 69, 99, 100, 101, 119, 122, 124, 130, 148, 149, 151, 157, 160, 161, 162, 163, 164, 165, 168, 172, 173, 174, 175, 192, 206, 214, 215, 221, 230, 242, 298, 307, 326, 351, 359
Arhats 1, 5, 14, 28, 36, 97, 102, 106, 107, 158, 165, 167, 168, 176, 180, 202, 250, 275, 278, 286
Arhatship 36, 52, 206, 207, 275, 276
Ârya 59, 230, 294
Âryas 67, 69, 230
Asvagit 1
Avabhâsa 119
Avabhâsaprabha 3
Avalokitesvara 2, 341, 342, 343, 344, 345, 346, 347, 348, 349, 350
Âvarta 367
Avîki 5, 7, 78, 281, 282, 284, 292, 301

B
Bali 3
Bauhinia 285
Benares 47, 59
Bhadra 160, 215
Bhadrapâla 2, 302
Bhadrika 1
Bhaishagyarâga 2, 179, 180, 181, 182, 184, 185, 186, 187, 213, 311, 312, 317, 324, 328, 329, 330, 332, 340, 360
Bhaishagyarâgasamudgata 332, 360
Bhaishagyariga 186
Bhâradvâga 1, 15
Bhîshmagargitasvararâga 297, 298, 299, 301

Bhîshmasvara 302
Bimba 357
Boddhisattvas 319
Bodhi 25, 67
Bodhisattva 2, 5, 6, 13, 17, 18, 21, 22, 55, 57, 60, 148, 149, 161, 168, 185, 186, 187, 191, 192, 193, 194, 207, 208, 209, 210, 211, 212, 213, 214, 215, 219, 220, 221, 222, 223, 224, 226, 227, 228, 235, 237, 239, 242, 243, 245, 246, 247, 249, 250, 252, 259, 261, 263, 269, 273, 275, 281, 282, 284, 286, 287, 288, 289, 292, 293, 297, 298, 299, 300, 301, 302, 303, 305, 311, 312, 317, 318, 319, 320, 321, 322, 323, 324, 325, 326, 328, 329, 330, 331, 332, 333, 334, 336, 337, 338, 339, 340, 341, 342, 343, 344, 345, 346, 350, 359, 361, 362, 364, 365, 366
Bodhisattva-course 5
Bodhisattvas 2, 4, 5, 8, 9, 10, 11, 13, 14, 16, 17, 19, 20, 21, 24, 26, 27, 28, 43, 47, 48, 49, 51, 53, 54, 56, 58, 66, 67, 68, 75, 76, 77, 83, 84, 90, 91, 95, 106, 108, 112, 119, 120, 122, 123, 124, 125, 127, 130, 146, 147, 148, 149, 150, 155, 160, 161, 162, 164, 166, 172, 173, 175, 176, 179, 186, 187, 189, 192, 194, 197, 203, 208, 213, 214, 215, 216, 219, 223, 226, 227, 228, 230, 231, 235, 236, 237, 238, 239, 240, 241, 242, 243, 244, 245, 246, 247, 248, 249, 250, 255, 259, 260, 261, 262, 264, 265, 266, 267, 268, 277, 282, 284, 286, 289, 292, 293, 297, 298, 301, 302, 305, 306, 307, 308, 309, 310, 317, 318, 321, 323, 325, 327, 328, 330, 331, 332, 333, 334, 335, 339, 340, 351, 359, 360, 361, 362, 363, 364, 365, 367, 369, 370
Bodhisattvaship 243
Brahma 3, 46, 59, 134, 135, 136, 137, 138, 139, 140, 141, 211, 292, 322, 326, 337, 344
Brahma-angels 135, 136, 141, 142, 143, 145, 153, 262
Brahmadhvaga 148
Brahmakâyika 3, 131, 326
Brahman 144, 338, 345
Brahmans 17, 55, 85, 137, 145, 217, 224, 229, 291, 352
Brahmas 17, 55, 97
Brahmavihâras 117
Buddha 12, 14, 16, 19, 22, 23, 25, 26, 27, 29, 33, 34, 36, 37, 38, 39, 40, 44, 45, 46, 48, 53, 54, 55, 56, 57, 59, 60, 65, 66, 68, 69, 75, 76, 78, 79, 80, 81, 83, 91, 96, 97, 98, 104, 105, 107, 108, 114, 115, 119, 120, 121, 122, 123, 124, 125, 126, 135, 138, 139, 140, 141, 148, 160, 161, 162, 163, 164, 166, 172, 173, 174, 176, 181, 189, 192, 193, 194, 196, 197, 203, 207, 222, 232, 233, 240, 246, 248, 256, 258, 262, 267, 269, 272, 284, 291, 293, 295, 305, 306, 308, 317, 321, 332, 333, 340, 344, 349, 352, 354
Buddha field 4
Buddha-field 124
Buddha-fields 4, 5, 6, 7, 176, 193, 194, 196, 306, 331, 334
Buddhahood 182
Buddha-knowledge 9, 66, 143, 147, 151, 152, 155, 163, 171, 188, 224, 238, 244, 255, 261, 264, 265, 266, 268, 327, 358, 369
Buddha-laws 7
Buddhas 2, 4, 5, 7, 13, 15, 16, 17, 18, 20, 22, 23, 25, 26, 27,

28, 31, 34, 37, 38, 39, 41, 43,
44, 45, 46, 47, 48, 49, 50, 51,
54, 55, 56, 57, 58, 59, 75, 76,
81, 95, 107, 108, 116, 119,
122, 123, 124, 125, 142, 145, 146,
147, 148, 155, 158, 160, 161, 162,
163, 165, 166, 172, 173, 174, 175,
176, 179, 189, 193, 194, 195, 200,
214, 215, 226, 228, 229, 238, 246,
260, 261, 264, 277, 291, 292, 293,
301, 303, 307, 308, 309, 310, 312,
313, 319, 320, 323, 325, 328, 329,
336, 337, 343, 344, 346, 354, 355,
360, 362, 364, 365
Buddhaship 23, 60, 211
Buddha-vehicle 8
C
Celestial cars 138, 140
D
Deodar 42
Devadatta 206
Devarâga 206
Devarâgu 206
Devasopâna 206
Dhâranî 259
Dharanîdhara 2
Dharanindhara 350
Dhâranîs 261
Dharma 47, 205
Dharmadhara 3
Dharmamati 15
Dharmaparyâya 4, 14, 16, 17, 18,
19, 55, 146, 147, 148, 179, 180, 181,
182, 184, 185, 186, 187, 191, 192,
193, 198, 199, 200, 213, 215, 216,
219, 224, 227, 228, 229, 230, 235,
247, 251, 259, 260, 263, 266, 267,
268, 269, 273, 275, 276, 277, 281,
282, 284, 290, 292, 293, 297, 299,
300, 301, 302, 305, 307, 308, 311,
315, 318, 319, 320, 325, 326, 327,

328, 329, 330, 334, 336, 337, 338,
350, 351, 352, 353, 355, 356, 357,
361, 362, 363, 364, 365, 366, 367,
369
Dharmaparyâyas 101, 251,
252
Dharmaprabhâsa 161, 162, 164
Dharmarâga 49, 102
Dhârmika 205
Dhritarâshtra 3
Dhritiparipûrna 57
Dhvagâgrakeyûra 331
Dîpankara 18, 23, 250
Druma 3
E
Evil One 10, 54, 119,
230, 329, 335, 362
Exposition of Infinity 19, 4, 16
Exposition of the Infinite 19
F
Five perfections 263, 264
G
Gadgadasvara 331, 332, 333, 334,
336, 337, 338, 339, 340
Galadharagargitaghos-
hasusvaranakshatrarâ-
gasankusumitâbhigña 351, 352,
353, 354, 355, 356, 357, 358, 359
Gambudvîpa 180, 181, 274,
298, 329, 364, 365
Gâmbûnada 124, 125
Gandharva 3, 344
Gandharvakâyikas 3
Gandharvas 3, 4, 6, 16, 20, 30, 58,
136, 179, 187, 212, 282, 292, 305,
306, 317, 323, 346, 361, 370
Ganges 8, 12, 20, 22, 28, 30, 45, 80,
97, 98, 123, 126, 145, 147, 148, 149,
154, 155, 161, 172, 173, 189, 194,
197, 200, 201, 202, 206, 233, 235,
236, 239, 240, 241, 259, 262, 298,

305, 311, 312, 317, 319, 328, 331,
332, 337, 339, 343, 344, 357, 367
Garuda 3, 4, 338
Garudas 4, 6, 16, 58, 136,
179, 187, 212, 282, 290, 305,
306, 317, 323, 346, 361
Gâtakas 37
Gautamî 214, 215
Gavâmpati 1
Gayâ 1, 165, 244, 245, 247, 249
Ghee 266, 327
Ghoshamati 15
Gina 9, 10, 12, 13, 19, 21, 22,
23, 27, 28, 30, 40, 49, 57, 58, 76,
95, 96, 98, 104, 106, 116, 121,
123, 124, 126, 127, 130, 133,
136, 152, 154, 155, 165, 166,
172, 173, 183, 188, 200, 201,
203, 233, 234, 270, 289, 302,
303, 346, 350, 354
Ginas 5, 9, 11, 12, 22, 24, 28, 31,
41, 42, 44, 45, 48, 53, 54, 75, 120,
126, 127, 142, 154, 155, 156, 158,
174, 175, 183, 257, 261, 262, 294,
309
Gñânâkara 132
Gñânamudrâ 331
Gñanolkâ 331
Great Exposition 4, 16
Gridhrakûta 1, 197,
208, 256, 333, 335, 361
Guhagupta 2
Gyotishprabha 3
H
Hârîtî 313
Himâlaya 109, 114, 293
I
Indra 46, 59, 211,
292, 326, 337, 344
Indradatta 2
Indradhvaga 148

Indras 105
Isle of Jewels 150, 151
Îsvara 3, 46, 292, 345
K
Kâlodâyin 165
Kakravâla 195
Kakravartin 132, 146, 211, 345
Kâla 165, 195, 196, 332
Kâlânusârin 318
Kalpa 78, 131
Kalpas 17, 18, 19, 21, 22, 57,
58, 76, 78, 119, 120, 122, 123,
124, 125, 126, 127, 131, 132,
133, 152, 206, 237
Kamaladalavimalanaksha-
trarâgasankusumitâbhigña
331, 332, 333, 334, 335, 340
Kampaka 315, 319, 327
Kândâlas 219
Kandra 3
Kandraprabhâsvararâga 300
Kandrapradîpa
(name of a Samâdhi) 331
Kandrârkadîpa 21
Kandrasûryapradîpa 14, 15,
16, 17, 18, 19
Kandravimala-
sûryaprabhâsasrî 317,
318, 320, 321, 322
Kapilavastu 245, 247
Kapphina 1, 165
Karakas 219
Karketana 191
Kâsyapa 99, 100, 101,
102, 107, 108, 111, 119,
120, 165, 167
Kâsyapa of Gayâ 1
Kâsyapa of Nadî 1
Kâsyapa of Uruvilvâ 1
Kâtyâyana 124
Kaundinya 165

Kesinî 313
Ketus 176
Kharaskandha 3
Kinnara 3, 338
Kinnara king 3
Kinnaras 4, 6, 16, 20, 58, 136, 179, 187, 212, 282, 290, 305, 306, 317, 323, 346, 361
Kitradhvaga 346
Kotis 2, 3, 4, 7, 8, 9, 11, 12, 16, 18, 19, 23, 25, 26, 27, 30, 31, 32, 37, 38, 43, 44, 48, 54, 55, 68, 74, 76, 81, 106, 120, 122, 123, 125, 126, 130, 134, 135, 137, 139, 141, 143, 145, 146, 147, 149, 152, 153, 232, 234, 240, 249, 250, 252, 253, 255, 256, 257, 259, 260, 261, 262, 263, 264, 265, 266, 267, 268, 269, 270, 278, 279, 283, 291, 295, 298, 299, 300, 301, 303, 305, 306, 307, 308, 309, 311, 313, 317, 318, 320, 323, 326, 331, 332, 333, 334, 339, 340, 341, 344, 346, 355, 358, 360, 361, 363, 365, 367, 369
Kshatriyas 85
Kubera 337, 345
Kumbhândas 313
Kunda 165
Kundina 165
Kuntî 313, 314, 315
Kûtadantî 313
L
Lambâ 313
Lotus of the True Law 17, 18, 19, 55, 146, 147, 148, 155, 191, 192, 193, 198, 199, 204, 207, 209, 277, 299, 300, 301, 307, 311, 318, 319, 320, 325, 326, 327, 328, 331, 334, 336, 337, 338, 340, 351, 352, 353, 355, 356, 357, 361, 362, 364, 365, 366, 367
M
Madhura 3
Madhurasvara 3
Magadha 4
Mahâ 83, 91, 99, 108, 121, 123, 125, 165
Mahâbhigñâgñanâbhibhû 129, 130, 132, 133, 134, 136, 138, 139, 140, 142, 143, 145, 146, 147
Mahâdharma 3
Mahâ-Kâsyapa 1
Mahâ-Kâtyâyana 1
Mahâ-Kaushthila 1
Mahâkâya 4
Mahâ-Maudgalyâyana 1
Mahânâman 1
Mahânanda 1
Mahâpragâpatî 1
Mahâpratibhâna 2, 191, 192, 193, 194, 213
Mahâpûrna 4
Mahâratnapratimandita 56
Mahârddhiprâpta 4
Mahârûpa 129
Mahâsambhava 297
Mahâsattva 2, 5, 6, 13, 18, 57, 186, 191, 192, 193, 194, 219, 220, 221, 224, 226, 227, 228, 237, 239, 242, 243, 245, 247, 249, 250, 259, 261, 263, 269, 273, 275, 281, 282, 284, 292, 293, 298, 299, 300, 301, 302, 305, 311, 312, 317, 318, 319, 320, 321, 322, 323, 324, 328, 329, 331, 332, 333, 334, 336, 337, 338, 339, 340, 341, 342, 343, 344, 345, 346, 350, 359, 361, 362, 364, 365, 366
Mahâsattvas 2, 5, 68, 90, 148, 179, 186, 219, 227, 235, 236,

237, 238, 239, 242, 243, 246,
250, 259, 260, 261, 268, 302,
305, 307, 308, 317, 318, 319,
321, 332, 339, 340, 360, 361,
364, 367, 370
Mahâsthâmaprâpta 2, 297,
298, 299, 300, 301, 302
Mahâtegas 4
Mahâtegogarbha 351
Mahâvyûha 119
Mahesvara 3, 46, 292, 345
Mahisattvas 259
Mahivikrâmin 2
Maitrâyanî 159, 160
Maitrâyanîputra 1
Maitreya 2, 5, 6, 13, 23, 239,
242, 243, 245, 247, 275
Makutadantî 313
Mâlâdhârî 313
Manasvin 3
Mandâra 191
Mandâras 257
Mandârava 191, 195, 196,
260, 285, 318
Mandâravas 4, 6, 16, 19, 59,
262, 288
Mañgughosha 11, 234
Mañgûshakas 4, 6, 16, 288
Mañgusrî 2, 5, 6, 9, 13, 19,
207, 208, 209, 219, 220, 221,
224, 226, 227, 228, 229, 230,
231, 305, 332, 333, 334, 336, 340
Mañgusvara 12, 13
Manobhirâma 125
Manogña 3
Manogñasabdâbhigargita 172
Manogñasara 3
Mâra 54, 119, 131, 230, 329,
330, 362, 367
Mârakâyikas 329, 362
Mâras 17, 54, 55, 97, 137, 230

Meghadundubhisvararâga
336, 337
Meghasvarapradîpa 149
Meghasvararâga 149
Meru 281, 292, 293, 347
Merukalpa 149
Merukûta 148
Mudgala 126
Mukilinda 195
Musâragalva 204
Musâragalvas 341
N
Nadî 165
Nâga 3, 208, 209, 210, 211,
290
Nâgas 3, 4, 6, 16, 20, 30, 58,
136, 152, 179, 187, 212, 233,
282, 283, 290, 291, 292, 294,
305, 306, 317, 323, 329, 346,
347, 361
Nakshatrarâga 2, 328
Nakshatrarâgâditya 351
Nakshatrarâgasan-
kusumitâbhigña 332
Nakshatraragâvikrîdita 331
Nakshatrararâga-
sankusumitâbhigña 317, 318,
319, 320, 321, 322, 323, 324,
325, 326, 327, 328, 329, 330
Nanda (an Arhat) 1;
(a Nâga king) 3
Naradatta 2
Nârâyana 335
Nirgranthas 219
Nirvâna 5, 14, 17, 18, 21, 22,
28, 29, 30, 36, 38, 40, 47, 53,
57, 60, 67, 68, 69, 76, 78, 83,
84, 90, 96, 102, 105, 107, 108,
112, 113, 115, 116, 117, 131,
143, 149, 150, 151, 152, 155,
158, 167, 168, 169, 170, 181,

230, 250, 251, 256, 278, 297
Nityaparinirvrita 148
Nityodyukta 2
Niyutas 321
Noble Truths 14, 297
P
Padmaprabha 55, 56, 57
Padmasrî 2, 336, 337, 338, 339, 340, 359
Padmavrishabhavikrâmin 57
Parivrâgakas 219
Paryâya (=Dharmaparyâya) 213
Paryâyas 232
Pilindavatsa 1
Prabhâsa
(also see Samantaprabhâsa) 166
Prabhûtaratna 192, 193, 195, 198, 200, 201, 207, 208, 236, 237, 260, 306, 307, 330, 334, 335, 336, 340, 346, 370
Pradânasûra 2, 312, 332, 340
Pragñâkûta 207, 208, 211, 212
Prasâdavatî 331
Pratyekabuddha 105, 114, 326, 329, 339, 344
Pratyekabuddhas 7, 25, 27, 28, 29, 30, 36, 66, 67, 68, 75, 77, 106, 107, 112, 147, 152, 179, 226, 250, 264, 282, 286, 291, 292, 325, 326, 327
Pratyekabuddhaship 162, 206, 207
Pratyekagina 114
Priyadarsana (an Æon) 351
Pûrna 1, 159, 160, 164
Pûrnakandra 2
Purushottamas 39
Pushpadantî 313
R
Râgagriha 1
Râhu 3

Râhula 1, 2, 171, 174, 175, 214
Rasmiprabhâsa 119, 121
Rasmisatasahasra-paripûrnadhvaga 215
Ratipratipûrna 125
Ratna 176
Ratnakandra 2
Ratnâkara 2
Ratnaketurâgas 176
Ratnamati 15
Ratnapâni 2
Ratnaprabha 2, 3
Ratnaprabhâsa 122
Ratnasambhava 122
Ratnategobhyudgata 361
Ratnâvabhâsa 162, 164
Ratnavisuddha 192
Revata 1
Riddhivikrîdita 331
Rishipatana 59
S
Sadâparibhûta 298, 299, 300, 301, 302
Saddharma-pundarîka
(see Lotus of the True Law); (name of a Samâdhi) 331
Sâgara 3, 208, 209, 210, 211
Sâgarabuddhidhârin 172
Sâgaravaradhara-buddhivikrîditâbhigña 171, 172, 174, 175
Saha 149, 307
Sahâmpati (see Brahma) 3, 59, 326
Saha-world 193, 195, 199, 212, 213, 235, 236, 237, 243, 250, 267, 307, 308, 317, 319, 332, 333, 334, 335, 338, 339, 340, 344, 345, 346, 361
Saikshas 60
Sakra 3

Index 379

Sakridâgâmin 326
Sâkya 121
Sâkyamuni 149, 191, 195, 196,
197, 198, 199, 207, 208, 210, 212,
236, 237, 242, 249, 260, 266, 303,
305, 306, 307, 328, 331, 332, 333,
334, 336, 339, 340, 346, 361, 365,
366, 369, 370
Sâkyas 24, 245, 247
Sâkyasimha 23
Sâla 350
Sâlendrarâga 359
Samâdhi 318, 323, 331
Samâdhis 331, 332
Samantabhadra (see
Samantaprabhâsa) 361, 362,
364, 365, 366, 367
Samantagandha 3
Samantaprabhâsa 165, 166
Sambhava 129
Sangha 47
Sangrahas 117
Saptaratnapadma-
vikrântagâmin 174
Sâri 40, 47, 57, 58
Sâriputra 1, 25, 26, 28, 29, 30, 31,
32, 33, 34, 35, 36, 37, 39, 48, 49, 51,
52, 55, 56, 57, 58, 59, 60, 61, 63, 64,
66, 67, 68, 69, 75, 77, 78, 80, 82, 83,
210, 211, 212
Sârisuta 27
Sarvabuddhasandarsana 336
Sarvagunâlankâravyûha 356
Sarvalokabhayâgitakkham-
bhitatvavidhvamsanakara 149
Sarvalokadhâtûpadravod-
vegapratyuttîrna 148
Sarvapunyasamukkaya 331
Sârvarthanâman 2
Sarvarûpasandarsana 318,
323, 339, 340

Sarvarutakausalya 331
Sarvasattvapâpagahana 355
Sarvasattvapriyadarsana
214, 318, 319, 320, 321, 322,
323, 324, 329
Sarvasattvatrâtri 135
Sarvasattvogahârî 313
Sasiketu 122
Satatasamitâbhiyukta 2,
281, 282, 284, 290, 292, 293
Senâpati 345
Sikhin (name of Brahma) 3;
(name of a Brahma-angel) 141
Simha 2
Simhadhvaga 148
Simhaghosha 148
Simhakandrâ 302
Siva 337
Six Perfections 14, 204, 297
Srîgarbha 17
Srotaâpanna 326
Stûpa 43, 185, 191, 192, 193,
195, 197, 198, 199, 201, 206,
207, 236, 269, 272, 306, 307,
335, 340, 346, 370
Stûpas 5, 12, 22, 42, 43, 44, 123,
124, 125, 126, 162, 192, 267, 268,
269, 322, 323
Subhavyûha 351, 352, 353, 355,
356, 357, 358, 359, 360
Subhûti 1, 83, 121, 122
Sudharma (a king of the
Kinnaras) 3; (an angel) 139
Sudharmâ 285, 288
Sûdras 85
Sugata 8, 9, 10, 11, 12, 13, 14,
20, 21, 22, 23, 27, 28, 30, 31, 32,
48, 55, 64, 76, 81, 84, 95, 98,
105, 126, 127, 129, 130, 133, 136,
155, 159, 161, 162, 165, 166, 169,
170, 171, 175, 179, 191, 227, 243,

248, 249, 255, 261, 263, 275,
283, 289, 295, 297, 309, 311,
317, 321, 336, 337, 344, 357, 362
Sugataketanâ 302
Sugatas 8, 10, 11, 12, 20, 27, 42,
43, 44, 52, 126, 172, 231, 284
Sukhâkara 350
Sumati 15
Sumeru 135, 136, 138, 142,
195, 201, 223, 281, 292, 293, 325
Sundara-Nanda 1
Supratishthitakâritra 237
Sûrânta 55
Sûrya 3
Sûryagarbha 2
Sûryâvarta 332
Susamsthita 2
Susârthavâha 2
Sûtra 19, 24, 49, 77, 78, 79, 80, 81,
82, 155, 179, 182, 183, 184, 188,
189, 201, 202, 203, 204, 205, 207,
209, 213, 216, 217, 221, 222, 223,
226, 227, 231, 232, 233, 234, 269,
270, 271, 273, 278, 279, 281, 284,
287, 289, 293, 294, 295, 297, 302,
303, 309, 310, 315, 330, 364
Sûtrânta 181, 183, 307, 312,
313, 330, 362, 366, 367
Sûtrântas 120, 232, 325, 326, 366
Sûtras 36, 37, 38, 81, 82, 188,
201, 203, 217, 230, 232, 294,
310, 325, 326
Suvikrântavikrâmin 2
Suvisuddha 162, 164
Svâgata 165
T
Takshaka 3
Tâl 352
Tâlas 335
Tamâlapatrakandana-
gandhâbhigña 148
Tamâlapatrak-
andanagandha 125, 126
Tathâgata 5, 13, 14, 15, 16,
17, 18, 26, 29, 32, 33, 34, 35,
36, 41, 51, 54, 55, 56, 57, 58,
60, 64, 65, 66, 67, 68, 69, 82,
90, 91, 98, 99, 100, 101, 102,
104, 106, 107, 111, 112, 113,
115, 119, 122, 124, 125, 129,
130, 132, 133, 134, 136, 137,
139, 140, 143, 145, 146, 147,
148, 149, 150, 151, 152, 159,
160, 161, 162, 165, 166, 168,
170, 171, 172, 173, 174, 175,
177, 179, 180, 181, 184, 185,
186, 187,192, 193, 194, 195,
196, 197, 198, 199, 203, 206,
207, 208, 210, 212, 213, 214,
215, 220, 224, 226, 227, 228,
229, 230, 231, 232, 233, 236,
237, 239, 242, 243, 245, 246,
247, 249, 250, 251, 252, 253,
259, 260, 261, 263, 266, 267,
268, 269, 271, 273, 274, 275,
277, 291, 293, 297, 298, 299,
301, 302, 305, 306, 307, 308,
317, 318, 319, 320, 321, 322,
323, 324, 325, 326, 327, 328,
329, 330, 331, 332, 333, 334,
335, 336, 337, 339, 340, 346,
351, 352, 353, 354, 355, 356,
357, 358, 359, 361, 364, 365,
366, 367, 369, 370
Tathâgatas 2, 5, 6, 9, 14, 15, 25,
26, 28, 29, 34, 35, 36, 37, 41, 43,
44, 55, 56, 77, 83, 102, 107, 113,
123, 130, 134, 149, 150, 152, 159,
160, 165, 167, 174, 176, 180, 183,
184, 186, 193, 194, 196, 197, 198,
199, 203, 209, 214, 227, 230, 231,
234, 236, 237, 242, 243, 250, 253,

282, 286, 292, 293, 294, 298, 299, 300, 301, 306, 307, 308, 311, 312, 328, 331, 357, 369, 370
Tathâgatas (the sixteen) 148
Tathâgataship 44, 231
Tîrtha 217
Tishya 76
Trailokavikrâmin 2
Tushita-gods 365

U
Upananda (an Arhat), 1; (a Nâga king), 3
Uragasâra 318, 319, 322
Ûrnâ 357
Uruvilvâ 165
Utpalaka 3
Uttaramati 2

V
Vagrapâni 345
Vaidehî 4
Vaigayanta 288
Vaigayantî 172
Vairokanarasmi-pratimanditarâga 359
Vairokanarasmiprati-mandita 331, 333, 334, 351
Vaisravana 3, 313
Vaisyas 85
Vakkula 165
Vakula 1
Vallakî 283
Varaprabha 17, 18, 21, 22, 23
Vardhamânamati 2
Vârshikâ 315, 327
Varunadatta 2
Vâshpa 1
Vâsuki 3
Vemakitri 3
Vilam'â 313
Vimala 211, 212, 331; (name of a Samâdhi) 351

Vimalâbhâsa 351
Vimaladattâ 320, 351, 352, 354, 355, 356, 358, 359; (name of a Samâdhi) 331
Vimalagarbha 332, 351, 352, 354, 355
Vimalâgranetra 22
Vimalanetra 17, 351, 352, 354, 355
Vimalanirbhâsa 351
Vimalaprabhâ 332
Vimatisamudghâtin 15
Vinialadattâ 352
Vinirbhoga 297
Vipasyin 160
Viraga 55, 56, 57
Virûdhaka 3, 313
Virûpâksha 3
Viseshamati 2, 15
Visishtakâritra 237, 305, 308, 332, 370
Vistîrnavatî 359
Visuddhakâritra 237
Vivaras 321
Vyûharâga (name of a Samâdhi) 331; (name of a Bodhisattva) 332

Y
Yama 65, 195, 207, 338, 348
Yasaskâma 18, 23
Yasodharâ 2, 214, 215
Yoga 5
Yoganas 12, 79, 110, 116, 123, 125, 131, 136, 150, 156, 191, 195, 196, 197, 206, 313, 332
Yogins 5, 78